THE SECRETS OF SKINNY CHICKS

How to Feel Great in Your Favorite Jeans
—When It Doesn't Come Naturally

KAREN BRIDSON

McGraw·Hill

New York   Chicago   San Francisco   Lisbon   London   Madrid   Mexico City
Milan   New Delhi   San Juan   Seoul   Singapore   Sydney   Toronto

Library of Congress Cataloging-in-Publication Data

Bridson, Karen.
    The secrets of skinny chicks : how to feel great in your favorite jeans — when it
doesn't come naturally / Karen Bridson.
        p.   cm.
    ISBN 0-07-146901-X (book : alk. paper)
    1. Weight loss.   2. Reducing diets.   3. Reducing exercises.   4. Thin
people—Attitudes.   5. Women—Health and hygiene.   I. Title.

RM222.2B78136   2006
613.2'5—dc22   2006002716

This book is dedicated to those "Unskinny Chicks"
of the world who long to feel fit and fabulous
in their own skin

and

To Skinny Chick Laurie Channer, who helped
solidify the idea for this book when she admitted one day, "It's not
that I don't want a bagel on the way
to work; they smell good to me too. It's just that I
already had breakfast and I know how much
I can eat and stay the size I am."

1 2 3 4 5 6 7 8 9 10 11 12 13 14 15   DOC/DOC   0 9 8 7 6

ISBN-13: 978-0-07-146901-2
ISBN-10:   0-07-146901-X

Interior design by Think Design Group LLC

McGraw-Hill books are available at special quantity discounts to use as premiums and
sales promotions, or for use in corporate training programs. For more information, please
write to the Director of Special Sales, Professional Publishing, McGraw-Hill, Two Penn
Plaza, New York, NY 10121-2298. Or contact your local bookstore.

This book is printed on acid-free paper.

Contents

Acknowledgments

THERE ARE A NUMBER of people I'd like to thank for helping to make this book happen. First, I'd like to thank my agent, Dawn Michelle Frederick, who believed in this idea from the start and threw her own passion behind getting it published. Next, I'd like to thank my editor Michele Matrisciani, who took the idea and ran with it. Michele, I also can't thank you enough for having and fighting for the same woman-friendly, responsible vision I had for this book. You made me feel truly free to write as the former chubby chick I am.

I'd also need to thank fitness trainer Jay Blahnik, dietitian Dominique Adair, and Jake Jakicic Ph.D., for taking time out of their intensely busy schedules to provide comments and feedback about the women profiled in this book (and those who didn't make it in). I can't thank the three of you enough. If I can ever repay you for your generosity of time and expertise, please let me know.

A thank-you just doesn't seem like enough for the next batch of people I want to thank, the women who were interviewed to be in this book. To Shelley Michelle, Jillian Ann, Kim Lyons, Kristia Knowles, Alex Barker, Katie Katke, Ann Currell, Julia Beatty, Lisa Ray, Menina Fortunato, Erin Kirk, Cathy Stanbrook, Sherry Boudreau, Danielle Gamba, Monika Schnarre, Sazzy Varga, Anna Wyatt, Diana Bernier, Josie Radocchia, Naomi Jay, Carla Collins, Kristen Cheh, Ariane Resnick, and Amanda Williams—words are not enough. You ladies put up with endless questioning and probing. Just when you thought I was done with you, I'd come back for more. Thank you for your patience, your candor, and your willingness to share with the women of the world the truth about what it takes to have those fit and fabulous bodies of yours. Thank you.

To my husband, Bob, thank you for believing in me, supporting me, for encouraging me in my career, for understanding my passion for writing and women's health, and for giving me our angel boy (and for taking him so much so I can write!). I love you. Next, I must thank my rockin' monkey sister Khadijah for watching my little boy for endless hours while I worked feverishly on this book. To be truly free, a woman needs a room of one's own and you gave that to me. Thank you. Thank you also to my cofeminist-in-crime, Laura, for helping to keep my feminist feet on the ground while writing a book on women's diet and exercise. Thanks also to Dr. Susan Goldstein for getting as excited about this book as I was and helping me believe in myself. Thanks also to all the women in my life whose eyes widened at hearing about this book and reminded me of how much women want and need a book like this one. Finally, a hearty thank-you goes out to health education and behavior Ph.D. student Anna Price, who offered her trained pair of eyes to provide me with feedback on the manuscript. You rock, Anna.

Introduction

SKINNY CHICKS. WE ALL know at least a few of them. Those tiny-butt girls in their size 6 (or smaller) jeans strutting around with complete confidence. They don't have to so much as think about covering up bulging bellies or standing "just so" to minimize the girth of their thighs. Their bodies are firm, their clothes fit perfectly, and they seem *so* comfortable in their own skin that they don't even appear to give a second thought to whether their bums look big. Meanwhile, for most of the rest of the female world, the nonskinny chicks, weight and bulges and food and bathing-suit season are, to some degree or another, a problem.

I am fortunate enough to have lived in both worlds and, in essence, continue to keep one foot on both sides of the line. I often call myself a fat chick who runs every day. I used to weigh forty-five pounds more than I do now and was completely out of shape. Wearing black from head to toe and teasing my hair out as much as possible (hey, it was the 1980s) was my way of averting attention from the size of my flabby, unfit, gradually widening body. My self-esteem was in the gutter, I couldn't bear to see myself naked in the mirror, and I'd keep my head up the whole time I sat in the bathtub because looking down at the rolls of fat beneath my breasts horrified me.

I reached the point where I didn't want to get even one pound bigger. So I turned it all around. I started running in my bedroom, graduated to laps in my parents' tiny basement, and after long, hard work eventually ran my first 10K race. I started eating much more healthily, and, slowly but surely, thirty pounds came off. I was thrilled. My self-esteem soared, and I was a new woman. I discovered what it was like to have to ask a salesperson to bring a smaller pair of pants to me in the changing room, I felt the joy of being able to get up off of the ground with ease, and I caught myself looking at my naked lower body in the mirror and actually liking what I saw. Feeling good in my own skin became addictive, and I never wanted to end up back where I'd been before. And I did stick with it. Today, I've run five marathons and have made women's health and fitness (in particular, helping women on this same journey) a major focus of my life.

But my voyage into the world of health has a more recent chapter. Over the past five years I have shed another fifteen pounds off of my frame. While I was strong and fit and healthy fifteen pounds ago, I wanted to see just how fit and fabulous I could get. I studied my personal trainer manuals and serious exercise magazines for details on what the chicks with fabulous bods actually did to look the way they do. What I hadn't expected, however, was just how hard it would be. As I shed more and more weight, I was really surprised by what it took to get down another size. And the more I read about what other women with 24-inch waists did to get their fabulous forms and the more I talked to them myself, the more I marveled at just how ill-informed the rest of the world is about what these women with fabulous bodies do to look *that* great.

Most skinny chicks don't starve themselves on lettuce and cabbage-soup diets, but most of them are not blessed with naturally fast metabolisms either. Being a skinny chick is hard work, and the women I spoke to spend lots of time, energy, and thought mastering their skinny chick lifestyle. (Note: none of the women profiled in this book has had liposuction or other surgeries to help them achieve their slim frame.) Behind every pair of size-5 jeans is a woman who exercises daily and counts her calories. She is conscious of what she needs to fuel her body properly and how to feel good about herself every day, even when she slips up.

And so, this book pulls back the curtain and exposes once and for all the truth about what it takes to get fit and fabulous when it doesn't come naturally. These skinny chicks have lived in secrecy for long enough. It's time for the rest of the women of the world to know—and know in detail—what it is these women are doing and, more importantly, how we can do it too. And we can.

Now, this book is meant to empower women. It's not just another diet book telling women they need to be thin. I do think women should work to be within a healthy range for the sake of their own self-esteem, mental health, and physical health. But teaching a woman how to be a skinny chick is not necessarily the point of this book. You can use it to get a fabulous body, just like the women profiled inside. And if you think that's what you want to do, I encourage you to do it. But for most of you reading this book, I hope it provides all the information you've ever wanted to have about what it takes to be thin but healthy (finally exploring this end of the thin-fat scale) so that once and for all you may be able to make peace with *your* emotional and physical "healthy place" on the fitness spectrum.

You may look at these women who work out two or more hours a day and eat just 1,600 calories most days and say, "I will never, ever be willing to live my life that way." And that's just fine because for the most part, we are all in the same boat. We don't have the time, energy, or, in some cases, the money to spend on health foods and gym memberships. That's why I wrote this book.

We will inspect fifty secrets of skinny chicks and figure out ways to implement them into a "Skinny Chicks Plan for Real Women." The skinny chicks we meet throughout this book will inspire and encourage you to integrate many of the secrets they live by into your own life. These women were picked for this book because they have to work to keep their bodies in the fabulous shape they are in. (They are not the kind of women who have super-fast metabolisms, can eat whatever they want and not exercise, and still look the way they do.) You may not want to go to the wall with each tip the way these gals do, but know that living your life this way, to whatever degree you are comfortable, will help you to be healthier and happier. If you are at an unhealthy weight, I hope this book helps you on your way to getting fit. For you, *that* may mean a size 8 or it may mean a size 14. Skinny is, after all, a state of mind. But it's imperative that you get moving and start eating well. Too many of us today are eating far, far more than we need to and exercising far, far less than we should.

The skinny chicks in this book will show you the thin end of healthy; it's up to you to decide how close you want to get to that for your own body type and lifestyle. Or perhaps you don't have a weight problem at all and would just like to lose that last, stubborn five, ten, or fifteen pounds. The Skinny Chicks Secrets will help you do just that. Ultimately, what I hope all women will take away from this book is the information needed to choose what point on the fitness spectrum is right for them. This book is about demystifying the lives of skinny chicks. It's about choice. And, ultimately, it's about being inspired to take action.

Note: Before starting any diet or exercise regimen, consult your doctor.

PART 1

Deciding to Make That Change

Our Eating-Disordered, Unhealthy World

WOMEN ARE KILLING THEMSELVES trying to get thin. An estimated ten million North American women suffer from anorexia nervosa and bulimia. Without treatment, up to 20 percent of these women will die. That's potentially two million women each year. Eating disorders have the highest mortality rate of any psychological disease. While it is clear most women suffering from these disorders have emotional problems going deeper than a desire to be thin, it's often Western society's glorification of a gaunt frame that starts these women down this deadly path.

At the other end of the spectrum, an estimated twenty-five million American women suffer from binge eating

> I started undereating, overexercising, pushing myself too hard, and brutalizing my immune system. The amount of time I spent thinking about food and being upset with my body was insane.
>
> —Courtney Thorne-Smith, actor and star of "According to Jim" and "Ally McBeal"

disorder (BED), in which a person binges without purging or using laxatives afterward. This disorder is a contributing factor to the obesity epidemic sweeping North America. Approximately 127 million adults in the United States are overweight, 60 million are obese, and 9 million are severely obese. Obesity is the second leading cause of preventable death in the United States.

But it's not just people at these two extremes of the spectrum who have unhealthy relationships with food. It's estimated that 80 percent of North American women are dissatisfied with their appearance. And they spend $40 billion a year on diets and related products in an effort to do something about that. However, an estimated 35 percent of "normal" dieters progress to pathological dieting, or nonstop dieting, that can lead to eating disorders and cause damage to the metabolism. Of those, 20 to 25 percent go on to have partial- or full-syndrome eating disorders. And these problems are also on the rise outside of North America, where disordered eating had been less of a problem in the past. Ultimately, for far too many of us, food is not simply something we use to nourish our bodies. Food is at the core of a lot of emotional and physical pain.

Given that the stakes are as high as they are—life or death— showing women how to navigate the muddy waters of food and exercise is very serious business. While a book called *The Secrets of Skinny Chicks* may sound like yet another contribution to the eating disorder problem, that's actually the opposite of my intention. Rather, my goal for this book is to give women the information they have been denied for so long and to empower them to use this information to make the best lifestyle choices for themselves. Women are hurting themselves trying to figure out how to look like these skinny chicks. Too many of us have been flailing around in the dark, without access to the truth, trying to get the bodies we have always wanted. This book is about empowering women with information so they can make informed choices about what point on the fitness spectrum is right for them. But before we get into a discussion of diet and exercise secrets, it's critical that we take time to learn more about how this journey can go terribly, terribly wrong.

A Closer Look at Anorexia Nervosa

Anorexia nervosa is a very serious, potentially life-threatening problem that is characterized by self-starvation and excessive weight loss. According to the National Eating Disorder Association (NEDA), the four main symptoms of this disorder include the refusal to maintain a body weight at or above a minimally normal weight, an intense fear of weight gain or being "fat," feeling "fat" or overweight despite dramatic weight loss, and loss of menstrual periods.

NEDA Warning Signs of Anorexia Nervosa

* Dramatic weight loss (Two pounds lost per week is considered safe, more than that can be a problem.)
* Preoccupation with weight, food, calories, fat grams, and dieting to the extent that it interferes with your life and causes you to miss opportunities
* Refusal to eat certain foods, progressing to denying yourself whole categories of food (e.g., no carbohydrates)
* Frequent comments about feeling "fat" or overweight despite weight loss
* Anxiety about gaining weight or being "fat"
* Denial of hunger
* Development of food rituals (e.g., eating foods in certain orders, excessive chewing, rearranging food on a plate)
* Consistent excuses to avoid mealtimes or situations involving food
* Excessive, rigid exercise regimen—despite weather, fatigue, illness, or injury—in a need to burn off calories
* Withdrawal from usual friends and activities

* In general, behaviors and attitudes indicating that weight loss, dieting, and control of food are becoming *primary* concerns

As a result of the cycle of self-starvation, the body doesn't get the essential nutrients it needs to function properly. Ultimately, the body is forced to slow down all of its processes to conserve energy. This slowing down results in very serious medical problems, including an abnormally slow heart rate and blood pressure, reduction in bone density, muscle loss and weakness, severe dehydration (leading to kidney failure), fainting, weakness, hair loss, dry skin, and growth of a downy layer of hair called lanugo all over the body, which can keep body temperature regulated.

A Closer Look at Bulimia

Characterized by a cycle of bingeing and compensatory behaviors, such as self-induced vomiting designed to undo the effects of the bingeing, bulimia is a very serious, potentially life-threatening eating disorder. It involves eating large amounts of food (more than a person would typically eat at one meal), often in secret. Then, the person tries to get rid of those calories through vomiting, laxative abuse, or overexercising. According to NEDA, symptoms of bulimia include repeated alternating episodes of bingeing and purging, feeling out of control and eating beyond the point of comfortable fullness during a binge, and frequent dieting.

NEDA Warning Signs of Bulimia
* Evidence of binge-eating, including disappearance of large amounts of food in short periods of time or the existence of wrappers and containers indicating the consumption of large amounts of food

Deciding to Make That Change

* Evidence of purging behaviors, including frequent trips to the bathroom after meals, signs and/or smells of vomiting, presence of wrappers or packages of laxatives or diuretics
* Excessive, rigid exercise regimen—despite weather, fatigue, illness, or injury—in a need to burn off calories
* Unusual swelling of the cheeks or jaw area
* Calluses on the back of the hands and knuckles from self-induced vomiting
* Discoloration or staining of the teeth
* Creation of complex lifestyle schedules or rituals to make time for binge-and-purge sessions
* Withdrawal from friends and usual activities

Ultimately the recurrent binge-and-purge cycles of bulimia can take their toll on the digestive system and lead to electrolyte and chemical imbalances in the body, affecting the heart and other major organ functions. It can also lead to gastric ruptures, inflammation of the esophagus from vomiting, tooth decay and staining from stomach acid, chronic irregular bowel movements, peptic ulcers, and pancreatitis.

A Closer Look at Binge Eating Disorder (BED)

Binge eating disorder (BED), also known as compulsive overeating, is diagnosed in situations in which a person binge eats again and again but does not engage in any activities that compensate for the binge. The disorder is characterized by frequent episodes of eating large quantities of food in short periods of time. People suffering from this disorder eat when they are not hungry and eat in secret. They also can be of a normal or heavier than average weight. It's estimated that between 1 and 5 percent of the general population suffers from BED. The disorder can lead to many of the same health problems associated with clinical obesity, including high blood pressure, high cholesterol levels, heart disease, type 2 diabetes, and gallbladder disease.

NEDA Binge Eating Disorder Warning Signs

* Frequent episodes of eating large quantities of food in short periods of time
* Believing that your eating behavior is out of control
* Feeling ashamed of or disgusted by the behavior
* Eating when not hungry
* Eating in secret

Anorexia Athletica

Many of the women in this book exercise a great deal. Therefore, it's important to talk about the serious problem of compulsive exercise, also known as anorexia athletica. Even though anorexia athletica is not recognized as an official medical diagnosis, according to the National Eating Disorder Information Centre (NEDIC) this term is being used more and more within the health-care community to identify people with a preoccupation with food and weight who exercise compulsively in an attempt to gain a sense of power, control, and self-respect.

Symptoms of Anorexia Athletica (NEDIC)

* Exercising beyond the requirements for good health, which could mean burning more than 3,500 calories a week from exercise (Note: Burning more than this number of calories per week can be healthy for some people, but since this does go beyond the requirements for good health, it can also be a warning sign.)
* Being fanatical about weight and diet

* Stealing time from work, school, and relationships to exercise
* Focusing on challenge and forgetting that physical activity can be fun
* Defining self-worth in terms of performance
* Rarely or never being satisfied with athletic achievements
* Always pushing on to the next challenge
* Justifying excessive behavior by defining yourself as an athlete or insisting that your behavior is healthy

Experts say exercising to burn up to 3,500 calories per week is perfectly healthy. Going beyond that can be healthy too, as long as it doesn't become an obsession that negatively affects your job, relationships, and other life commitments.

"Flirting" with Eating Disorders

Most of us do not suffer from eating disorders, and most of us never will. But the millions of women around the world who end up suffering from disordered eating at both ends of the spectrum probably thought it wouldn't happen to them either. And in this weight-conscious, superficial world, where thinking about what you eat becomes essential to some degree, there is a risk of starting down a slippery slope. NEDA says the following can be an indication of what it called "disordered eating":

* Do you avoid eating meals or snacks when you are around other people?
* Do you constantly calculate numbers of fat grams and calories?
* Do you weigh yourself often and find yourself obsessed with the number on the scale?

* Do you exercise because you feel like you have to, not because you want to?
* Are you afraid of gaining weight?
* Do you ever feel out of control when you are eating?
* Do your eating patterns include extreme dieting, preferences for certain foods, withdrawn or ritualized behavior at mealtime, or secretive bingeing?
* Has weight loss, dieting, and/or control of food become one of your major concerns?
* Do you feel ashamed, disgusted, or guilty after eating?
* Do you worry about the weight, shape, or size of your body?
* Do you feel like your identity and value is based on how you look or how much you weigh?

NEDA says if you answer "yes" to any of these questions, you could be dealing with disordered eating. These attitudes and behaviors can take their toll on your mental and physical well-being, so if you suspect that's the case with you, you should talk to your doctor, a counselor, or a family member or friend about possibly getting some help. Being conscious about diet and exercise can be very healthy, but the line between what's healthy and what's not is very fine.

A Closer Look at Obesity

For the last twenty years doctors and scientists have noticed an alarming increase in obesity in North America. Overweight is defined by a Body Mass Index (BMI) of 25 or more, obesity is 30 or more, and severe obesity is 40 or more. The American Obesity Association says obesity is a complex, chronic disease involving environmental (social and cultural), genetic, physiologic, metabolic, behavioral, and psychological components.

Health and Social Effect of Obesity (Source: American Obesity Association)

* Obesity increases the risk of illness from approximately thirty serious medical conditions.
* Obesity is associated with increases in deaths from all natural causes.
* Onset of obesity-related diseases, such as type 2 diabetes, is being reported in children and adolescents with obesity.
* Individuals with obesity are at higher risk for impaired mobility.
* Overweight or obese individuals experience social stigmatization and discrimination in employment and academic situations.

Our "Super-Sized" World

Eating disorders are so rampant in our society partially because our eating world has become so disordered. Alongside technological advances came a two-headed monster: less and less need for or opportunity to exercise and faster, less nutritious, and more fattening take-out "meals." We are less active than ever before and eating worse than ever. Is it any surprise, then, that we're struggling with weight? Our dinner plates are larger than they've ever been, our portions are out of control, and the caloric content of many foods bought on the run are astronomical.

According to the book *Fast Food Nation*, by Eric Schlosser, Americans spent just $6 billion on fast food in 1970. In 2001, that number had jumped to $110 billion. That's more than is spent on higher education, personal computers, computer software, or new cars. A generation ago, Schlosser says, 75 percent of the money used to buy food was spent on home meals. Today half is spent on restaurants. The typical American today consumes three hamburgers and four orders of french fries each week. Most Americans eat between 10 to 30 percent more than they need to. And it's a growing problem outside of North America as well.

According to Schlosser, between 1984 and 1993 the number of fast-food restaurants nearly doubled in Great Britain, as did obesity rates. Even in China, the proportion of overweight teenagers doubled during the 1990s. And, sadly, in many developing nations obesity coexists with malnutrition. The American Obesity Association calls the problem of obesity a global epidemic.

My Friend's Story

As a closing note to this chapter on how concern about diet and exercise can go horribly wrong, I'd like to share a story about my friend Nina, who suffered from bulimia. At twenty-one years old, Nina was a brilliantly talented artist studying to become a medical illustrator at a prestigious art school. She was beautiful, she was funny, and she was the Gin Rummy champion of our dorm house. We had suspected Nina had an eating disorder, but because she wasn't thin enough to ring any serious alarm bells, we expressed concern but let her parents take care of it.

Not long after her parents pulled her out of school to get help for her bulimia, Nina collapsed while running on their treadmill. After three years of bingeing and purging, her heart was damaged and just stopped. When her father found her, he did CPR and managed to bring her back to life. She was rushed to the hospital and put on life support. Later, she "progressed" from unconsciousness into a catatonic state. From there, she lay for months in a hospital bed, flailing her arms and legs like a baby and relearning how to walk and talk. After months and months of rehabilitation, Nina did learn how to walk and talk again, but she's not the same Nina. I would estimate her mental age at about seven years old.

She can no longer draw, she doesn't remember her friends, and she drags her left leg when she walks. The only good thing is that she's gained about fifty pounds and seems completely uninterested in her weight or body image. It's too late for much to be done for Nina. I only hope that her story will help compel others to keep their diet and exercise habits healthy and to get help immediately if things start to go off the rails.

Resources to Help with Eating Disorders

The National Eating Disorders Association, nationaleatingdisorders.org, 800-931-2237

The American Anorexia Bulimia Association, 212-575-6200

The American Psychological Association, http://helping.apa.org

The National Women's Health Information Center, http:// womenshealth.gov, 800-994-9662

Staying on the Healthy Track

Most of us will not develop an eating disorder. But in this toxic environment of ours, teeming with fast foods and a trend toward inactivity, it can be all too easy to fall into unhealthy lifestyles, whether it be eating too much or not enough. We need to learn about moderation. That's a trick the skinny chicks know by heart. Food is our friend. We simply need to learn how to have a healthy relationship with the things we put into our bodies for nourishment. Throughout this book we will learn more about how to do just that.

Body Image, Self-Esteem, and Loving Yourself

YOU ARE STANDING IN a changing room in the bathing suit section of your local department store. You've just snapped on one of the few bathing suits you could find that seemed to have figure-flattering potential. With fluorescent lights blazing, you face a wall of mirrors that allows views of every angle. Taking a deep breath, you finally allow your eyes to take a good hard look at your reflection. What do you see? How do you feel about what you see? If you are like most women, your eyes will go right to your midsection: waist, hips, butt, and thighs. Critique of every pucker, dimple, bulge, and curve will likely follow. Anxiety, frustration, and sadness may then seep in.

To lose confidence in one's body is to lose confidence in oneself.

—Simone De Beauvoir, author of *The Second Sex*

Depends on the day, like a mood body ring.

—Skinny Chick and comedian Carla Collins, on the state of her body image and self-esteem

While bathing suit season can provide the opportunity for this heightened, intense test of our self-esteem and body image (which are, sadly, entwined for so many women), the effects of a lowered sense of self and the ability to love your body are felt by many women each and every day. Self-esteem problems are rampant among women and an estimated 80 percent of us suffer from poor body image. Ultimately women with low self-esteem and poor body image do not believe that they are as smart, funny, beautiful, talented, capable, and sexy as they really are. The tragedy of this is that, as a result, women with low self-concept may turn away from or miss out on opportunities (both personal and professional), allow themselves to be treated poorly, and lead lives that are in many ways less fulfilling than they deserve.

When looking at the commonalities of the skinny chicks, whom we will meet in the coming chapters, I first realized that these women don't hate themselves. They don't throw fits in the dressing room or judge their entire beings on the size of the jeans they wear that month. In fact, they think so much of themselves that they spend time taking care of themselves, which they do first and foremost. They make time for exercise and nutrition and treat themselves like princesses. They put themselves before other mundane things in life, which so many of us don't do. But we are worth it, no matter if the bathing suit fits or not.

So what's to be done about this epidemic of poor self-concept? While problems of this nature at the extreme end of severity require nothing less than professional guidance, which goes beyond the authority of this book, I believe by implementing, to some degree, the secrets described in this book, most women can learn to love themselves, cellulite and all, a whole lot more.

Body Image, Self-Esteem, and Self-Concept

What exactly are we talking about when we use these terms? First, *body image* is the picture you have in your mind of your size, shape, and general appearance and how you think and feel about it. That image can be positive or negative. On the other hand, *self-esteem* refers to how you like and regard yourself in general. Unfortunately, for many women body image and self-esteem are so closely related that a negative body image steadily erodes the core of their self-esteem. For many of us, if we do not like our bodies, we don't like ourselves. While ideally these two things should remain separate—your self-esteem should *not* be dictated by your body image—because they so often are intertwined, I will refer to them collectively as *self-concept.*

How we feel about our bodies and ourselves is something that begins to form in childhood, when we first look around to others to get a sense of ourselves and how we fit into the world. Unfortunately, many children, particularly girls, are bombarded early in life by negative feedback and images that result in their thinking less of themselves than they should. Everything from being told you were fat as a child, to being abused, to seeing glorified pictures of unrealistically thin models on television or in print can contribute to this poor self-concept. We naturally compare ourselves to each other and are often overly critical of ourselves when we focus on what we look like. Ultimately, this self-criticism can make women underestimate their power and value. And it can be a vicious cycle, with low self-concept preventing us from starting to participate in activities that can change the way we feel about ourselves. This includes embarking on a new healthy lifestyle.

Making That Change

A lowered self-concept may have you believing that you will never love your body, feel sexy in your own skin, or like what you see when you stand naked in front of the mirror. It can make you think being fit and fabulous is out of your reach, so you shouldn't even bother trying. So how do you break through this negativity to do something about it? And how can a book focused on skinny chicks possibly help with someone's self-concept? Well, for starters, virtually all of the skinny chicks profiled in this book report having a very high self-esteem and very positive body image. And because they are the experts and we're trying to learn from their example here, it's worth taking a look at how they have achieved this.

While many of the girls profiled admitted they have at different times of their lives felt lowered levels of self-concept, most report that having taken control of their bodies with exercise and healthy eating has had an enormously positive effect on how they feel about themselves. They feel strong, healthy, and powerful. While they are not all perfectly happy with every little thing about their bodies, generally they report feeling pretty darn good about themselves. And science supports this finding. A number of studies have shown exercise increases emotional stability, self-confidence, self-sufficiency, persistence, self-esteem, and optimism.

So now we are presented with a chicken-and-egg scenario. How do you get to this improved self-concept that comes with taking control of your health when poor self-concept is what's standing in the way of your getting started? Well, this is where you've got to have a little talk with that part of yourself that *does* love *you*. Everyone has that little voice deep inside that says you are fabulous. You've just got to focus on it, cultivate it, and help it be heard. Then, you've got to "fake it until you make it." Just get started. This approach is also supported by what science tells us.

Studies have actually shown that self-esteem programs, focused on trying to improve people's self-esteem through exercises and counseling, actually don't work. Dr. Harold Stevenson, professor of psychology at the University of Michigan, says self-esteem comes from accomplishments, not the other way around. "Self-esteem often comes from an awareness that the requirements of a sought-after goal have been mastered," he says. So getting started with a healthy new life may be the best way to turn your self-esteem around.

I hope I've made a compelling enough case here for just what wonderful improvements to your self-concept can be found through taking control of your health. You need to focus on the benefits of making this change in your life and use that leverage to get yourself started. The benefits of living a healthier life will start to show themselves almost immediately, which should help you to stay on track once your initial enthusiasm begins to wane and when you slip up from time to time along the way.

How Exercise Changed My Self-Concept

I started running fifteen years ago because I was more than thirty pounds overweight and my self-esteem and body image were in the toilet. My only real goal at that time was to shrink my butt down to a size so that I could stop being embarrassed by it and covering it under loose, dark clothing. And while this ultimately did happen, what I hadn't expected was the incredible improvements to my self-concept. I used to be the kind of woman who couldn't leave the house without makeup on and my hair done. I took particular care to wear clothing that hid my body, choosing various shades of black most often. Ultimately, I was in hiding. I was hiding behind the makeup and hair and cloaks of black.

But as I waded further and further into a healthy lifestyle, running a few times a week and eating much, much more healthfully than I had previously, the pounds started to drop off and my ability to love myself blossomed. And my new habits didn't just result in my looking at myself in the mirror and actually liking what I saw—even when I was only wearing my panties, although that was a huge part of it. Beyond that, I had grown to be so proud of myself for taking control of my life and making changes. I felt strong and empowered. I began running fun runs around town and would cross the finish lines with my head held high and my shoulders back, and I'd actually strut around for the rest of the day. It was through running those first "races" that I started to notice I was changing in other ways as well.

I began to appreciate the way my face looked when it was flushed red from exercise, which was much better than the fake look of blusher! Because sweat caused my eye makeup to run down my face, I began to run without makeup. And later, looking at myself in the mirror and seeing the real Karen looking back (someone I hadn't seen since childhood), I realized that I was actually pretty, sans cosmetics. I remember crossing the finish line of my first marathon and looking down at my thighs, which were still very fleshy but strong as hell and bending down to kiss each one. I thanked them for letting me finish that race. I saluted them, cellulite and all. Later I tattooed my first marathon time on my bikini line so that every time I got naked I'd be reminded of just how fabulous my body is because it is strong and capable and beautiful.

Ultimately my body image and self-esteem went through the roof, which fueled me further and helped me maintain the exercise and eating habits I had developed. (There's that chicken-and-egg thing again!) And while I still have my moments when I think my butt is too big (something most women will likely never lose), most of the time I look at my body and like what I see. Ultimately that has led to my feeling a whole lot more confident in general. This change in self-concept that comes with a healthy lifestyle is in large part what has made me positively evangelical about exercise. I want to convert all the women I can into exercisers because so many women suffer needlessly from poor self-concept. Spread the word: taking control of your body can mean taking control of your mind. And with that, beautiful things can happen.

Skinny Is a State of Mind: What's Right for You?

ONE OF MY PET peeves is seeing skinny chicks with shriveled, barely there calf muscles. Even when they are propped up atop stiletto heels (which causes these muscles to flex), these naturally thin gals can't hide the fact that they don't even walk around much on a regular basis. That's the only way, I figure, that these muscles could have shrunken from view almost completely: near total inactivity. While not being able to see a muscle that should by all rights be visible is annoying to me as a fitness coach and avid exerciser, what is more irksome is that, because these women are thin, people with untrained eyes mistakenly think they are healthy.

I have to work very hard to look the way I do. I want the girls out there to know that.

—Rock singer Gwen Stefani

It's my job as an actress to look good. Women should just relax and not worry about it.

—Actor Sarah Michelle Gellar

Unfortunately, women who are a little "chubby" by society's standards are immediately pegged as unhealthy when they may in fact be nearly at peak physical health. I have often reflected on this at the finish line of marathons when I see women who are by no means thin finishing well ahead of people who *look* like they are more fit. The reality is that these heavier women have hearts and lungs and muscles of steel. *And* they enjoy their food too. While their health, in some cases, may stand to be improved if they cut back on calories a bit and get their weight down some, ultimately these women are a testament to the fact that you can't necessarily judge someone's level of health by their girth—or lack thereof. Plenty of naturally skinny chicks make terrible food choices, never exercise, and do all sorts of other things that make them unhealthy; yet because our society equates thinness with beauty and, therefore, to some extent, with health, they are initially deemed healthy. That's not to say that women who are at the thin end of healthy can't be visions of health too. They absolutely can, as we'll see later in this book. But it's important to remember, too, that a woman can be just as fit and fabulous in size 12 or 14 jeans as she can be in a size 4. It's about being and feeling strong and healthy. It's about feeling good in your own skin and choosing what is right for you.

Finding Your Healthy Weight

The universally accepted standard for determining a healthy weight range is known as the Body Mass Index, or BMI. A BMI reading of 18.5 up to 24.9 is considered healthy. Go below that and you are in the low category, moving into an area that can lead to health problems. Go above that range and you move into the overweight category. For most people, there is a healthy weight range of as much as forty pounds. This leaves a pretty broad definition of what's healthy. Now, the BMI is not a diagnostic tool on its own, therefore it can't be used independently to determine if a person is healthy or not. It's also been criticized for not accounting for muscle mass; the BMI says a bodybuilder with nearly no body fat is overweight if their weight goes above a certain level. But for the average person, the BMI does provide a good starting point for figuring out what range is a healthy range. Take a good look at Figure 3.1 and find your healthy range.

After you've found your healthy weight range on the BMI, it's a good idea to measure your body fat percentage or body density (BD). This will tell you how much of your body is

FIGURE 3.1 Body Mass Index

	Weight (Pounds)															
	100	110	120	130	140	150	160	170	180	190	200	210	220	230	240	250
5'0"	20	21	23	25	27	29	31	33	35	37	39	41	43	45	47	49
5'1"	19	21	23	25	26	28	30	32	34	36	38	40	42	43	45	47
5'2"	18	20	22	24	26	27	29	31	33	35	37	38	40	42	44	46
5'3"	18	19	21	23	25	27	28	30	32	34	35	37	39	41	43	44
5'4"	17	19	21	22	24	26	27	29	31	33	34	36	38	39	41	43
5'5"	17	18	20	22	23	25	27	28	30	32	33	35	37	38	40	42
5'6"	16	18	19	21	23	24	26	27	29	31	32	34	36	37	39	40
5'7"	16	17	19	20	22	23	25	27	28	30	31	33	34	36	38	39
5'8"	15	17	18	20	21	23	24	26	27	29	30	32	33	35	36	38
5'9"	15	16	18	19	21	22	24	25	27	28	30	31	32	34	35	37
5'10"	14	16	17	19	20	22	23	24	26	27	29	30	32	33	34	36
5'11"	14	15	17	18	20	21	22	24	25	26	27	28	30	32	33	35
6'0"	14	15	16	18	19	20	22	23	24	26	27	28	30	31	33	34
6'1"	13	15	16	17	18	20	21	22	24	25	26	28	29	30	32	33
6'2"	13	14	15	17	18	19	21	22	23	24	26	27	28	30	31	32
6'3"	12	14	15	16	17	19	20	21	22	24	25	26	27	29	30	31
6'4"	12	13	15	16	17	18	19	21	22	23	24	26	27	28	29	30

Height

BMI Interpretation

Under 18.5	Underweight
18.5–24	Normal
25–29	Overweight
30 and above	Obese

made up of muscle and bone and how much is fat. You can be in a healthy weight range but still have an unhealthy percentage of body fat or a body composition that can be improved. However, measuring body fat percentage or BD is a lot more difficult than using the BMI. Your body fat percentage can be measured in a number of ways. The two most effective means, *hydrostatic weighing* (done in a pool) and a *DEXA body scanner*, both require expensive, hard-to-find equipment.

However, other methods exist, including using fat calipers, standing on a body fat scale which sends electric currents through the lower half of your body (the current moves more slowly through muscle and faster through fat), or using body measurements and calculations. I recommend having a personal trainer at a local fitness club or community center test your body fat percentage via equations and, perhaps, fat calipers. Purchasing a body fat percentage scale is another option, but the reliability of some of these products is uncertain. Or, you can do a calculation to determine your body fat percentage or BD. The calculation is as follows:

BD for women = 1.168297 − (0.002824 × abdomen circumference measurement in cm) + (0.0000122098 × abdomen circumference in cm, to the power of two) − (0.000733128 × hips circumference in cm) + (0.000510477 × height in cm) − (0.000216161 × age)

Estimating Body Fat from Circumference Measures, Personal Trainer Manual: The American Council on Exercise, 1996.

Next:

Percentage of body fat = (495/BD) − 450

* Abdominal measurement should be taken at exactly your belly button.
* Hips measurement should be taken at the widest point of your hips.

* Use a cloth or fiberglass, not elastic, measurement tape and pull the tape only tight enough to hold it in place and not tight enough to make an indentation in the skin.

The following are some specific categories of body fat percentage that are used to describe the women in this book and that you can use to determine your range of body fat health as well.

General Body-Fat Classification Categories		
CLASSIFICATION	WOMEN (% BODY FAT)	MEN (% BODY FAT)
Essential fat	10–13%	2–5%
Athletes	14–20%	6–13%
Fitness	21–24%	14–17%
Healthy	25–31%	18–24%
Obese	32% and higher	25% and higher

Personal Trainer Manual, American Council on Exercise, 1997.

A State of Mind

So according to the BMI, there's a forty-pound range that's healthy for you. That's a pretty big range. So are you only "skinny" if you're at the low end of this range? Hardly. Being fit and fabulous is truly a state of mind. I know women at the high end of their range who work out regularly, eat really well, and feel great in their skin. They are proud of and comfortable in their bodies. They feel sexy and fit and strong. They have embraced their womanly curves and for them, a size 14 is skinny, thank you very much.

On the other hand, I know women at the other end of the spectrum who are quite thin and still focus on the size of their thighs. By many other people's standards these women are perfectly proportioned. But because they don't believe it, it's simply not true. Nothing *is*; it's only how you *perceive it to be*. That's why so much of this journey into a healthy lifestyle is about what's going on above your neck not below your waist. To feel fit and fabulous, no matter how healthy you may truly be, you have to believe it. It's all a state of mind. That said, you won't be able to convince yourself that you are fit and fabulous if you truly feel heavy and unhealthy and have been inactive. You can be fit and fabulous at any healthy weight as long as you are eating well and exercising regularly. So learn what your healthy range is, take steps to get there if you aren't already, then dance naked in your room every night until you believe it!

Factors Affecting Your Weight

Infants recognize themselves in the mirror at about the age of two. Just a few years later, female children start to dislike what they see in that mirror. A British study conducted in 2003 reported that girls are dieting from as young as nine years old. This is a tragedy. It would be nice if we could not care about what we eat or never force ourselves to get off the couch. But while a society in which children are putting themselves on diets is just not healthy emotionally or physically, neither is a life of sloth and gluttony. So this healthy body issue is a fight we're going to have to face one way or the other.

That said, we need to keep some factors in mind while making our way down the road to a healthy lifestyle. First, there is something called a *fat gene*, known to scientists as HOB1, that gives people a genetic tendency toward obesity. I believe I have it, and scientists have proven many other people do, too. If you are one, having this gene will affect what weight you can get down to easily. However, it's important to remember that scientists stress there are few obese people in places like rural China, even though the obesity gene exists there also. Only in toxic food environments, where bad food is plentiful, does the obesity gene show its strength.

That fat gene affects us through our metabolism, or the rate at which we burn energy. Everyone has a different metabolism, which largely accounts for the range of caloric intakes you'll see in the skinny chick profiles. Your metabolism can be affected by a number of factors, from thyroid disorders, to postpregnancy problems related to thyroid, to your age, to your dieting history. As you age, your metabolism slows. If you've dieted in extreme ways in the past, your metabolism may have slowed to protect your body. Ultimately, it's up to you to find out by trial and error where your metabolism is. See how much food and exercise you need to be the size you want to be. While medication can help with thyroid problems and you can speed up your metabolism with a healthy lifestyle if it's been unhealthy in the past, age will slow your metabolism no matter what you do. Exercise and good nutrition can help a great deal with this, but ultimately, you need to consider your age when deciding what weight is ideal for you.

Next, your particular body type may dictate that you can only get a certain body part down so far before it's a problem. I remember reading actress Courtney Cox Arquette saying that to get her butt down to the size she liked she had to let her face get gaunt. Everyone has a different body. You may always have a bigger butt proportionally than you would like, but that may just be a fact of life that you've got to accept. What's important is that you get your body into a healthy weight and body fat percentage range. And it's important to remember, too, that a study at Virginia Tech University found stress may play a role in increasing storage of body fat in the abdominal area and can actually lead to increased hunger. So stop stressing about your bod and learn to love it. Work it and feed it right, but love it.

It's also important to remember that many women have a warped sense of what size they are. In fact, studies have shown that up to 80 percent of women overestimate their size. (In it's severe form, this is a serious psychological problem known as *body dysmorphia* or, in males who are obsessed with getting bigger muscles, *muscle dysmorphia*.) These conditions can be dangerous because you may not recognize it when you have reached a very healthy weight. This is part of why objective methods of judging your size and weight, like BMI and body fat percentage, can be critical tools as you move down the road toward that healthy body.

Making the Best Use of the Secrets of Skinny Chicks

The next section of this book presents some pretty hard-core examples of how to get your body into tip-top shape. Some of these women have even pushed the envelope, moving into the low category of BMI, meaning they must not lose any more weight or they could start to see some negative health repercussions. While these particular girls are still healthy, they remain conscious that they can't push further. Nor do they want to. I'm presenting them in this book because they have the bodies of the typical Hollywood starlet, and I want you to know the truth about what it takes to look that way.

For some women, this may be the body type you are after. If so, go ahead, follow the diet and exercise regimes of these women and fine-tune things until you get down to your goal weight. But for most of the women reading this book, you'll probably want to take a closer look at the regimes of the women with a little more meat on their bones. These women, too, are all very fit, but their lifestyles are more realistic. Still, I encourage you to only use their health regimes as information with which to make a decision about just how much exercise and what diet decisions are right for you.

Remember, thin women are thinner than they've ever been before. The average model's weight is 23 percent lower than the average woman, while twenty years ago it was only 8 percent lower. Some of the women in this book work out more than two hours a day. If you know that your lifestyle will never allow for this, this is your opportunity to make peace with the fact that you will likely never get down to the size 2 pants that some of these girls wear. Let the knowledge of the details of their diet and exercise regimes empower you to make that informed decision.

Perhaps even working out every day isn't in the cards either. Then adjust your expectations accordingly. And if you find that eating just 1,400 or 1,600 calories a day is just too restrictive over the long haul, even with making smart, bulky food choices, then embrace that fact as well, accept it, and honor your decision to let go of the unrealistic goals you may have set for yourself while on previous diets. This book is a tool for you to use to finally, once and for all, discover the diet and exercise regime that's right for you, using the real tricks of the trade, and ultimately loving yourself at your best—whatever that means to you!

PART 2

The Secrets Unveiled

Meet the Skinny Chicks

AT LAST YOU MEET the skinny chicks. The following are profiles of twenty-one women who all have the fit and fabulous bods so many women covet. They range in size and shape, some are cover girls and fitness models, others are just "real chicks" with "real" jobs, but all of them are healthy, strong, and feel great in their favorite jeans. While some of these women, thanks to genetics, come by slimmer frames more easily than others, all of these gals work hard at eating well and exercising often.

These women can't be just written off as those who can eat anything they want, sit on their butts, and still stay slim. In researching this book, I expected to come

> **People tell me all the time how lucky I am to be slim. LUCKY?! It's work, but it's worth it.**
>
> —Skinny Chick Diana Bernier

across more women like that, but I came across few (they weren't right for this book because I only wanted women who had to work at it). The truth is, based on my search for women to profile, most skinny chicks actually do live a life that is supportive of having a slim frame, meaning most of them work at it through appropriate food intake and exercise. So, here we are; take a good, hard look at the details of food and exercise involved in each girl's life. There's a lot to learn from these women.

Each profile is concluded with comments from John Jakicic, Ph.D., chair of the Department of Health and Physical Activity and director of the Physical Activity and Weight Management Research Center at the University of Pittsburgh, in Pittsburgh, Pennsylvania; award-winning and internationally renowned fitness trainer Jay Blahnik; and registered dietitian and women's health expert Dominique Adair.

PROFILE (1) Shelley Michelle

Claim to fame: She was Julia Roberts's body double in the film *Pretty Woman* and has doubled for hundreds of other Hollywood stars, including Kim Basinger and Madonna.

Age: 37 years

Height: 5' 8"

Weight: 122–125 pounds

Dress size: 8

Measurements: 36" bust, 26" waist, 34" hips

Body mass index: 19 (in "normal" range)

Body fat percentage: Estimated at 16–19 percent (in "athlete" range)

Hometown: Los Angeles

Children: One

Daily calorie intake: 1,549

Daily calorie expenditure from exercise: Up to 750

Shelley's Typical Daily Menu

Breakfast: 1 cup of low-fat yogurt (155 calories) with 1 tablespoon of granola (25 calories) and one sliced medium apple (80 calories) Total: 260 calories

Snack: One protein bar, such as Apex or Herbalife (150 calories) Total: 150 calories

Lunch: 2 ounces of chicken, grilled or slow-roasted, without bone or skin, (90 calories) with vegetables (150 calories) Total: 240 calories

Snack: One protein bar (150 calories) Total: 150 calories

Snack: One protein bar (150 calories) Total: 150 calories

Dinner: 3 ounces of skinless chicken (160 calories) with 2 tablespoons of low-fat mayonnaise (70 calories) combined with a vegetable dish (150 calories) cooked in 1 tablespoon of olive oil (119 calories) and a green salad with light vinaigrette dressing (100 calories) Total: 599 calories

Total daily calories: 1,549

Uncovered! Secret Number 1

Burn all the calories you eat.

Sample Weekly Workout

Monday: 1 hour lower-body strength training (200 calories burned), 1½ hours of circuit training (500 calories burned)

Tuesday: 1 hour upper-body strength training (200 calories burned), 1½ hours of martial arts (500 calories burned)

Wednesday: 1 hour core training with stability ball (210 calories burned), 2-hour ballet class (400 calories burned)

Thursday: 2 hours of yoga (400 calories burned), 1 hour of full-body circuit training (350 calories burned)

Friday: 1 hour of Pilates (210 calories burned), 1½ hours of full-body weight training (400 calories burned)

Saturday: 1 hour of cardio of choice (450 calories burned), 1½ hours of core strengthening, abs, hips, and back (150 calories burned)

Sunday: Rest

Uncovered! Secret Number 2

Add weight training to your regime.

Shelley's Fitness Facts

Food philosophy: I believe in moderation. Everything in moderation. If I want to have a dessert, I will go ahead and do it—I just won't do it every day.

Foods avoided: Pasta, bread, potatoes, and rice

Supplements taken: Flaxseed oil used on salads and pregnancy vitamins

Total daily water intake: I'm constantly drinking all day—a minimum of eight 8-ounce glasses.

Cheating: I still will have some pasta or something bad like that once every couple of months if I am really feeling like it.

Approach to holidays/temptations: I try to combine foods wisely (proteins and healthy carbohydrates) and keep things proportional.

Advice to others: On holidays, don't stuff yourself. Go ahead and eat what you want to eat but don't overdo it. And in the following few weeks, make sure you stay away from those simple carbs and eat lots of veggies to make up for it.

What the Experts Think of Shelley's Regimen

Dr. John Jakicic says: Shelley appears to be in a healthy state based on BMI and physical activity that is reported. She should be careful not to reduce lower than a BMI of 19.

Personal trainer Jay Blahnik says: Her program seems well rounded and very complete.

Registered dietitian Dominique Adair says: Shelley should eat more real food and fewer substitutes, like protein bars, and she should get more fruits and vegetables.

Claim to fame: Actor and former Ford Supermodel of the World, former star on "The Bold and the Beautiful," and appeared on "The King of Queens" and "Charmed" television shows

Age: 34 years

Height: 6' 1¾"

Weight: 150 pounds

Dress size: 8

Measurements: 36" bust, 26" waist, 36" hips

Body mass index: 20.5 (in "normal" range)

Body fat percentage: Estimated at 21 percent (in "fitness" range)

Hometown: Toronto and Los Angeles

Children: None

Daily calorie intake: 1,698

Daily calorie expenditure from exercise: Up to 320–600

Monika's Typical Daily Menu

Breakfast: One protein shake consisting of 1 cup of soy milk (150 calories), 1 ounce protein powder (115 calories), 1 tablespoon of peanut butter (95 calories), one banana (92 calories), and 1 tablespoon of flaxseed powder (75 calories) Total: 527 calories

Snack: One medium apple (80 calories) Total: 80 calories

Lunch: Spinach, mushroom, and cheese omelet made from four egg whites (66 calories), ½ cup of fresh spinach (39 calories), two fresh mushrooms (10 calories), two slices soy cheese (70 calories), and 1 tablespoon of olive oil (119 calories) Total: 304 calories

Snack: One handful of almonds (204 calories) Total: 204 calories

Rejoice in fresh new tastes.

Dinner: 5 ounces of skinless, boneless roasted chicken (277 calories) with salad (14 calories) mixed with 1 tablespoon (or 2 ounces) goat cheese (152 calories) and 1 tablespoon of nuts (40 calories) and drizzled with a homemade dressing of balsamic vinegar, 1 teaspoon olive oil, and blueberry jam (100 calories) Total: 583 calories

Total daily calories: 1,698

Sample Weekly Workout

Monday: Run 4 miles (600 calories burned)

Tuesday: 90 minutes of power/flow yoga (320 calories burned)

Wednesday: Run 4 miles (600 calories burned)

Thursday: 90 minutes of power/flow yoga (320 calories burned)

Friday: Run 4 miles (600 calories burned)

Saturday: 90 minutes of power/flow yoga (320 calories burned)

Sunday: Run 4 miles (600 calories burned)

Monika's Fitness Facts

Food philosophy: Shop only in the outer perimeter of the grocery store. No deep-fried food and keep it as organic as possible.

Total daily water intake: 2 liters

Cheating: On weekends, chocolate and popcorn

Approach to holidays/temptations: Let loose!

Advice to others: Learn to love your body, flaws and all. Remember that everyone cheats on their eating plan. Don't use the word *diet*. Learn that eating healthy is a lifestyle. Treating your body well will not only lengthen your life but make it more enjoyable. Love the body that you were given and treat it with the utmost respect.

Stop seeing it as "dieting."

Sticking to the plan: I stick to my plan by remembering how terrible I feel when I eat junk.

Exercise philosophy: Every day it's important to get some form of exercise. I don't feel great unless I have exercised that day.

What the Experts Think of Monika's Regimen

Dr. John Jakicic says: Monika appears to be healthy based on BMI and exercise behaviors. I like her philosophy of being active at some level every day.

Personal trainer Jay Blahnik says: Appears to be healthy based on BMI and exercise behaviors. I like her philosophy of being active at some level every day.

Registered dietitian Dominique Adair says: Monika has a terrific attitude toward food.

PROFILE 3 Kim Lyons

Claim to fame: A well-known fitness model and competitor, named Ms. Galaxy 2000 in Physique and Overall Competition, has a B.S. in human development and nutrition

Age: 31 years

Height: 5′ 3″

Weight: 117 pounds

Dress size: 2

Measurements: 34″ bust, 25″ waist, 36″ hips

Body mass index: 20.7 (in "normal" range)

Body fat percentage: 9 percent during competitions, 13–15 percent off season (in "competitive athlete" range)

Hometown: Hermosa Beach

Children: None

Daily calorie intake: 1,390

Daily calorie expenditure from exercise: Up to 550–950

Kim's Typical Daily Menu

9 A.M.: 1 cup slow-cooked oatmeal (145 calories) topped with 1 teaspoon of regular jam (25 calories) Total: 170 calories

11 A.M.: Egg white veggie omelet made from 6 egg whites (99 calories) with unlimited vegetables (50 calories) and one slice of fat-free cheese (31 calories) Total: 180 calories

2 P.M.: One skinless chicken breast (280 calories) with 1 cup of brown rice (200 calories) Total: 480 calories

5 P.M.: 3 ounces flank steak (175 calories) with vegetables (180 calories) Total: 355 calories

8 P.M.: 1 cup of fat-free cottage cheese (150 calories) Total: 150 calories

Before bed: 1 cup of sugar-free hot chocolate (55 calories) Total: 55 calories

Total daily calories: 1,390

Sample Weekly Workout

Monday: Run 20–40 minutes (200–400 calories burned), biceps weight exercises (60 calories burned), 1 hour body-sculpting class (350 calories burned), 20 minutes walking (100 calories burned)

Tuesday: 45 minutes to 1 hour weight-training workout: triceps, legs, buttocks, and abs (300–350 calories burned)

Wednesday: 20–40 minute hike (120–240 calories burned), 45 minutes to 1 hour weight-training workout: shoulders, legs, and abs (300–350 calories burned), 20-minute run (200 calories burned)

Thursday: Rest

Friday: 20–40 minutes Rollerblading (240–480 calories burned), 45 minutes to 1 hour weight-training workout: chest, legs, abs, and buttocks (300–350 calories burned), 20 minutes Rollerblading (240 calories burned)

Saturday: 20–40 minutes running (200–400 calories burned); 45 minutes to 1 hour weight-training workout: back, legs, buttocks, and abs (300–350 calories burned); 20 minutes biking (150 calories burned)

Sunday: Rest

Uncovered! Secret Number 5

Exercise more days than not.

Kim's Fitness Facts

Food philosophy: If God didn't make it, don't eat it.

Supplements taken: Nitrotech protein powder, Glutamine, Multi Vitamin pack, zinc, Juice Plus

Total daily water intake: 1 gallon

Uncovered! Secret Number 6

Drink water like there's no tomorrow.

Approach to holidays/temptations: Eat healthy on your own, splurge a LITTLE at special events.

Sticking to the plan: I make it a top priority and schedule it into my daily routine. I allow myself to take breaks when I need them, but over all I have just learned that being in shape is the greatest feeling and well worth the work!

Exercise philosophy: Commitment is everything. It is mind over matter. If you believe in yourself and want something bad enough you can do anything.

Advice to others: Stop making excuses and just do it.

What the Experts Think of Kim's Regimen

Dr. John Jakicic says: Kim appears to be healthy based on BMI and physical activity patterns. Her body composition is in the range of what you would expect for a female athlete of this nature but should not be encouraged for most women as this may be unattainable and not realistic for most.

Personal trainer Jay Blahnik says: Kim's exercise routine is very balanced and sensible.

Registered dietitian Dominique Adair says: Her diet is better than average. Could replace protein bars with natural foods.

PROFILE ④ Lisa Ray

Claim to fame: Two-time cover model for *Muscle and Fitness* magazine and appeared on four other fitness covers, including *Oxygen* and *Fitness RX*; earned a master's degree in physical therapy from Central Michigan University; Faremon Fitness Model Search winner

Age: 31 years

Height: 5′ 7″

Weight: 118 pounds

Dress Size: 4

Measurements: 34″ bust, 24″ waist, 35″ hips

Body mass index: 18 (just below "normal" range)

Body fat percentage: Estimated at 16 percent (in "athlete" range)

Hometown: Harbor Beach, Michigan

Children: None, one much-loved dog

Daily calorie intake: 1,658

Daily calorie expenditure from exercise: Up to 520

Lisa's Typical Daily Menu

Breakfast: ½ cup of slow-cooked oatmeal (73 calories) mixed with ½ teaspoon of natural peanut butter (20 calories), 11½ grams of chocolate-flavored protein powder (46 calories) with Splenda Total: 139 calories

Snack: One Zone bar (210 calories) Total: 210 calories

Lunch: Mixed greens salad made with 1 cup of broccoli, tomatoes, cauliflower, and spinach (100 calories); 4 ounces of grilled, skinless chicken (222 calories); and 2 tablespoons of olive oil and vinegar dressing (119 calories) Total: 441 calories

Uncovered! Secret Number 7

Eat high-bulk, low-calorie foods.

Snack: One protein shake made with 1 cup of low-fat soy milk (100 calories), 3 tablespoons of protein powder (92 calories), and four frozen strawberries (15 calories) Total: 207 calories

Dinner: Stir-fry made from 5 ounces of skinless, roasted chicken (277 calories); 1½ cups of broccoli, peapods, mushrooms, zucchini, and peppers (150 calories); and ½ cup of brown rice (107 calories). Season with 3 tablespoons of low-sodium soy sauce (25 calories) Total: 559 calories

Snack: 1 cup of broccoli (25 calories) with 3 tablespoons of hummus (77 calories) Total: 102 calories

Total daily calories: 1,658

Sample Weekly Workout

Monday: 20 minutes of high-intensity running (250 calories burned), 45-minute full-body weight workout (270 calories burned)

Tuesday: 30 minutes of moderate-intensity elliptical workout (210 calories burned), 30-minute weight workout focused on legs (180 calories burned)

Wednesday: 40 minutes of moderate-intensity stationary biking (280 calories burned), 30-minute weight workout focused on arms (180 calories burned)

Thursday: 20 minutes of high-intensity running (250 calories burned), 30-minute weight workout focused on back (180 calories burned)

Friday: 30 minutes of moderate-intensity elliptical workout (210 calories burned), 30-minute weight workout focused on abs (180 calories burned)

Saturday: 40 minutes of moderate-intensity stationary biking (280 calories burned)

Sunday: Rest

Lisa's Fitness Facts

Food philosophy: Have everything in moderation, good balance, don't deprive yourself of everything—enjoy your life, too.

Supplements taken: Multivitamin, calcium, protein powders, and caffeine (usually in the form of coffee)

Total daily water intake: 2 liters, including Contrex brand, which is French water fortified with calcium and magnesium

Cheating: On weekends, indulge in a couple of glasses of wine, baked tortilla chips and salsa with low-fat cottage cheese, and sushi. One to two real cheat days per month.

Exercise philosophy: Variety is the key to sticking with a workout plan. I like to do something different each time, even if it's just slightly different. And just like diet, everything in moderation. You shouldn't have to kill yourself working out two to three hours a day to look good and feel good.

Other tips: I really try to avoid making unplanned food stops. I almost always plan ahead as far as my day goes and have some sort of snack with me if I know I will be out for more than a few hours. I either have a protein bar or some nuts or fruit with me wherever I go. If I absolutely have to stop somewhere I try to at least stop at a convenience store instead of fast food and pick up the best choice possible.

Uncovered! Secret Number 8

Don't make unplanned food stops.

What the Experts Think of Lisa's Regimen

Dr. John Jakicic says: Lisa's physical activity is in a healthy range. However, she is at the low end of healthy and should not lose any weight.

Personal trainer Jay Blahnik says: Her exercise program seems reasonable and well balanced.

Registered dietitian Dominique Adair says: Her choices are healthy, but her calories are on the low side for someone this active.

PROFILE 5 Josie Radocchia

Claim to fame: Fitness instructor and high school teacher

Age: 44 years

Height: 5′ 8″

Weight: 125 pounds

Dress Size: 4

Measurements: 33″ bust, 26″ waist, 36″ hips

Body mass index: 19 (low end of "normal" range)

Body fat percentage: Estimated at 18 percent (in "athlete" range)

Hometown: Kitchener, Ontario

Children: None

Daily calorie intake: 1,971

Daily calorie expenditure from exercise: Up to 629

Josie's Typical Daily Menu

Breakfast: A third of a pineapple (76 calories) with about ¼ cup of blueberries (20 calories); one spelt (type of grain) bun (190 calories) with about a teaspoon of organic butter spread (50 calories); and one smoothie, made with 2½ ounces silken tofu (47 calories), 1 cup of plain yogurt (154 calories), and ⅓ cup of raspberry-strawberry combination (16 calories) Total: 553 calories

Snack: Two dry figs (97 calories) and 1 cup of grapes (114 calories) Total: 211 calories

Lunch: One regular, medium tortilla (52 calories) with ½ can reduced-sodium salmon (126 calories) and alfalfa sprouts (1 calorie), about twenty small carrots (76 calories), and 2 cups of salad consisting of romaine or green leaf lettuce (16 calories) and 1 tablespoon of regular Italian dressing (54 calories) Total: 325 calories

Snack: One apple (81 calories), one small plain yogurt (77 calories) with about twenty almonds (150 calories) Total: 308 calories

Before workout: One energy bar (229 calories). Total: 229 calories

Dinner: 4 ounces of skinless, grilled chicken breast (222 calories), 1 cup of broccoli (30 calories), 1 cup of corn (132 calories) Total: 384 calories

Before bed: 1 cup of plain yogurt (154 calories) with 1 tablespoon of pumpkin seeds, sunflower seeds, and crushed walnuts mixture (26 calories) plus 1 teaspoon of dried cranberries (10 calories) Total: 190 calories

Total daily calories: 1,971

Uncovered! Secret Number 9

Get enough protein.

Sample Weekly Workout

Monday: 60-minute BodySTEP high-intensity aerobic class (483 calories burned)

Tuesday: Rest

Wednesday: 55-minute indoor cycling class (629 calories burned)

Thursday: 60-minute BodyFLOW (tai chi/yoga/Pilates) stretch class (211 calories burned)

Friday: Rest

Saturday: 60-minute BodyPUMP total body strength-training class (350 calories burned)

Sunday: Rest

Josie's Fitness Facts

Food philosophy: Everything in moderation.

Total daily water intake: 9–10 cups a day

Cheating: Sundays when I visit my Italian parents.

Approach to holidays/temptations: I have a little bit of whatever I want.

Sticking to the plan: I just make it part of my overall routine. I plan my meals ahead of time and shop to fit the plan.

Uncovered! Secret Number 10

Plan meals and shop to fit your plan.

What the Experts Think of Josie's Regimen

Dr. John Jakicic says: Josie's BMI and physical activity appear to put her at a healthy level. She appears to have a good perspective of the commitment that is necessary as well as a philosophy of moderation.

Personal trainer Jay Blahnik says: Josie appears to have well-balanced nutritional and exercise programs.

Registered dietitian Dominique Adair says: Great variety, balance, and nutrient density.

Claim to fame: Actress and model, appearing in numerous films, television shows, and commercials, including TV's "Nip/Tuck" and commercials for Herbal Essences, Bowflex, and 6 Star Systems; personal trainer with a master's degree in physical therapy; a spokesperson for the Ab-doer and the Exer-gym

Age: 35 years

Height: 5′ 11″

Weight: 144 pounds

Dress Size: 6

Measurements: 36″ bust, 25″ waist, 36″ hips

Body mass index: 20.1 (in "normal" range)

Body fat percentage: Estimated at 11–13 percent (in "competitive athlete" range)

Hometown: Orlando, Florida

Children: None

Daily calorie intake: 1,905

Daily calorie expenditure from exercise: Up to 800–1,250

Kristia's Typical Daily Menu

Breakfast: Two Morning Star brand veggie sausage patties (158 calories), ½ cup of slow-cooked oatmeal (73 calories), and ½ cup regular cottage cheese (100 calories) Total: 331 calories

Snack: One apple (80 calories), one medium banana (109 calories), and 1 tablespoon of peanut butter (95 calories) Total: 284 calories

Lunch: Turkey wrap made from 4 ounces turkey cold cut (200 calories), one medium wrap (120 calories), one slice veggie cheese (50 calories), and 1 tablespoon of low-fat mayonnaise (36 calories) and one piece of fruit (100 calories) Total: 506 calories

Snack: One protein bar (200 calories), one medium banana (109 calories), and 1 tablespoon of peanut butter (95 calories) Total: 404 calories

Dinner: 6 ounces grilled salmon (230 calories) and salad with 1 tablespoon of olive oil dressing (150 calories) Total: 380 calories

Total daily calories: 1,905

Sample Weekly Workout

Monday: 45–90 minutes of swimming (450–900 calories burned), 1 hour of full-body weight training (350 calories burned)

Tuesday: 45–90 minutes of running (450–900 calories burned)

Wednesday: 45–90 minutes of biking (450–900 calories burned), 1 hour of full-body weight training (350 calories burned)

Thursday: 45–90 minutes of swimming (450–900 calories burned)

Friday: 45–90 minutes of biking (450–900 calories burned), 1 hour of full-body weight training (350 calories burned)

Saturday: 45–90 minutes of running (450–900 calories burned)

Sunday: Rest

Kristia's Fitness Facts

Food philosophy: Dieting is not a lifestyle; eating healthy for life can be achieved.

Supplements taken: Multivitamin, calcium, B complex

Total daily water intake: 64–80 ounces

Cheating: One each week, indulging in pizza and cookie dough

Sticking to the plan: Take it one day at a time. If you fall off the horse, get back on.

Exercise philosophy: Exercise is like brushing your teeth. You have to do it every day, and the benefits are well worth the time.

Uncovered! Secret Number 11

Avoid sugar and refined wheat.

Uncovered! Secret Number 12

Have a cheat day once a week to eat what you want.

Uncovered! Secret Number 13

Adopt a "no excuses" mindset.

What the Experts Think of Kristia's Regimen

Dr. John Jakicic says: Kristia appears to be healthy based on BMI and activity level reported. Good philosophy of exercise. Her body composition appears to be at the level of a female athlete training at the level reported. However, most females will not be able to commit to this level of activity and thus the low level of body fatness is probably not realistic for most females.

Personal trainer Jay Blahnik says: Her workout routine is very balanced.

Registered dietitian Dominique Adair says: Many of her choices are health supportive.

PROFILE (7) Anna Wyatt

Claim to fame: Worked on a presidential campaign, as a model, and as a business manager

Age: 31 years

Height: 6′ 1″

Weight: 138 pounds

Dress size: 4

Measurements: 32″ bust, 25″ waist, 35″ hips

Body mass index: 19.2 (in "normal" range)

Body fat percentage: Estimated 18 percent (in "athlete" range)

Hometown: Charlotte, North Carolina

Children: Two

Daily calorie intake: 1,515

Daily calorie expenditure from exercise: Up to 210–500

Anna's Typical Daily Menu

Breakfast: Stoneyfield Farms Organic Yogurt drink (150 calories)
Total: 150 calories

Preexercise snack: One protein bar (230 calories) Total: 230
calories

Postexercise snack: Body for Life shake (200 calories) and 12
almonds (87 calories) Total: 287 calories

Lunch: Turkey sandwich made from two slices of whole-wheat bread
(138 calories), 2 ounces turkey (117 calories), tomato (8 calories),
mustard (3 calories), and spinach (10 calories) Total: 276 calories

Snack: One granola bar (150 calories) Total: 150 calories

Dinner: Michelina's Lean Gourmet turkey or chicken meal (250
calories) Total: 250 calories

Snack: One mini bagel (72 calories) with 1 tablespoon of almond
butter (100 calories) Total: 172 calories

Total daily calories: 1,515 calories.

Uncovered! Secret Number 14

Eat smaller meals throughout the day.

Sample Weekly Workout

Monday: 1 hour of yoga (210 calories burned)

Tuesday: 1 hour of weight circuit training with a trainer (485 calories
burned)

Wednesday: 1 hour of cardio of choice (500 calories burned)

Thursday: 1 hour of weight circuit training with a trainer (485 calories
burned)

Friday: 1 hour of cardio with a trainer, mixing treadmill, stepper, and
stationary bicycle (500 calories burned)

Saturday: 1 hour of yoga (210 calories burned)

Sunday: Rest

Anna's Fitness Facts

Food philosophy: I don't believe in diets; instead, I eat well. I eat small meals throughout the day, when I am hungry, and I stop eating when I'm not hungry anymore.

Total daily water intake: 10–12 glasses a day

Cheating: Sundays—pizza and dessert

Approach to holidays/temptations: I allow myself to enjoy but not indulge because most of the time, I follow a strict diet. I know that I eat clean so those times aren't going to really do any harm if I have a few cookies.

Sticking to the plan: I enjoy the working out and the science of feeding my body well. So, because it's fun for me, it's pretty easy. I'm a single mom, and I absolutely need all the extra energy I can get, as well as optimal health because it's all on my shoulders. I'm not willing to lag. That's pretty good motivation.

Uncovered! Secret Number 15

Concentrate on how eating well and exercising make you feel.

Exercise philosophy: Move it or lose it. But more importantly, it's not about being skinny; that's a nice side effect. I move my body to stay healthy and to have energy. If I don't, I feel like a lug. Our bodies are gifts and amazing machines that need to be tuned up, and exercise will do that.

What the Experts Think of Anna's Regimen

Dr. John Jakicic says: Anna appears to be healthy based on exercise and BMI. Her exercise routine is not excessive and is something that most individuals could realistically perform. This is a good example of a level of activity a person could progress to in order to improve health and control body weight.

Personal trainer Jay Blahnik says: Her workout routine is very impressive and appears very well balanced.

Registered dietitian Dominique Adair says: Anna could increase fiber, vitamins, and minerals by replacing bars, shakes, and entrees with vegetables and fruit.

PROFILE (8) Kristin Cheh

Claim to fame: Award-winning artist, 1999 Miss New Jersey USA Pageant competitor, and an event host for *Maxim* magazine events

Age: 26 years

Height: 5′ 3″

Weight: 98 pounds

Dress size: 2P

Measurements: 34″ bust, 22″ waist, 33″ hips

Body mass index: Below 19 (in "normal" range)

Body fat percentage: Estimated at 18 percent (in "athlete" range)

Hometown: Edison, New Jersey

Children: None

Daily calorie intake: 1,905

Daily calorie expenditure from exercise: Up to 250

Kristin's Typical Daily Menu

Breakfast: Two packets of instant, plain oatmeal (206 calories) and one can of Ensure (250 calories) Total: 456 calories

Lunch: 2 tablespoons of natural peanut butter (187 calories) and 1 tablespoon of peach jam (50 calories) on two slices of potato bread (200 calories), four vanilla Oreo cookies (170 calories), 1 cup of orange juice (113 calories) Total: 720 calories.

Uncovered! Secret Number 16

Work in the yummy stuff.

Snack: 1 cup of low-sugar plain yogurt (75 calories) and one Nature's Finest granola bar (180 calories) Total: 255 calories

Dinner: 3 ounces of grilled chicken breast (166 calories); one plain, medium-sized baked potato (136 calories); and twelve string beans (42 calories) Total: 344 calories

Uncovered! Secret Number 17

Get a portion size wake-up call.

Dessert: 1½ cups of watermelon sorbet (130 calories) Total: 130 calories

Total daily calories: 1,905

Sample Weekly Workout

Monday: 45-minute free-weight, full-body workout (135 calories burned) plus extensive unmonitored walking (100+ calories burned)

Tuesday: Extensive unmonitored walking (100+ calories burned)

Wednesday: 50-minute free-weight, full-body workout (150 calories burned) plus extensive unmonitored walking (100+ calories burned)

Thursday: Extensive unmonitored walking (100+ calories burned)

Friday: 1 hour free-weight, full-body workout (180 calories burned) plus extensive unmonitored walking (100+ calories burned)

Saturday: Extensive unmonitored walking (100+ calories burned)

Sunday: Extensive unmonitored walking (100+ calories burned)

Kristin's Fitness Facts

Food philosophy: I try to eat healthy and never eat anything fried. The more protein I can get the better. Eating fresh food is always best, like fruits and steamed veggies. Never completely deprive yourself of your favorite things. Mine is the Oreo cookies.

Total daily water intake: 16 ounces

Cheating: Every day can be a cheat day . . . just in moderation.

Approach to holidays/temptations: Holidays are meant for you to enjoy. As always, everything in moderation . . . there are plenty of healthy foods that you can eat around the holidays.

Sticking to the plan: I have grown to really enjoy the things that I used to hate eating, like Ensure, veggies, and natural peanut butter. I actually crave healthy food now rather than what I used to eat . . . like sugar!

Advice to others: You must stick to your plan but allow yourself your favorite foods; the key is in moderation. If you like chocolate you can't sit down and eat three pieces of chocolate cake. Have one piece or a piece of chocolate candy. Feel good about your goals you set and stick to them. Don't stop at your first good result. Use it only as a stepping-stone to future goals. In order for you to get that smokin' body you have to take in what your body craves on the inside to make itself look good on the outside. Once you begin to train yourself to eat better, you will crave the healthy food rather than the junk. Trust me, it is true.

Uncovered! Secret Number 18

When you reach your goal, keep it going.

What the Experts Think of Kristin's Regimen

Dr. John Jakicic says: Kristin is apparently healthy based on her BMI. It's difficult to determine if activity includes sufficient cardio activity to maintain or improve cardiorespiratory fitness.

Unmonitored walking may be sufficient to burn calories but needs to be at an adequate intensity to also maximize improvements in cardiorespiratory fitness.

Personal trainer Jay Blahnik says: I like that she walks a lot, but she may want to add one or two cardio workouts that challenge her cardiovascular system.

Registered dietitian Dominique Adair says: Her food philosophy—"Every day can be a cheat day"—is terrific.

PROFILE (9) Sazzy Varga

Claim to fame: Appeared in *Playboy* magazine, on the TV show "Baywatch" and on Sci Fi and Lifetime channels; is cofounder of the Tibetan Photo Project, a collection of photos taken by Tibetans in exile

Age: 30s

Height: 5′ 7″

Weight: 128 pounds

Dress size: 6

Measurements: 35″ bust, 25″ waist, 35″ hips

Body mass index: 20 (in "normal" range)

Body fat percentage: Estimated in the 20s when not shooting, 16 percent when shooting (between "athlete" and "fitness" ranges)

Hometown: Tomahawk, Wisconsin

Children: One

Daily calorie intake: 1,422

Daily calorie expenditure from exercise: Up to 350

Sazzy's Typical Daily Menu

Breakfast: 1 cup of coffee with Splenda and a bit of milk powder (10 calories), ½ cup of Raisin Bran cereal (88 calories) with ½ cup of fat-free milk (50 calories) Total: 148 calories

Lunch: 1 cup of coffee (4 calories), 3 ounces of skinless grilled chicken breast (117 calories) with 1 ice-cream scoop of rice (160 calories) with some butter spray (50 calories) Total: 331 calories

Dinner: One calorie-free glass of Crystal Light, 4 ounces of skinless grilled chicken breast (183 calories), 1 ice-cream scoop of pasta (196 calories) with 1 cup of homemade tomato sauce (90 calories) and 2 cups of broccoli (60 calories) with butter spray (100 calories) Total: 629 calories

Snack: 8 cups of air-popped popcorn (244 calories) with water sprayed on it lightly and pepper and a 4-ounce glass of white wine (70 calories) Total: 314 calories

Total daily calories: 1,422

Sample Weekly Workout

Monday: 45-minute bike ride (350 calories burned)

Tuesday: Rest

Wednesday: 30 minutes running on treadmill (270 calories burned)

Thursday: 30 minutes floor, Pilates-style exercises (105 calories burned)

Friday: Rest

Saturday: 30 minutes of weight training (91 calories burned)

Sunday: Rest

Sazzy's Fitness Facts

Food philosophy: Calories in, calories out.

Total daily water intake: Not nearly enough

Cheating: I cheat smart. Again, if I want the chocolate chip cookie, I know that I will have to cut back elsewhere to stay in my calorie zone or else burn more calories.

Healthy eating advice: I try to keep a "clean" food environment at home, with bad foods locked away or out of the house altogether. It helps if everyone in the house is on the same page. I was married to a bodybuilder for years, and we ate virtually the same way.

Uncovered! Secret Number 19

Live in healthy environments.

Approach to holidays/temptations: Again, the key is moderation. Just keep saying calories in, calories out. Want five of Mom's awesome gingerbread men? (And, yes, my mom's are the best). Then how are you going to get rid of those little guys later? Skiing, ice skating, a snowball fight with my nieces, and whatever it takes to get moving.

Uncovered! Secret Number 20

Have a holiday/vacation game plan.

Sticking to the plan: I am in control of my eating, it is not in control of me. I can choose to be in shape or overweight all by what I eat and how much I move. I also research (nutritional information for) restaurants I go to. I think if more people did, they would pass on the Whopper and fries.

Uncovered! Secret Number 21

Research restaurants.

Other tips: Emotions can wreak havoc on diet, both in over- and undereating, which cause a myriad of health problems and often, then, fuel depression because of bad body image. It is always better to deal with emotional issues directly, as not only do they affect weight but they can cause other health problems as well.

Uncovered! Secret Number 22

Sort out your emotional problems.

What the Experts Think of Sazzy's Regimen

Dr. John Jakicic says: Sazzy appears to be healthy based on BMI and activity level. Moderate level of activity is realistic and achievable for most individuals.

Personal trainer Jay Blahnik says: Her exercise program is pretty light. She could work out *and* eat more.

Registered dietitian Dominique Adair says: She makes healthy food choices.

PROFILE 10 Diana Bernier

Claim to fame: Marathon runner, registered nurse, and mother of three

Age: 40 years

Height: 5′ 9″

Weight: 133 pounds

Dress size: 4

Measurements: 34″ bust, 27″ waist, 32½″ hips

Body mass index: 19.5 (low end of "normal" range)

Body fat percentage: Estimated at 15 percent (in "athlete" range)

Hometown: Long Island, New York

Children: Three (ages seven, ten, and fourteen)

Daily calorie intake: 1,780–2,059

Daily calorie expenditure from exercise: Up to 800

Diana's Typical Daily Menu

Breakfast: One package of instant oatmeal (171 calories), half of a banana (46 calories), ¼ cup of fat-free milk (38 calories), and 2 cups of coffee (4 calories) with light cream (10 calories) Total: 269 calories

Lunch: Half a bagel (125 calories) with 3 ounces of tuna fish (100 calories) and 1 teaspoon of mayonnaise (50 calories), an apple (81 calories), and 8 ounces of milk (150 calories) Total: 506 calories

Snack: ¾ cup of Cracklin' Oat Bran cereal (225 calories), ¾ cup of fat-free milk (113 calories), and 2 tablespoons of almonds (62 calories) and coffee (4 calories) with light cream (5 calories) Total: 409 calories

Dinner: 5 ounces of grilled salmon (197 calories) or skinless chicken (229 calories) with 2 cups of raw vegetable salad (30 calories) with 2 tablespoons of full-fat dressing (136 calories), ¾ cup of white rice (153 calories) with 1 teaspoon of butter (50 calories), 1 cup of steamed broccoli (30 calories) or asparagus (77 calories), occasionally a slice of bread (80 calories) with 1 teaspoon of butter (50 calories), and occasionally a 4-ounce glass of white wine (70 calories) Total: 656–888 calories

Total daily calories: 1,780–2,059

Sample Weekly Workout

Monday: 25 minutes free-weight, full-body workout (75 calories burned), 10 minutes of sit-ups and push-ups (80 calories burned)

Tuesday: 8-mile run at high intensity (600 calories burned)

Wednesday: 8-mile run at high intensity (600 calories burned), 10 minutes of sit-ups and push-ups (80 calories burned)

Thursday: 8-mile run at high intensity (600 calories burned)

Friday: 40 minutes elliptical trainer at moderate intensity (362 calories burned), 25 minutes of free-weight, full-body workout (75 calories burned), 10 minutes of sit-ups and push-ups (80 calories burned)

Saturday: 6-mile run at intermediate pace (500 calories burned), 10 minutes of sit-ups and push-ups (80 calories burned)

Sunday: 10-mile run at somewhat hard pace (800 calories burned)

Diana's Fitness Facts

Food philosophy: Eating healthy food and not overeating is the key to maintaining weight and feeling good. Occasional bingeing is OK, but try to get back on track.

Total daily water intake: At least 10 glasses daily

Cheating: I love dessert but usually avoid it. Even runners have to be careful! But occasionally I have a cheat day when I'll have more than one serving of dessert.

Sticking to the plan: It's just a part of my life, there's no other way to do it. It's like asking me how I manage to brush my teeth. I try to exercise in the morning so I don't have to think about squeezing it in later, but I will if I have to! People tell me all the time how lucky I am to be slim. LUCKY?! It's work, but it's worth it. I've learned what I need to do to keep my weight where it is (what my metabolic rate will allow).

Uncovered! Secret Number 23

Learn what your body's metabolic rate will allow.

Exercise philosophy: It's what makes everything in my life better. I respect myself for it, and I think others do as well. It's not always easy, but nothing that is worth achieving is ever easy.

Fitness tip: I have a weight "buffer zone." I have an orange-light number (which means I need to be careful because I'm two to three pounds over my ideal weight zone) and my red-light number (this is bad, where I'm five pounds over). Red means I must cut back on the amount I'm eating for at least three days.

Uncovered! Secret Number 24

Keep weight within a set range.

Advice to others: Anyone can exercise four times a week. I am just as busy as everyone else. It's a matter of choice. Discipline will come once you get into a routine and realize how good it makes you feel. Positive self-talk is very important. For example, right now I feel like eating something, but it's late at night and I know that I'll be asleep soon and will be glad in the morning that I passed up snacking. I use positive self-talk to make sure I stay disciplined.

Other tips: I portion out foods ahead of time in order to avoid overindulging.

Uncovered! Secret Number 25

Learn positive self-talk.

Uncovered! Secret Number 26

Portion foods out.

What the Experts Think of Diana's Regimen

Dr. John Jakicic says: Diana appears to be healthy and fit based on the information provided. Her level of exercise is not excessive for an individual who runs marathons. Her Fitness tips, Advice to others, and Other tips would be very helpful to others, too.

Personal trainer Jay Blahnik says: Her workout routine is great, but she could include some alternative cardio to balance the running.

Registered dietitian Dominique Adair says: Her choices and food distribution are good.

Claim to fame: Whistler Mountain downhill ski enthusiast, accomplished account executive, and mother of two grown daughters

Age: 47 years

Height: 5′ 5″

Weight: 126 pounds

Dress size: 7

Measurements: 37″ bust, 29″ waist, 37″ hips

Body mass index: 21 (in "normal" range)

Body fat percentage: Estimated 26 percent (low end of "healthy" range)

Hometown: Vancouver, British Columbia

Children: Two daughters, ages seventeen and twenty-two

Daily calorie intake: 1,767

Daily calorie expenditure from exercise: Up to 360–1,800

Cathy's Typical Daily Menu

Breakfast: 1 cup of green tea (2 calories) and 1 cup of fat-free soy milk (100 calories) with a Kinetix meal replacement protein/vitamin mix (230 calories) Total: 332 calories

Snack: One Starbucks grande nonfat latte (160 calories) Total: 160 calories

Lunch: 1 cup of chicken soup (100 calories), one slice of whole-grain bread (79 calories) with ½ can of tuna (97 calories) mixed with 1 tablespoon of mayonnaise (99 calories), a glass of water, and a cup of herbal tea (2 calories) Total: 377 calories

Snack: ¼ cup of trail mix (173 calories) and 1 cup of fat-free soy milk (100 calories) Total: 273 calories

Dinner: Salad with ¼ cup of feta cheese (99 calories), dried fruit, pine nuts, pumpkin seeds (50 calories), 2 tablespoons of olive oil and balsamic vinegar dressing (99 calories), 4 ounces of barbecued chicken (222 calories), 1 cup of green beans (83 calories), a glass of wine (70 calories) Total: 623 calories

Before bed: 1 cup of herbal tea (2 calories) Total: 2 calories

Total daily calories: 1,767

Uncovered! Secret Number 27

Get a total daily intake wake-up call.

Sample Weekly Workout

Monday: 45 minutes of circuit training on hydraulic machines at Curves for Women (360 calories burned), 1 hour of Pilates (210 calories burned)

Tuesday: 45 minutes of circuit training on hydraulic machines at Curves for Women (360 calories burned)

Wednesday: 45 minutes of circuit training on hydraulic machines at Curves for Women (360 calories burned)

Thursday: 45 minutes of circuit training on hydraulic machines at Curves for Women (360 calories burned)

Friday: 45 minutes of circuit training on hydraulic machines at Curves for Women (360 calories burned)

Saturday: Skiing 5 hours on mountain in winter (1,800 calories burned)/waterskiing 5 hours in summer (1,800 calories burned)

Sunday: Skiing 5 hours on mountain in winter (1,800 calories burned)/waterskiing 5 hours in summer (1,800 calories burned)

Cathy's Fitness Facts

Food philosophy: Everything in moderation. Stay away from sugars.

Supplements taken: Detox multivitamin, Greens + supplement and Milk thistle liver detox supplement

Total daily water intake: 7 glasses a day

Cheating: Yes, of course. I love pasta with cream sauces; I love wine, in fact I love food, period. Cheat days would mainly be dinners on the weekend.

Approach to holidays/temptations: Exercise more, drink more water, and avoid the sugars. I order a salad with either chicken or fish when eating out at restaurants.

Uncovered! Secret Number 28

Think ahead about risky outings.

Sticking to the plan: It has become a habit. You have to stick with something you enjoy and be committed. Before you know it, it is just a part of your daily life and an expected part of your schedule.

Other tips: I'm almost 50 years old, so I try not to compare my body to people in their 20s.

Uncovered! Secret Number 29

Accept and act upon the fact that your body is unique.

What the Experts Think of Cathy's Regimen

Dr. John Jakicic says: Apparently healthy based on BMI and activity level. Depending on the intensity and amount of cardio activity in her circuit training, she may want to consider supplementing her current workout with some additional cardio exercise.

Personal trainer Jay Blahnik says: Cathy's diet looks pretty good. Her Curves workouts are very balanced and have a low injury risk, but, because they use hydraulics, she will have a hard time seeing improvements over time.

Registered dietitian Dominique Adair says: Overall good choices. Nice vegetable selection, lean proteins, and healthy fats. She may choose the meal replacement breakfast for convenience, but since all her other meals and snacks are foods, it is fine. To improve, she could toss in a few servings of fruit. She should consider a calcium supplement for bone health.

PROFILE 12 Alex Barker

Claim to fame: Accountant/recruiter and mother to a one-year-old

Age: 33 years

Height: 5′ 10″

Weight: 155 pounds

Dress size: 10

Measurements: 36″ bust, 29″ waist, 40″ hips

Body mass index: 22.5 (in "normal" range)

Body fat percentage: Estimated at 21–22 percent (at low end of "fitness" range)

Hometown: Oakville, Ontario

Children: One

Pregnancy weight gain: 53 pounds

Time to lose pregnancy weight: Four months

Daily calorie intake: 1,693–2,133

Daily calorie expenditure from exercise: Up to 660

Uncovered! Secret Number 30

Keep pregnancy weight gain under control.

Alex's Typical Daily Menu

Breakfast: 1 cup bran cereal (180 calories) with ¾ cup of 1 percent milk (75 calories), ½ cup of berries (35 calories), coffee with cream

(20 calories) with 1 packet Splenda, one small bottle of water Total calories: 310

Midmorning Snack: One protein/Atkins bar (240 calories) Total: 240 calories

Lunch: Turkey wrap made from 2 ounces cold cut turkey (100 calories) in a medium whole-wheat wrap (200 calories) with 1 tablespoon of honey mustard dressing (35 calories); small salad consisting of 2 cups lettuce (13 calories), 1 tomato (26 calories), ½ red pepper (15 calories), onion (10 calories), and 2–3 tablespoons of balsamic or poppy seed dressing (120–180 calories); and small piece of fruit (30–60 calories) Total calories: 549–639

Snack: ½ cup of pretzels (100 calories) and one piece fruit (50–80 calories) or ten rice crackers (100 calories) Total calories: 100–180 calories

Dinner: 4 ounces of grilled chicken (200 calories) or fish (130 calories) with large salad (same as lunch, 184–244 calories) or vegetables, typically steamed broccoli or asparagus (50–90 calories) Total calories: 364–534

Snack: Frozen dessert bar (230 calories) or 2–3 cups of microwave, regular popcorn (130 calories) Total: 130–230 calories

Total daily calories: 1,693–2,133

Sample Weekly Workout

Monday: Run 4 miles at 6 miles per hour (500 calories burned), 20 minutes free-weight exercises for back and free-weight exercises for triceps (90 calories burned), 10 minutes of ab work, including crunches on exercise ball (50 calories burned)

Tuesday: Run 5 miles at 6 miles per hour (600 calories burned)

Wednesday: Run 4 miles at 6 miles per hour (500 calories burned), 20 minutes of free-weight exercises for shoulders and free-weight exercises for biceps (90 calories burned), 10 minutes ab work (50 calories burned)

Thursday: Run 4 miles at 6 miles per hour (500 calories burned), chest exercises using free weights and lunges for legs (100 calories burned)

Friday: Run 5 miles at 6 miles per hour (600 calories burned), 10 minutes ab work (50 calories burned)

Saturday: May run 4–5 miles (500–600 calories burned); may rest

Sunday: Rest

Alex's Fitness Facts

Food philosophy: My philosophy is basically low-carb, and I generally try to avoid too much processed food. I also eat small meals frequently throughout day. (Alex says she also makes a point of reading the labels on the foods she eats to see exactly what she is getting.)

Uncovered! Secret Number 31

Read labels.

Total daily water intake: 6–8 cups

Cheating: I frequently cheat on weekends and try to stay consistent during the week.

Approach to holidays/temptations: Go all out. You only live once.

Sticking to the plan: I know that when the weekend comes I can allow myself to cheat. You should avoid total deprivation of any food. I look at diet as not absolutely perfect but as long as I am generally on track, it is OK. I am harder on myself for missing a workout than the odd treat.

Other tips: It's important to cut off emotional eating. If something upsetting happens at work or if I am having a bad day trying to control a toddler, I find myself sometimes snacking mindlessly, almost as a coping mechanism. This doesn't happen that often but it is like a control thing. If you can't control everything else, how can you control your diet? I have to actually step back and look at what I am doing, question if I am really hungry. Then I exercise, go for a walk, have a bath, or call a friend to change my mindset.

Uncovered! Secret Number 32

Replace emotional eating.

What the Experts Think of Alex's Regimen

Dr. John Jakicic says: Alex's diet is apparently healthy based on BMI and activity program. A good, well-rounded exercise routine. She should be complimented for returning to prepregnancy body weight and maintaining her activity with the time commitments of a newborn.

Personal trainer Jay Blahnik says: Her exercise program is balanced between strength and cardio, which is great. But she should consider doing something for her cardio besides running. Running is great but can lead to injuries if you do it every day.

Registered dietitian Dominique Adair says: Her moderate approach to eating is healthy and well balanced.

PROFILE 13 Katie Katke

Claim to fame: Self-proclaimed healthy lifestyle coach, certified personal trainer and group fitness instructor, certified EMT, and fitness model featured in videos, on book covers, and on TV

Age: 42 years

Height: 5' 5"

Weight: 117 pounds

Dress Size: 0–2

Measurements: 36″ bust, 25″ waist, 35″ hips

Body mass index: 19.5 (low end of "normal" range)

Body fat percentage: Estimated at 12–15 percent (low, in "essential fat" range)

Hometown: San Clemente, California

Children: Five stepchildren, three grandkids, and two dogs

Daily calorie intake: 1,876

Daily calorie expenditure from exercise: Up to 300–914

Katie's Typical Daily Menu

Breakfast: One protein Fusion bar by Metagenics (240 calories) Total: 240 calories

Midmorning: 14 ounces café latte with nonfat milk (110 calories) Total: 110 calories

Lunch: 6 ounces of grilled fish (142 calories), ½ cup of carrots (49 calories), ½ cup of broccoli (15 calories), ½ cup of garbanzo beans (134 calories), and 1 ounce of feta cheese (75 calories) Total: 415 calories

Snack: Metagenics shake (120 calories) Total: 120 calories

Dinner: 8 ounces of tofu (329 calories), 1 cup of brown rice (215 calories), 1 cup of steamed broccoli (90 calories), and a salad made with 2 cups of lettuce (14 calories), cucumber, radishes, carrots, onion (all 40 calories), and 2 tablespoons of olive oil/vinegar/honey dressing (119 calories) Total: 807 calories

Dessert: 1 cup of sorbet (184 calories), 1–2 times per week Total: 184 calories

Total daily calories: 1,876

Sample Weekly Workout

Monday: 1-hour cycling class (754 calories burned), run 1 mile (100 calories burned), walk the dogs 1 mile (60 calories burned)

Tuesday: 1-hour weight-lifting full-body workout (350 calories burned), walk the dogs 1 mile (60 calories burned), walk up and down steep hill one time (60 calories burned)

Wednesday: 1-hour cycling class (754 calories burned), run 1 mile (100 calories burned), walk the dogs 1 mile (60 calories burned)

Thursday: Walk the dogs 1 mile (60 calories burned), 40 minutes uphill walking (240 calories burned)

Friday: 1-hour cycling class (754 calories burned), walk the dogs 1 mile (60 calories burned)

Saturday: 1-hour weight-lifting full-body workout (350 calories burned), walk the dogs 1 mile (60 calories burned), uphill walking–shorter distance (60 calories burned)

Sunday: Walk the dogs 1 mile (60 calories burned), walking uphill (60 calories burned)

Katie's Fitness Facts

Food philosophy: I just eat until I am not hungry. If I worry about counting calories, life is no fun.

Total daily water intake: Approximately 40 ounces

Supplements taken: Multivitamin, estrogen balancer, liver detox, CLA (weight loss support products), EPH-DHA, phytonutrients, and calcium

Uncovered! Secret Number 33

Try the healthy, safe weight-loss support products.

Cheating: I love to drink wine when I cook. I have a glass or two, three to five days per week. I make dessert for dinner parties about once a month.

Approach to holidays/temptations: Be happy. Have a bite if it looks that good.

Sticking to the plan: My health is important, always. It is a lifestyle. It feels good to be healthy.

Advice to others: Start. Continue. If you stop, start again, and remember how good you feel when you exercise and eat well. Learn to cook.

Uncovered! Secret Number 34

If you fall off the horse, get right back on.

What the Experts Think of Katie's Regimen

Dr. John Jakicic says: Apparently healthy based on BMI and activity level. Good philosophy.

Personal trainer Jay Blahnik says: Her exercise program is well balanced.

Registered dietitian Dominique Adair says: Katie's rejection of the diet mentality and reliance on hunger and fullness is very healthy.

PROFILE (14) Danielle Gamba

Claim to fame: *Playboy* model, stats in music videos, Oakland Raiderette (NFL cheerleader), *FHM* magazine Official Lingerie Model for USA, and pageant winner

Age: 22 years

Height: 5′ 3″

Weight: 105 pounds

Dress size: 2

Measurements: 34″ bust, 25″ waist, 34″ hips

Body mass index: Just under 19 (in "low" range)

Body fat percentage: Estimated at 19 percent (high end of "athlete" range)

Hometown: San Francisco

Children: None

Daily calorie intake: 1,560

Daily calorie expenditure from exercise: Up to 300

Danielle's Typical Daily Menu

Breakfast: One hard-boiled egg (75 calories), three egg whites (50 calories), and one slice of American cheese (86 calories) with three strawberries (15 calories) Total: 226 calories

Snack: One Balance protein bar (210 calories) Total: 210 calories

Lunch: 4 ounces of grilled salmon (158 calories) seasoned with lemon pepper and barbecue sauce (75 calories) and 2 cups of stir-fried frozen vegetables (90 calories) Total: 323 calories

Snack: One slice of wheat toast (79 calories) with ½ small can of tuna (97 calories) and 1 tablespoon of mayonnaise (99 calories) Total: 275 calories

Dinner: Shrimp cocktail made from nine grilled, medium-sized shrimp, cocktail sauce, minced garlic, and herb dressing (196 calories) and a handful of berries and melon (70 calories) Total: 266 calories

Snack: Two slices of prepackaged cheddar (190 calories) and a handful of berries and melon (70 calories) Total: 260 calories

Total daily calories: 1,560

Uncovered! Secret Number 35

Have healthy snacks on hand.

Sample Weekly Workout

Monday: 1-hour dance class at moderate intensity (300 calories burned)

Tuesday: May do 20 minutes of weights for upper and lower body (60 calories burned)

Wednesday: 1-hour dance class at moderate intensity (300 calories burned)

Thursday: Rest

Friday: 1-hour dance class at moderate intensity (300 calories burned)

Saturday: 1-hour dance class at moderate intensity (300 calories burned)

Sunday: Rest

Danielle's Fitness Facts

Food philosophy: Get creative to avoid boredom.

Total daily water intake: 8 or more glasses

Cheating: Once a week, usually pizza or sushi plus champagne

Approach to holidays/temptations: I regift all the treats I'm given! I know, that's bad, but it keeps me from eating them!

Sticking to the plan: I stay creative with how I prepare my food and exercise. I also keep a cupboard with all the "bad" foods in it, so I don't have to stare at it every time I go to eat something.

Advice to others: Everyone is different, so find what suits you the best in terms of diet/exercise preferences. Try to immerse yourself in healthy environments; it makes staying on track a lot easier.

Uncovered! Secret Number 36

Keep a "clean" food environment.

What the Experts Think of Danielle's Regimen

Dr. John Jakicic says: Danielle is apparently healthy based on BMI and activity level.

Personal trainer Jay Blahnik says: Her exercise schedule is great, but she could add more weight training.

Registered dietitian Dominique Adair says: Danielle makes some very good food choices, but she could use more complex carbohydrates and a vitamin.

PROFILE (15) Erin Kirk

Claim to fame: *FHM* magazine model, legal assistant, and part-time model; appears in Bud Light commercials; and placed second in Houston's Hottest Moms contest

Age: 27 years

Height: 5′ 5″

Weight: 120 pounds

Dress size: 2

Measurements: 33″ bust, 24″ waist, 33″ hips

Body mass index: 20 (in "normal" range)

Body fat percentage: Estimated at 20 percent (high end of "athlete" range)

Hometown: Alvin, Texas

Children: One

Daily calorie intake: 1,356–1,454

Daily calorie expenditure from exercise: Up to 70–250 calories

Erin's Typical Daily Menu

Breakfast: Low-fat granola bar (142 calories) and a 10-ounce Dr. Pepper (130 calories) Total: 272 calories

Lunch: Grilled chicken salad made from lettuce (15 calories), 4 ounces grilled chicken (200 calories), and 3 tablespoons of honey mustard dressing (180 calories) Total: 395 calories

Snack: Two mini-chocolate bars (86 calories) Total: 86 calories

Make salad your friend.

Learn how to have just one cookie.

Dinner: 5 ounces of grilled skinless chicken breast (250 calories); 1 cup of vegetables, generally corn, green beans, or peas (34–132 calories); and ½ cup of white rice (101 calories), all cooked with 1 tablespoon of olive oil (119 calories); one 8-ounce glass of lemonade (99 calories) Total: 603–701 calories

Total daily calories: 1,356–1,454 calories

Sample Weekly Workout

Monday: Run 2½ miles (250 calories burned)

Tuesday: 200 sit-ups (70 calories burned), full-body weight workout (110 calories burned)

Wednesday: Run 2½ miles (250 calories burned)

Thursday: 200 sit-ups (70 calories burned)

Friday: Run 2½ miles (250 calories burned)

Saturday: May run 2½ miles (250 calories burned)

Sunday: 200 sit-ups (70 calories burned)

Erin's Fitness Facts

Food philosophy: You have to teach your body to learn how you can eat and not gain weight. . . . If you eat fairly healthy five days a week, more than likely you will look great and feel great! I don't keep up with calories. Also, it's important to listen to your body. I do not overeat, ever. Once my stomach feels satisfied, I quit eating.

Total daily water intake: 5–6 glasses

Cheating: One meal every Saturday and Sunday. I usually eat Mexican food or Italian food on these days with one dessert.

Approach to holidays/temptations: During the holidays, I don't just eat because there is a ton of food there. I still eat until I'm satisfied.

Sticking to the plan: I am a creature of habit. During the week, I really like to stay on my regimen and keep in mind that I get to splurge when the weekend comes!

Exercise philosophy: Exercise to me is like basic hygiene. If you want your body to look like you take care of it, you have to work at it, just like brushing your teeth.

What the Experts Think of Erin's Regimen

Dr. John Jakicic says: Apparently healthy based on BMI and activity behavior. Demonstrates what a busy working mom is able to accomplish—good attitude and philosophy.

Personal trainer Jay Blahnik says: Her workout routine is fairly good, but she could add weight training.

Registered dietitian Dominique Adair says: Ideally she might take in fewer calories in refined sugar in her drinks and eat more fruits and vegetables.

PROFILE 16 Anne Currell

Claim to fame: Mother of three, regatta racer, and registered nurse

Age: 47 years

Height: 5′ 4″

Weight: 120 pounds

Dress size: 4

Measurements: 35" bust, 25" waist, 36" hips

Body mass index: 20.6 (low end of "normal" range)

Body fat percentage: Estimated at 17 percent ("athlete" range)

Hometown: Mississauga, Ontario

Children: Three

Daily calorie intake: 1,770–1,780 calories

Daily calorie expenditure from exercise: Up to 754–1,478 calories

Ann's Typical Daily Menu

Breakfast: 1 cup of Raisin Bran cereal (177 calories) with ½ cup of 1 percent milk (50 calories), plus 1 cup of tea (0 calories) with low-fat milk (5 calories) and 1 teaspoon of sugar (16 calories) Total: 248 calories

Snack: Doughnut holes, cookies, and other treats coworkers bring into work (300 calories) Total: 300 calories

Lunch: 2 cups of salad with lettuce, carrots, peppers, and celery (30 calories) with 2 tablespoons of low-fat dressing (70 calories); ½ cup low-fat yogurt (70 calories); and about ½ cup of blueberries (40 calories) or raspberries (30 calories), plus one Diet Coke (0 calories) Total: 200–210 calories

Snack: One peach (42 calories), 2 ounces nut and raisin trail mix (347 calories), and a cup of tea (0 calories) with low-fat milk (5 calories) and 1 teaspoon of sugar (16 calories), plus other snacks from coworkers (200 calories) Total: 610 calories

Dinner: One two-egg omelet (160 calories) with one slice of nonfat cheese (31 calories) or bunless veggie burger (140 calories) with mustard, ketchup, onion, tomato (together 20 calories), and one nonfat cheese slice (31 calories), plus a salad (30 calories) with 2 tablespoons of low-fat dressing (70 calories) Total: 291 calories

Snack: 2 cups of watermelon (100 calories) and a cup of tea (0 calories) with low-fat milk (5 calories) and 1 teaspoon of sugar (16 calories) Total: 121 calories

Total daily calories: 1,770–1,780

Sample Weekly Workout

Monday: 1-hour swim in the morning (600 calories burned); 1 hour of high-intensity weight training, circuit, or heavy weights (724 calories burned); 1-hour spin class (754 calories burned)

Tuesday: Run 12K at 5 min per kilometer in the evening (754 calories burned), paddle-pool workout for 1 hour at high intensity (724 calories burned)

Wednesday: 1-hour swim in the morning (600 calories burned), 1 hour of high-intensity weight training, circuit, or heavy weights (724 calories burned)

Thursday: Run 6K at 5 min per kilometer in the evening (377 calories burned), paddle-pool workout for 1 hour at high intensity (724 calories burned)

Friday: 1-hour swim in the morning (600 calories burned), 1 hour of high-intensity weight training, circuit, or heavy weights (724 calories burned)

Saturday: 1 hour core circuit (300 calories burned), 1 hour paddle pool (724 calories burned), run 6–20K (325–1,300 calories burned)

Sunday: 1 hour paddle pool (724 calories burned), 1 hour weights

Uncovered! Secret Number 40

Get addicted to exercise.

Ann's Fitness Facts

Food philosophy: I eat low-fat foods and try to limit bread, rice, potatoes, and pasta.

Total daily water intake: Very little. Mostly I don't drink any water. If I am at a regatta racing, I will drink a Gatorade-type drink, but otherwise not. Fluid is mostly from tea and Diet Coke.

Cheating: I cheat almost every day with snacks at work, and it varies from only a little (a couple of cookies) to a lot.

Approach to holidays/temptations: I often succumb. I never limit myself very strictly. I just try not to gorge.

Sticking to the plan: Have a concrete goal to work toward.

Advice to others: You have to do what you can live with, or you'll never stick to it.

What the Experts Think of Ann's Regimen

Dr. John Jakicic says: Ann's exercise is good and I like that she has a support group for her exercise. While her BMI is good, she does cheat a lot with snacks, but her exercise let's her get away with that for now. While she does not drink water (which isn't ideal), she does drink fluid, so that is better than nothing.

Personal trainer Jay Blahnik says: She appears to be exercising at an extremely elite level. I would suggest adding fruits and vegetables to her diet and she should be taking in more water than the average person, not less.

Registered dietitian Dominique Adair says: Some of Ann's choices are terrific, but her midmorning snack could be improved. She should also improve her water intake.

PROFILE 17 Julia Beatty

Claim to fame: Cohost for "Her Body," a fitness reality TV show; had lead role in movie *The Casino Job*; featured on "Elimidate" TV show and *National Lampoon's Dorm Daze 2*; and works as a runway model

Age: 28 years

Height: 5′ 8½″

Weight: 122 pounds

Dress size: 2

Measurements: 34″ bust, 24″ waist, 34″ hips

Body mass index: 18 (just below "normal" range)

Body fat percentage: Estimated at 19 percent (in "athlete" range)

Hometown: Jacksonville, Florida

Children: None

Daily calorie intake: 1,995

Daily calorie expenditure from exercise: Up to 672

Julia's Typical Daily Menu

Breakfast: Two eggs scrambled (150 calories) with 1 ounce of sharp cheddar cheese (100 calories), one slice of Canadian bacon (43 calories), one tomato (26 calories), and two mushrooms (10 calories) cooked with 1 tablespoon of butter (100 calories) plus one 8-ounce glass of apple juice (107 calories) Total: 536 calories

Snack: 6 ounces of cottage cheese (160 calories) Total: 160 calories

Lunch: 4 ounces of grilled chicken (222 calories) on a bed of romaine lettuce (14 calories) with 2 tablespoons of balsamic vinaigrette dressing (120 calories), and a diet soda (0 calories) Total: 356 calories

Snack: 4 ounces of low-fat yogurt (72 calories) Total: 72 calories

Dinner: 8 ounces of seared tuna (347 calories) cooked in 1 tablespoon of butter (100 calories), 2 cups of broccoli (180 calories), and 2 cups of salad (14 calories) with 2 ounces of balsamic vinaigrette dressing (120 calories) Total: 761 calories

Dessert: 6 ounces of chilled espresso custard (110 calories) Total: 110 calories

Total daily calories: 1,995

Sample Weekly Workout

Monday: 40 minutes on elliptical machine (400 calories burned), 1½ hours partial-body weight workout (272 calories burned)

Tuesday: 40 minutes on elliptical machine (400 calories burned), 1½ hours partial-body weight workout (272 calories burned)

Wednesday: 40 minutes on elliptical machine (400 calories burned), 1½ hours partial-body weight workout (272 calories burned)

Thursday: 40 minutes on elliptical machine (400 calories burned), 1½ hours partial-body weight workout (272 calories burned)

Friday: 40 minutes on elliptical machine (400 calories burned), 1½ hours partial-body weight workout (272 calories burned)

Saturday: 40 minutes on elliptical machine (400 calories burned), 1½ hours partial-body weight workout (272 calories burned)

Sunday: 40 minutes on elliptical machine (400 calories burned), 1½ hours partial-body weight workout (272 calories burned)

Julia's Fitness Facts

Food philosophy: I generally focus on foods included in the South Beach Diet. It teaches you to eat the right carbs and right fats. You'll look like you diet but eat like you don't.

Uncovered! Secret Number 42

Focus on the good things you do get to eat.

Supplements taken: Daily vitamin

Total daily water intake: 8–12 glasses

Cheating: You should only cheat when you know you have time to make up for it, or when you have planned ahead, say for a special event.

Approach to holidays/temptations: My approach to holiday temptations is to plan ahead. Approximately 2 weeks before the holidays you can pick up the power of your workout and diet. This way you can cheat a little bit.

Sticking to the plan: I stay on my eating and workout schedule using my inner strength and love for myself. It's important to sort out your emotional issues.

What the Experts Think of Julia's Regimen

Dr. John Jakicic says: Good cardio exercise. However, she is at the low end of a healthy weight range. She should examine if energy intake is sufficient based on level of exercise reported.

Personal trainer Jay Blahnik says: She should vary her cardio workouts to avoid injuries.

Registered dietitian Dominique Adair says: Her positive attitude about food and exercise is very health supportive.

PROFILE 18 Sherry Boudreau

Claim to fame: Elite personal trainer, aerobics instructor, and hairdresser; CNBF Fitness Champion 2002, ANBC Fitness Champion 2002, WNBF Ms. Exercise World Champion 2002, plus many other fitness competitions and titles

Age: 37 years

Height: 5′ 2″

Weight: 118 pounds

Dress size: 5

Measurements: 36″ bust, 26″ waist, 36″ hips

Body mass index: 19.5 (in "normal" range)

Body fat percentage: Estimated at 10 percent (low end of "essential fat" range)

Hometown: Coquitlam, British Columbia

Children: Three, ages five, ten, and eighteen

Daily calorie intake: 1,500–1,700

Daily calorie expenditure from exercise: Up to 400

Sherry's Typical Daily Menu

Breakfast: ½ cup slow-cooked oatmeal (73 calories), 1 tablespoon of walnuts (50 calories), and one cup of egg substitute (211 calories) Total: 334 calories

Snack: ⅓ cup of vanilla protein powder (100 calories) blended with ½ cup of blueberries (40 calories), water, and ice Total: 140 calories

Lunch: Grilled chicken salad made from 4 ounces chicken breast (183 calories) on salad (14 calories) mixed with 1 teaspoon of olive oil (50 calories) and raspberry vinegar (2 calories), with ½ cup of brown rice (107 calories) Total: 356 calories

Snack: Protein shake with ⅓ cup of vanilla protein powder (100 calories) blended with ½ banana (50 calories), water, and ice (150 calories) Total: 150 calories

Uncovered! Secret Number 43

Integrate a few meal replacements into your diet.

Dinner: ½ cup yam (79 calories), with 4 ounces of lean beef (327 calories), 1 cup of broccoli (90 calories), and 3 omega 3-6-9 capsules (essential fatty acids) Total: 496 calories

Snack: ⅓ cup of vanilla protein powder (100 calories) blended with one cup of peaches (73 calories) with water and ice Total: 173 calories

Total daily calories: 1,649

Sample Weekly Workout

Monday: 40 minutes weight training focused on back and biceps, 20 minutes of cardio of choice (400 calories burned)

Tuesday: 40 minutes weight training focused on chest and triceps, 20 minutes of cardio of choice (400 calories burned)

Wednesday: Rest

Thursday: 40 minutes weight training focused on shoulders and abdominals, 20 minutes of cardio of choice (400 calories burned)

Friday: 40 minutes weight training focused on legs, light walking on treadmill (300 calories burned)

Saturday: 30-minute walk with the kids (60 calories burned)

Sunday: 30-minute walk with the kids (60 calories burned)

Sherry's Fitness Facts

Food philosophy: Keep it clean, natural, and portioned.

Total daily water intake: 2–3 liters

Cheating: One day a week all day long, but I still make sure I choose one serving size.

Approach to holidays/temptations: Drink lots of water, and if you are going to cheat, do some cardio that day.

Sticking to the plan: Write everything you eat down in a journal, that way you won't forget what you ate or what you did for activity.

Uncovered! Secret Number 44

Keep a food diary.

Exercise philosophy: Train hard, eat clean, hydrate, rest, and then repeat.

Advice to others: Start today; tomorrow never comes. Keep smiling and stay positive. Make a plan on paper and set some goals, but baby step your way to the finish line. It's also really important to focus on what you have achieved to keep your eye on the ball and stay inspired. If you are constantly looking at your situations negatively, you will never see the good thing that is sitting right in front of you.

Uncovered! Secret Number 45

Set a goal, create a plan.

Uncovered! Secret Number 46

Focus on your successes and how they make you feel.

What the Experts Think of Sherry's Regimen

Dr. John Jakicic says: Sherry's exercise is moderate but sufficient for health benefits. However, body fatness is low and could potentially have a negative impact on health—this should be monitored and assessed.

Personal trainer Jay Blahnik says: A really well-balanced program.

Registered dietitian Dominique Adair says: Her philosophy of clean, natural, and portioned is terrific.

PROFILE 19 Susana Aguila

Claim to fame: Former competitive swimmer in Spain and mother of two children

Age: 28 years

Height: 5′ 2″

Weight: 105 pounds

Dress size: 0–2

Measurements: 33″ bust, 26″ waist, 33″ hips

Body mass index: 19 (in "normal" range)

Body fat percentage: Estimated at 20 percent (high end of "athlete" range)

Hometown: Andujar, Spain

Children: Two, ages three and four

Daily calorie intake: 1,266

Daily calorie expenditure from exercise: Up to 485

Susana's Typical Daily Menu

Breakfast: ⅓ of a cup of Mueslix cereal (100 calories) with ½ cup of 2 percent milk (61 calories), ½ an apple (40 calories), and 1 cup of orange juice (113 calories) Total: 314 calories

11:30 A.M. snack: Turkey sandwich made from two slices of omega bread (140 calories), one slice of turkey cold cut (40 calories), lettuce (1 calorie), tomato (8 calories), and onions (8 calories) Total: 197 calories

3:30 P.M. meal: 6 ounces of grilled salmon (245 calories) cooked with 1 tablespoon of olive oil (119 calories), with 2 cups of lettuce with 2 teaspoons of balsamic dressing (90 calories) Total: 454 calories

6:30 P.M. meal: 1½ cups of cantaloupe (70 calories) and 1 cup of 2 percent milk (122 calories) Total: 192 calories

Before bed meal: One medium plain baked potato (109 calories) Total: 109 calories

Total daily calories: 1,266 calories

Sample Weekly Workout

Monday: 1 hour of swimming (485 calories burned)

Tuesday: Rest

Wednesday: 1 hour of swimming (485 calories burned)

Thursday: 1 hour of swimming (485 calories burned)

Friday: 1 hour of swimming (485 calories burned)

Saturday: 1 hour of swimming (485 calories burned)

Sunday: Rest

Susana's Fitness Facts

Food philosophy: I am very particular about what I eat. I like to read the labels, find out what is in it. I know that cookies and things like that have a lot of sugar and salt and things that aren't good for my body. If I don't know the product, don't know what exactly goes into it, I don't like to eat it. I like natural, whole foods.

Uncovered! Secret Number 47

If man made it, avoid it.

Total daily water intake: 2 liters

Cheating: I don't have them often. When my body tells me I need something, about once or twice a week I will eat something like ice cream, but I only have two scoops.

Approach to holidays/temptations: In Spain it's very different. There may be one big party for the holidays but that's it, so there's not a lot of temptation. We don't make a party for everything the way we do in North America. The desserts are also different there. The ingredients are more natural and fresher.

Sticking to the plan: I like to be healthy. It helps me to be happy. If your body is healthy, you feel happy. I feel stronger and it's a great outlet for stress.

Advice to others: We should eat things that make us feel mentally good and healthy. We should eat fresh foods and read the labels and study what our bodies need.

What the Experts Think of Susana's Regimen

Dr. John Jakicic says: Susana appears to be healthy based on BMI and level of activity reported.

Personal trainer Jay Blahnik says: Better than average but she should vary her cardio.

Registered dietitian Dominique Adair says: Her focus on getting natural, whole foods is terrific, but she's on the low side calorie-wise.

PROFILE 20 Amanda Williams

Claim to fame: Student, Hilton Hotel Las Vegas Showgirl, model, and former zookeeper

Age: 27 years

Height: 5' 9"

Weight: 118 pounds

Dress size: 3–4

Measurements: 33" bust, 25" waist, 35" hips

Body mass index: 17–18 (just below "normal" range)

Body fat percentage: 18 percent (in "athlete" range)

Hometown: North Las Vegas, Nevada

Children: None

Daily calorie intake: 1,193–1,532

Daily calorie expenditure from exercise: Up to 270

Amanda's Typical Daily Menu

Breakfast: One bottle of low-fat Splenda Dannon yogurt drink (80 calories) with 2 cups of Post Select Great Grains cereal with Pecans cereal mixed into it (416 calories) Total: 496 calories

Lunch: Veggie wrap made with one medium whole-wheat wrap (120 calories) with lettuce (1 calorie), green peppers (6 calories), onions (6 calories), black olives (17 calories), cucumbers (8 calories), bean sprouts (8 calories), and tomatoes (13 calories) with 1 tablespoon of nonfat Miracle Whip dressing (13 calories); and one banana (100 calories) Total: 292 calories

Snack: 2 handfuls of mixed dried fruit (250 calories) containing banana chips, cranberries, apples, pineapple, and mango or 2

handfuls of pretzels (150 calories) or 100-calorie snack pack of Wheat Thins Total: 100–250 calories

Dinner: 4 ounces of grilled chicken (222 calories) with 1 cup of green beans (83 calories), or Campbell's Cream of Mushroom soup (494 calories) Total: 305–494 calories

Total daily calories: 1,193–1,532

Sample Weekly Workout

Monday: 30-minute medium-level Power 90 aerobics videos— compilation of aerobics, kickboxing, power yoga, and weight training (200 calories burned), 20-minute Windsor Pilates abdominal workout video (70 calories burned)

Tuesday: 30-minute medium-level Power 90 aerobics video (200 calories burned)

Wednesday: 30-minute medium-level Power 90 aerobics video (200 calories burned)

Thursday: 20-minute Windsor Pilates abdominal workout video (70 calories burned)

Friday: 30-minute medium-level Power 90 aerobics video (200 calories burned)

Saturday: 30-minute medium-level Power 90 aerobics (200 calories burned)

Sunday: Rest

Amanda's Fitness Facts

Food philosophy: I never live by a diet rule because it's not practical, so I just always try to stay conscious of what I am eating at all times no matter if I am at a party or on vacation.

Total daily water intake: As much as I can take. I hate water so I drink a couple of Crystal Lights every day.

Cheating: I cheat every day, even if it's just one cookie or a couple of Brachs mints. I have to have some candy.

Approach to holidays/temptations: Treat them as every other day, just eat very small amounts of things. I always eat my mother's chocolate cake when I go home but only one small piece and it's always just as good. Also I never bring home food gifts because I am too weak. If they are still wrapped, I just regift them.

Uncovered! Secret Number 48

Adopt a "skinny chicks" mindset.

Exercise philosophy: There is no way to stay toned without exercise, so it has to be done. Only afterwards does it ever feel worth it, but it always is.

Advice to others: You are beautiful the way you are. Diet only to stay healthy, not to conform to unrealistic standards. Work out with a buddy or meet them at the gym. You are always more likely to go and not find excuses not to. Find any way possible to stay motivated. A well-toned body is the best feeling in the world.

Uncovered! Secret Number 49

Create a support network.

What the Experts Think of Amanda's Regimen

Dr. John Jakicic says: Exercise appears to be appropriate. While BMI appears to be lower than what would be recommended, this should be considered taking into account her body fatness.

Personal trainer Jay Blahnik says: Her workout regimen is very complete even though it is all video-based.

Registered dietitian Dominique Adair says: Amanda's diet is well balanced.

Claim to fame: Actor, choreographer, dancer, model, dance instructor; guest star on "Star Trek: Enterprise"; backup dancer for Britney Spears and Beyoncé; appeared on "Alias," "MAD TV," and "Celebrity Fit Club" television shows

Age: 24 years

Height: 5′ 6″

Weight: 115 pounds

Dress size: 3–5

Measurements: 34″ bust, 25″ waist, 35″ hips

Body mass index: 18 (just under "normal" range)

Body fat percentage: Estimated at 19 percent (in "athlete" range)

Hometown: Residing in Burbank, California (raised in Coquitlam, British Columbia)

Children: None

Daily calorie intake: 2,021

Daily calorie expenditure from exercise: Up to 903

Menina's Typical Daily Menu

Breakfast: One packet of instant oatmeal (171 calories), 8 ounces of fresh orange juice (113 calories), one 3-inch-round bagel (157 calories) with a thin layer of strawberry cream cheese (25 calories) Total: 466 calories

Snack: One mozzarella cheese stick (80 calories), 15 salt 'n' vinegar chips (150 calories) Total: 230 calories

Lunch: Power smoothie from Robeks shop (180 calories) and a shrimp tempura roll (85 calories) Total: 265 calories

Snack: 1 cup of tortilla chips (130 calories) and 3 tablespoons of salsa (12 calories) Total: 142 calories

Dinner: 5 ounces of chicken breast (277 calories) with 1 tablespoon of barbecue sauce (10 calories), 1 cup of instant mashed potatoes

(223 calories), ½ cup of corn (83 calories), mixed green salad (14 calories) with 1 tablespoon of balsamic vinaigrette (60 calories), and an 8-ounce glass of grape juice (152 calories) Total: 819 calories

Snack: Eight strawberries (29 calories) and 2 tablespoons of whipped cream (70 calories) Total: 99 calories

Total daily calories: 2,021 calories

Sample Weekly Workout

Monday: Rest

Tuesday: 2-hour dance performance (543 calories burned), 1-hour full-body weight workout (360 calories burned)

Wednesday: 2-hour dance performance (543 calories burned), 1-hour yoga class (211 calories burned)

Thursday: 2-hour dance performance (543 calories burned), 1-hour Pilates class (211 calories burned)

Friday: 2-hour dance performance (543 calories burned), 1-hour full-body weight workout (360 calories burned)

Saturday: 2-hour dance performance (543 calories burned), 1-hour dance class (272 calories burned)

Sunday: 2-hour dance performance (543 calories burned), 1-hour full-body weight workout (360 calories burned)

Menina's Fitness Facts

Food philosophy: What you eat is how you will feel. In other words, if you eat healthy, you will feel healthy.

Total daily water intake: Bottles and bottles

Cheating: I have cheat days all the time. I am not going to lie. I like to sit in front of the TV with a bowl of ice cream or perhaps sit by the computer with a bag of chips. I have cravings from time to time, but I never let it get out of hand.

Approach to holidays/temptations: I tend to overeat on holidays, especially Christmas and Thanksgiving. It's only a couple times a year, so why not? I will just make sure I hit the gym the next day.

Uncovered! Secret Number 50

Have a plan for when weight goes up.

What the Experts Think of Menina's Regimen

Dr. John Jakicic says: Menina is extremely active but this is most likely not a problem considering her profession. While BMI appears to be lower than what would be recommended, this should be considered taking into account her body fatness. Based on photo, it appears that she is toned and has a healthy appearance.

Personal trainer Jay Blahnik says: Her diet is very well balanced and her program is very good.

Registered dietitian Dominique Adair says: Better than average.

Now you've met the skinny chicks. You've seen what they do each day on both the diet and exercise fronts to get the bodies they have, and we've pointed out each "secret" as we've come across them. These women don't diet; they maintain this lifestyle every day and have done so over the long haul. We have a lot to learn from them. Now that we've discovered the 50 secrets these women have in common, let's take a closer look at each one.

The Skinny Chick Plan for Real Women: Secrets 1 Through 25

5

NOW IT'S TIME TO learn all we can about the first twenty-five secrets of skinny chicks. In this chapter, we will define exactly what each secret means. You'll get background and context, a "Make It Happen Now: Real Chick Plan" for each secret, and a checklist for what you can actually do to make each secret happen for you. This is where you get the real goods on exactly how to integrate the advice of skinny chicks into your diet and exercise plans. So, let's get down to business and check out the first twenty-five secrets.

Secret Number 1:
Burn All the Calories You Eat

Low carb, high protein, forget the hype! The truth is that when it comes to the size of your buns, it's the number of calories you've burned compared to the number you've consumed that counts. It's simple math. One pound of fat equals 3,500 calories. Eat that much more than you need, and you gain a pound. Keep eating too much and the needle on the scale will keep on going up. On the other hand, cut down the number of calories you eat—down to what you *really* need—and the pounds will quickly slip away. Skinny chicks know all about it, as their daily calorie intake versus expenditures reveal.

While misinformation is everywhere about just how many calories we need, the truth is that women who are very active need fewer calories than is generally believed. And if you look closely, you'll see that, even with these very challenging fitness regimes, these buff babes generally don't consume more than 1,600 calories a day. So get smart and start counting those calories. For more information on figuring out how many calories you need, see Chapter 7.

Make It Happen Now: The Real Chick Plan for #1

First, take a good, hard look at what foods and beverages you typically consume. Start by taking careful notes, with pen and paper, of everything you eat and drink. That means *everything*—even the milk in your coffee counts! And no cheating! You'll only be cheating yourself. Look at food labels, use books or the Web to research the calorie content of foods that don't have labels, and then do the math. Tally the numbers at the end of each day. Maybe you will find that you are eating 2,300 calories a day and not doing very much exercise. The USDA recommends the average woman consume 1,600 calories, so you may want to try cutting down to that level for a while and see where that gets you. Or, you may decide to keep more calories and add more workouts. It's recommended that people get a minimum of thirty minutes of exercise on most (if not all) days, so if you aren't getting that much already, adding exercise may be the key. Then monitor what is working for you. Do you feel that you are getting enough food? Do you feel like you have enough energy? If you answer yes to these questions and are losing no more than one or two pounds a week (give yourself some time for this to start happening), then you are right on track. If you need more food, eat it. But if you find you aren't losing at that rate, consider cutting down on the food and/or increasing the exercise.

Read food labels carefully and don't discount teaspoon- or morsel-sized portions. A pinch here, a dash there. It really does add up. You may have to do some additional math to be sure you know exactly how many calories you are getting in the serving you are eating. And don't be afraid to ask for the nutritional information of the meals you eat in restaurants. You may want to keep your pen and paper, calculator, and calorie book with you at all times so you can easily keep on track. You can also buy handheld calorie "clicker" machines (available at sporting goods stores) that help you keep a tally or the more advanced computer programs that you can even use on your wireless portable devices. Skinny Chick Sazzy Varga says it's so important that women get educated about the calories in food. "This may seem like a lot of work at first, but it becomes second nature once you begin," says Sazzy, who says she keeps a "running mental ticker" of how many calories she eats each day.

The idea is to empower yourself with the facts about the foods you eat and a method of keeping track of it. By looking at the cold, hard data about the foods you eat, you'll soon see where you need to make adjustments (by reducing amounts of some foods or even eliminating some foods all together). For instance, I refuse to drink any of my calories. Diet cola tastes just as good to me and buys me another 150 calories I can "spend" somewhere else.

Other mental tips to help keep you on track include:

* That pizza pie you want to devour will bring you halfway toward gaining a whole pound!
* Think about how you'll eat that tempting treat but then won't feel full at all, because it's all calories and no substance. In the end you've wasted a good number of calories on it and are left with that many fewer calories for the rest of the day.
* If you've got a party or other food-centered event coming up, do the math ahead of time and plan around it. Eat light earlier in the day and make allowances for a certain number of calories while you are there. Keep track of the calories in your head as you go. (You can even call ahead to find out what foods will be served.)
* Stop to reflect that eating this particular thing will undo part of the work you have done in the previous days and weeks. The amount of calories in two cookies will mean an extra fifteen to twenty minutes of running. That forty-five-minute spin class won't even burn the amount of calories you consumed on your all-out binge. Think of the sweets and extra helpings in terms of workout time, and it will put your efforts into perspective.
* Check your typical calorie intake against your typical calorie burning and make adjustments if needed.
* See Chapter 7 for more details and tips on sticking to a low-calorie plan.

Calorie-Counting Grid *(use to help get yourself started)*

MEAL	CALORIE COUNTS	CALORIE TOTALS
Breakfast		
		Total Breakfast:
Snack 1		
		Total Snack 1:
Lunch		
		Total Lunch:
Snack 2		
		Total Snack 2:
Dinner		
		Total Dinner:
Snack 3		
		Total Snack 3:
		DAILY TOTAL:

Checklist

- ☑ Set up a system for counting calories (purchase computer program, use calculator and pen and paper, etc.).
- ☑ Research the calorie content of foods you eat regularly and build a database of that information for reference. (Computer programs can do this for you.)
- ☑ Research the calorie-burning value of various exercises, including your usual daily activities, and make a database of this information for your reference. (Again, computer programs can do this for you.)
- ☑ Set up a weekly exercise plan. (See Chapters 8 and 9 to see how to set up a cardio-resistance-stretch program.)
- ☑ Research the calorie content of foods on your "danger list," foods that you eat only occasionally and need to make accommodations for.
- ☑ Find some good low-calorie choices at the restaurants you like to dine in. (Subway and many other major restaurants provide online nutritional information so you can be better informed.)
- ☑ Check your typical calorie intake against your typical calorie burning and make adjustments if needed.
- ☑ Monitor your daily calories consistently to make sure you stay on track.
- ☑ Start with a maximum of 1,600 calories and work from there to see what's right for you.

Secret Number 2: Add Weight Training to Your Regime

For the longest time, fitness experts warned women against weight training for fear that they'd bulk up and not have the long, lean physique most women crave. However, we now know that it's actually difficult for women to build huge muscles like men. We simply don't have the hormones to do it. But by adding a weight-training regimen to your exercise plans, you can burn more calories lifting the weights and create muscle mass that will not only speed up your metabolism (the rate at which you burn calories) but require calories to maintain. That means the new muscle you build will eat calories for you! You'll end up with those cut upper arms; cute, sporty little calves; and long, slim legs. Weight training is a staple for skinny chicks who have to work at it, so make it a part of your week, too!

Make It Happen Now: The Real Chick Plan for #2

You don't need a lot of weight to make a lot of difference. A couple of 2-, 5-, or 8-pound hand weights are a great start. A good idea is to place them next to your TV or anyplace you spend a lot of time. That way you can just pick them up and do the sets you need whenever you think of it. An exercise band is another great way to do resistance/strength training. They only cost about $20 and can be used a number of ways. The idea with both hand weights and the exercise band is to challenge the muscle to make it longer and stronger. You also don't have to invest in heavy gym equipment or some expensive gym membership. Hand weights alone can work your entire upper body and, by throwing in some squats, lunges, and toe extensions, you can do your lower body, too. For more on this, see Chapter 9: Getting Long and Strong.

Checklist

☑ Read Chapter 9: Getting Long and Strong
☑ Decide whether you're going to build a small home gym or get a gym membership.
☑ If you're going the home-gym route, buy 2-, 5- and 10-pound free weights and an exercise band.

- ☑ Set up an area in your home where you will do your resistance training sessions. Ideally this should be a place where you often go—perhaps with a TV—to help you stick with your plan.
- ☑ Set up a weekly weights workout plan with at least two weights/resistance training sessions each week.
- ☑ Chose an exercise for every major muscle group in your body and create a program integrating all of those exercises. Each exercise should be done eight to twelve times and repeated for two sets.
- ☑ Be sure to learn proper technique and positioning before you start.

Secret Number 3: Rejoice in Fresh New Tastes

Here's where we're going to focus on widening our horizons. If you write down what you eat each day for a week, you'll probably notice that you tend to eat the same foods over and over. That's pretty typical of most people. There may be twenty or so different meals, or even fewer, that you cycle through your weeks. This is convenient in many respects—including keeping on top of the calorie content. However, if these twenty meals, or even a good portion of them, are not the most healthful choices, it's probably time to consider retiring a few meals and introducing some new ones.

Shake up your food world and discover new, healthier favorites that you will want to go back to time and time again. The skinny chicks know this trick. They are always on the hunt for healthy, yummy new foods that will make eating well enjoyable. This can include anything from a brand-new vegetable that you can't believe you haven't tried before to a complicated recipe that tastes so good you can serve it to guests. By shaking up your "food wardrobe," you'll soon find eating well isn't so hard after all.

Make It Happen Now: The Real Chick Plan for #3

At our friends' home one night for dinner, I discovered that I absolutely adore the taste of brussel sprouts and turnips. It seems silly, but after thirty years of thinking that my favorite vegetables were conventional favorites like green beans and potatoes, now I *know* that my favorites are actually brussel sprouts and turnips! And I've discovered that I love beets, eggplant, and artichoke, too.

When you're looking to shake up your food wardrobe, you have to start in the veggie section of your grocery store. These foods will make you feel full for next to no calories, and they are full of vitamins and minerals. So, every time you go to the grocery store, try a new vegetable, look up some recipes, and see if you like it. Next, try out some new whole-grain or healthier grain products, like spinach pasta and old-fashioned oatmeal. For virtually every fatty, sugary, high-calorie meal or food item, there is a healthier, lower-calorie option. You just need to shop around and not be afraid to try new things. Go around to all of the sections of the grocery store and see what they've got. You may not like the new item, but it's also possible that you'll end up liking it better than something else you eat all the time.

Checklist

☑ Head to the produce section of your grocery store and pick at least one new vegetable to try each time you shop.

☑ Look up new recipes to cook the vegetables to see if you like them.

☑ Don't let one bad veggie turn you off. Keep trying new ones.

☑ Try new fruits, too.

☑ Check out the healthier options in the bakery and grain-products section.

☑ Try different cuts and kinds of chicken and fish if you don't eat them already.

- ✓ Try replacing beef-centered meals with leaner cuts of meat.
- ✓ Test out lower-fat versions of milk and cheese if you haven't already. Try soy milks as well to see if you like them.
- ✓ As you find new meals and foods that you love, drop old standards that are less healthy from your meal rotation.

Secret Number 4: Stop Seeing It as "Dieting"

This is a big one. This is one of the pillars of this book. Being on a "diet" is seen as a bad thing these days and for good reason. Being on a diet means you are depriving yourself, often severely, of most of the foods you enjoy for a short period of time in a desperate effort to trim your body down to the size you want. The key part of this is that diets come to an end. They have to. They are usually too strict for anyone to safely stick to for the long term, even if you have the willpower (not likely) to do so. The official word now is that diets don't work simply because, even if you lose weight while on one, you just put it right back on when you go off it.

This was a big part of why I wanted to write this book. I wanted to share with the women of the world the secrets of women whose job it is to look good all the time. While these women do clamp down hard on occasion for special jobs or events, they keep their bodies in pretty tip-top shape year-round. What they do, they do all the time. They don't diet. They don't see what they do as dieting. They see it as a healthy diet, in the sense of the word referring to the way people eat. Skinny Chick Anna Wyatt says, "I don't believe in diets. Instead, I eat well in small portions when I'm hungry. And I stop when I'm not hungry anymore." Skinny Chick Monika Schnarre says, "Don't use the word *diet*. Learn that eating healthy is a lifestyle." While healthy eating may feel much more restrained than the way you've eaten in the past, it's crucial that you begin to see this new way of eating as part of a healthy lifestyle that will be with you for a lifetime.

Make It Happen Now: The Real Chick Plan for #4

Changing the way they think about their diet is hard for a lot of women. Whenever we begin a "health kick," we always see it in the context of dieting because that's what it always meant in the past. But skinny chicks know that dieting won't work for them, because they have to look great all the time and can't afford to have their weight yo-yoing up and down. They have had to find something they can live with for the long term. It's a healthy diet, not dieting. So in order to really incorporate this secret into our lives, we've got to shake the whole idea of being on a diet. If you think what you are doing is too strict for you to stick with for a lifetime, ease things up a bit. There is no point in white-knuckling it for a while only to collapse and say, "To hell with it, I give up" and go back to what you were doing before. You've got to find a balance you can live with.

In the beginning it might be best for you to eat more than you will ultimately. It can be shocking to drop down to 1,600 calories or less. (Never go below 1,200 calories; that's the minimum you need to sustain your body and get all the right nutrients.) To start, drop down as far as you can, and you may well find that, once you begin to see results, you want to trim more calories from your day. This will also be the case as you learn to "spend" your calories on smarter choices like veggies, instead of pasta. On the other hand, there may be particular times when you want to really buckle down to speed up the weight loss process. This is fine as long as you've got your eye on the goal, which is to get back to a manageable diet and level of exercise that you can sustain over a long period of time.

Checklist

- ✔ Replace the word *diet* with the phrase *healthy lifestyle*.
- ✔ Correct anyone who is referring to your new, healthy lifestyle as a diet.
- ✔ Add more calories if you are feeling too deprived to stick with your plan for life. But be sure to try choosing healthier options first.
- ✔ Seriously consider taking off ("cheating") one day a week so you can enjoy the foods you love.
- ✔ Repeat to yourself, "I am eating this way as a part of a healthy life, for my whole life."
- ✔ Resist any temptation to buckle down too hard for short periods of time. This can throw you off course completely.
- ✔ If you fall off the horse, get right back on again. Figure out what made you fall off and come up with ways to avoid that in the future.

Secret Number 5: Exercise More Days than Not

Feeling fit and fabulous requires exercise, period. The human being was not meant to spend the amount of time sitting on its buns that we do these days. Technological advances have made our lives a lot easier and more productive in many ways, but they have stopped us from being as physical as is required to stay in good shape. Therefore, we've got to add that movement back into our lives. Just to increase your health and well-being, you must exercise at a moderate intensity for an accumulated total of thirty minutes on most days, according to the Departments of Agriculture and Health and Human Services *Dietary Guidelines for Americans* released in 2005.

But, as you can see, the women in this book are working out at least an hour, six days a week. In some cases, it's two hours or more. The *Dietary Guidelines for Americans*, in fact, recommends ninety minutes of exercise daily just to maintain earlier weight loss. (Be sure to read the Make It Happen Now section to find out how you can make this happen even in your busy, hectic life.) Most of us lead such sedentary lives that we must consciously add an exercise regimen to burn off our extra calories and keep our bodies at a healthy weight. Reducing the number of calories we eat alone is a slow, painful way to get weight off and keep it off. By adding exercise, you can eat substantially more and still look terrific. Exercise speeds up your metabolism (the rate at which you burn calories), builds sexy muscle, and makes you feel terrific inside and out. It's also important to balance the types of exercise you do, with cardiovascular activity, weights, and stretching all working together to make you fit and fabulous.

Make It Happen Now: The Real Chick Plan for #5

Two hours of exercise a day! How the heck are you going to fit that into your week? Well, for starters, it's up to you to decide whether you even want to. And, depending on the type of exercise you choose, one hour of exercise six days a week can get you into terrific shape just as well as two hours a day. It's your call when it comes to what you can squeeze into your life. But keep in mind that there is more room for exercise in your day than you may realize. First, many skinny chicks get up before the sun to squeeze an hour of exercise in before the day begins. You may love that extra hour of sleep, but perhaps you'd love a size-6 butt more! Perhaps that's where you can add some exercise to your day.

Next, can you run, walk, or cycle to work? That's another terrific way to get some exercise, perhaps only adding a short amount of time to your commute. It's worth looking into. That way, you can also add some exercise on your way home at the end of the day, when you are stressed and need some endorphins. You can also take your running shoes to work and walk or run at lunchtime. Eat your lunch meal at your desk after you're finished your workout. (If you take workout clothes, a towel, and a hairdryer to work, you can get yourself fit for business again in no time).

Next, you can plan to hit the gym or put on your running shoes and hit the pavement the minute you get home from work. Add it onto your workday as though it were just another business meeting. If going home after work to change is likely to derail you because the couch and the TV are just too tempting, then don't go home. Have your clothes in your car or in a bag with you and go straight there. Also be sure to carry a snack with you, so you aren't starving for dinner and make that pit-stop at home after all.

For those with children, take your kids to the gym and put them in the free babysitting that many clubs provide. Another great way to exercise with kids in tow is to pop them in a single or double Babyjogger and go for a run. Give the kids some books and food and talk to them the whole way. It's a great way to spend time together while burning those extra calories.

Checklist

☑ Take a look at your typical daily schedule and see where you can fit in some exercise.

☑ Take a look at your typical weekly schedule and figure out how many days each week you can commit to exercise.

☑ Set up a weekly exercise plan and post it on your refrigerator or in some other highly visible place.

☑ Read Chapters 8 and 9 to figure out what cardiovascular and resistance exercises are best for you.

☑ Set up a no-fail plan of exercise that fits around your life.

☑ Resolve to make exercising more days than not just a fact of your new life.

☑ Stick to your plan and don't let excuses start to interfere with your exercise plans. (Treat these workouts like business meetings. Would you "no-show" for an important meeting with your boss? Probably not. Invest at least that same level of dedication in yourself.)

☑ When you have to miss a workout, find a way to replace it. (Perhaps work out longer the next day or even head out for a run after dark when the kids are in bed. Knowing that you will have to work out doubly hard the next day is a terrific incentive to stick to your original workout plans.)

Secret Number 6: Drink Water Like There's No Tomorrow

One gallon of water. That's a lot of water. But that's how much Skinny Chick Kim Lyons drinks every day. And if you look closely, she's not the only one who is drinking and drinking and drinking. There are many good reasons the skinny chicks can't get enough water (and other noncaffeinated and non-alcoholic beverages).

Drinking enough water is of particular importance to women who exercise because they lose a lot of liquid when they sweat. It can be dangerous to exercise and not replace the liquid. Dehydration causes the body to hold on to unnecessary sodium stores, which in turn makes the body hold on to up to TEN POUNDS of unneeded fluids. That will make you quite puffy and bloated. Water is also a natural appetite suppressant and it helps the body to metabolize fat. Also, you sweat out sodium and potassium, which can make you feel sick or, in extreme cases, can actually cause death.

For the average exerciser, it is recommended that you drink at least eight glasses of water a day. You should also drink one cup an hour before you exercise and drink another half cup of water for every fifteen minutes of exercise. Caffeine and alcohol dehydrate you, which means for every cup of these beverages you drink you have to drink another cup of nonalcoholic or noncaffeinated beverage just to replace what you've lost.

The best way to know if you are getting enough fluids is to check the color of your urine. If it's pale yellow or clear, you're doing well. If it's yellow or dark yellow, get drinking, girl! Bottom line: you could flush away up to ten pounds of excess fluids and puffiness just by drinking enough. So get drinking!

Make It Happen Now: The Real Chick Plan for #6

How are you going to squeeze eight glasses or more of water into your day? It can be hard, especially if you're not a big fan of water. Get yourself a funky water container that you can reuse and take with you throughout your day. (You always see the celebrities carrying water bottles wherever they go. Now it's your turn to clutch a water bottle under your arm everywhere you go. How glamorous!) Actually, having a reusable bottle will allow you to save money by refilling it whenever and wherever you want.

Does the taste of plain water make you gag past a certain point? No problem! Just sprinkle some Crystal Light or similar low- or no-calorie tasty mix and give your water a yummy splash. You can also water down your juices or even just add a splash of juice to liven up your water. Changing your caffeinated coffee or tea to decaf is another great way to get more fluids into your body. Also, more and more great calorie-free juices are available at corner stores and grocery stores. Any noncaffeinated beverage, even if it's not low calorie, is also a great way to get more fluids into your body. So there's no excuse.

Checklist

- ✓ Buy at least one funky water bottle that you can refill and carry with you throughout your day.
- ✓ Fill that bottle and take it with you everywhere.
- ✓ Consider buying some yummy calorie-free drink mix to spice up that water when you need to.

- ☑ Consider buying cases of bottled water to ensure you always have some fresh fluids on hand.
- ☑ Try out the sparkling water varieties and those flavored with a splash of lemon or lime.
- ☑ Drink, drink, drink! Make sure you drink at least ten 8-ounce glasses each day.
- ☑ Stay clear of alcoholic and caffeinated beverages. But if you do have any, then also drink an equal amount of water for every cup. (You need this much just to replace the fluids you lost from drinking these dehydrating beverages.)

Secret Number 7: Eat High-Bulk, Low-Calorie Foods

This is a secret that could be easy to miss reading over the skinny chicks' daily diets. You see them eating all sorts of veggies and fruit and whole grains, and you know that these are healthy foods, but not everyone realizes all the reasons why these foods are so healthy. An important part of it is that these foods have a lot of fiber, or are more "fibrous." Fiber, also known as bulk or roughage, is the part of a plant that humans can't actually digest. In fact, fiber passes through the body virtually unchanged. One of the biggest benefits of high-fiber foods from a weight management standpoint is how full they make you feel. This is because these foods take longer to chew (giving your body a chance to recognize that it's full and, therefore, leading to less overeating), they make meals seem bigger and the food linger in your stomach longer (making you feel more full), and they also tend to be less calorie-dense than other foods. We'll discuss this further in Chapter 7; The Lowdown on Food, but what you should keep in mind is that high-fiber foods will make you feel like you are eating tons of food (in a good way!) while keeping you feeling full and not taking in further calories.

Make It Happen Now: The Real Chick Plan for #7

Buying food that is as close to its natural state as possible is the best way to incorporate this secret into your life. This is a big part of why diets like The Zone, which steer people clear of carbohydrates like white bagels, are as successful as they are. When on these diets, people make much smarter choices because those refined foods are on the no-no list. (I think outlawing bagels is the fastest way to start everyone obsessing about bagels, so I don't like to see any foods completely crossed off your list. But you get the idea.) By choosing a whole-grain bagel you will feel full longer than if you ate the bagel made from white, processed flour. So, look around at the food choices you usually make and see if there are better choices you could be making.

Shopping in the outside aisles at the grocery store is a great way to keep refined, processed purchases to a minimum. Whole foods that haven't been processed—fruits, vegetables, whole grains—will go bad a lot faster than the processed products, so they are traditionally placed around the edges of the store so staff can move them in and out more quickly. The inside aisles hold all the processed stuff. Only if you find products with 3 grams of fiber or more in those inner isles should you be pausing to shop there!

Checklist

☑ Think about what vegetables you love to eat and make a point of picking some up on a regular basis.

☑ Make sure to have some of your favorite fruits on hand, particularly the more fibrous fruits like oranges, mango, and pineapple.

☑ Beware of canned fruits and vegetables that come packed with sugar and/or salt.

✓ Take a look at the breads and other baked goods you eat and shop around for some whole-grain versions. They taste just as good!

✓ Make a point of planning meals that are as high bulk but low calorie as possible, such as stir-fries, vegetable casseroles, and fruit salads.

✓ When you are eating out, select the whole-grain options and pick meals with vegetables on the side instead of pastas or rice.

Secret Number 8: Don't Make Unplanned Food Stops

On my way to my doctor's office I always pass by this cinnamon bun place that smells so very, very good. Those chewy, cinnamon rolls, dripping with icing . . . yum. Cinnamon rolls are one of my favorite foods. But I never stop to have some. The calorie count is off the charts, and even the smaller buns would mean I'd have to skip a meal that day. It's just not worth it to me. But still, that smell can get to me. So, what I try to do is conjure up negative associations with this smell. This is actually a very common approach used by hypnotists and behavior modification experts working with people who are trying to break habits or change other kinds of unwanted behaviors. These can be anything from trying to quit smoking to easing the pain of contractions in childbirth. Advertisers do this, too, by creating associations between their client's product and positive feelings.

My survey of the skinny chicks revealed that almost all of them refuse to stop walking to eat something bad, even if it smells good as they walk by. For starters, these foods are usually very unhealthy, and these women like to stick to their healthy eating plans. These unplanned food stops also throw a wrench in their meal plans for the day. Skinny chicks take the time to think about what they are going to eat each day, and stopping to eat when they hadn't planned for it can throw their whole eating day off.

Make It Happen Now: The Real Chick Plan for #8

This may be a hard one for people who have really made a habit of this. If there is something that you really can't live without, perhaps you should plan for it and work the rest of your daily calories around it, as we'll talk about more in Secret #16. Again, these treats tend to be quite high in calories and will likely make the rest of your day quite restrictive, so I wouldn't advise doing it often. I think that those of us who would change our plans and walk into the cinnamon bun store have the impression that most people would do the same, and that this is a natural and normal way of living. But now you know the truth—the skinny chicks who have to work at having great bodies simply don't do it. They know there is every reason *not* to do it. These women realize what a calorie trap these treats can be. So make a resolution: unplanned food stops are simply not an option.

Checklist

☑ Think about the unplanned food stops you tend to make.

☑ Where are the high-risk food vendors in your life? Can you change your daily walking or driving routes to avoid them?

☑ Decide if there is one treat that you just can't give up. If so, find out the calorie damage and find a way to work it into your weekly calorie intake.

☑ Resolve to stop stopping. Realize that this is not something skinny chicks do, at least not the gals who have to work at it. Resolve to be like the skinny chicks and feel inspired by their willpower. If you need to, inhale that great smell as you walk past, and imagine that you've eaten it. Then be proud of the fact that you didn't and think about how firm your abs feel today.

- ☑ Remind yourself that if you had that treat you wouldn't feel as good about yourself, you'd feel sluggish afterward, and you'd pay for it in the end with weight gain, more exercise, or less real food later on.
- ☑ Add up the amount of money you save each time you don't buy the snack and use the money toward something terrific—like skinny jeans.

Secret Number 9: Get Enough Protein

Because protein and fat take a lot longer for your body to digest than carbohydrates, they help to provide a steadier stream of fuel to your body. For this reason, it's an excellent idea to try to add some protein and healthy fats to all of your meals. You can eat dough and sugar until the cows come home but you won't feel full unless you are getting enough protein. Skinny chicks know this. You won't find one girl in this book who isn't getting adequate protein. While protein can be high in calories, the skinny chicks know it's critical to helping them stick to their healthy eating plan. Without the lean, low-fat protein they eat, they would continue to feel hungry even after they've had all they need.

Although results are mixed, some government-funded studies have shown that people with higher levels of calcium, something that can be found in high levels in dairy-derived protein sources, had more control over their body weight. Also, protein is critical to building those muscles and repairing muscles after workouts because your body uses protein to fill in the microscopic tears in muscles that exercise creates. For more information on protein, see Chapter 7.

Make It Happen Now: The Real Chick Plan for #9

This should be an easy one. It's not too painful to chow down on a nice, healthy skinless chicken breast, is it? But the real challenge will likely be finding out how much protein you need and then figuring out how to get it every day. First, you need to learn the appropriate amount of low-fat protein that is right for your body. The 2005 Food Guidelines Pyramid recommends women nineteen years and over incorporate 5 to 5½ ounces of protein into their diets each day. One ounce of protein is about the size of one-third of a deck of cards, so the amount you need daily is smaller than two decks of cards. This protein can come in the form of chicken, fish, other lean cuts of meat, beans, eggs, or tofu. (One egg, ¼ cup of dry beans, and ½ cup of tofu are all equal to one 1-ounce serving.) Food packaging and kitchen scales can also help you figure out how much of each protein source equals one ounce. So, you need to think about your day and think about when and how you will fit this protein in. Plan, plan, plan!

You may have every intention of making a good, lean cut of meat the center of your dinner plate when you get home at night, but having foods like this on hand and cooking them for dinner can be more work and require more energy than many of us have at the end of the day. That box of cereal looks a whole lot more convenient when you come home hungry at the end of the day. Therefore, it's important to plan ahead. On the weekend, plan your menus for the whole week and buy all the ingredients you will need, including the protein sources. In the case of chicken, you can divide the breasts into separate freezer baggies and have individual servings ready to pop in the oven when you get home. Or, you can cook them ahead of time and store them in individual servings in the freezer. Stock your shelves with cans of tuna and cook some hard-boiled eggs and have them waiting in a bowl in the fridge. Keep a few protein bars and shakes in your cupboard. Be prepared and you won't fall into the carb trap.

Checklist

✓ Determine how much protein you need each day (see Chapter 7).

✓ Decide what kinds of lean protein you enjoy most and have them available in a convenient form at all times.

✓ Go wild and try some new kinds of protein, like yummy protein powder, protein bars, or hummus!

✓ Remember that one ounce of protein is about the size of one-third of a deck of cards. Use that visual measurement to help guide you at home and when eating out.

✓ If you like fish, make it your new best friend. If you don't, find other lean protein sources to love.

✓ Package chicken, turkey, and other frozen meats in single-serving bags in the freezer.

✓ Always have some hard-boiled eggs in the fridge for a nice, filling, healthy snack.

✓ Plan how many servings of protein you will have each day.

✓ Keep track of the protein servings you eat throughout the day.

Secret Number 10: Plan Meals and Shop to Fit Your Plan

Without a doubt, an argument can be made for having spices and rice and other staples in your pantry. But do we really need to stuff our cupboards full of cookies and other indulgent foods that really won't be a part of any meal? Often these high-calorie snack foods are just sitting there waiting to be eaten between meals, which gets many of us into trouble. For this reason it's critical to plan your meals ahead of time and shop to fit that menu. It's OK to buy snack food, as long as it is something tasty and healthy. And if you're buying a "cheat" snack food, put more thought into it than just buying a box and shoving it in the pantry where it can "call" to you. (Do you really want to put temptation like that in your house?) Remember that basically all the groceries you buy should be part of a planned meal. Otherwise, they're just sitting there begging to be eaten and will not help you stick to your healthy eating plans.

Make It Happen Now: The Real Chick Plan for #10

Start looking at the labels on the food in your pantry and decide if any of it is the kind of food you want to keep around. If you could care less about it anyway, get rid of it. Why set yourself up for temptation? If there's something you just love and have a hard time saying no to, decide how you will incorporate it into your new, healthy lifestyle. Remember skinny chicks don't deprive themselves, but everything in moderation will help you satisfy your cravings while not pushing you over your daily calorie allotment. Begin planning your meals by setting up a one-week menu cycle. Maybe one night is chicken night, another night is fish . . . that sort of thing. Make these decisions based on what you like to eat and when. Next, make a list of ingredients you will need. You may just need to shop once a week, or several times a week, but stick to the list of items you need for those meals. That way, if you start to go hunting for something to munch on, you'll think twice because it's a major component of tomorrow night's meal!

Breakfast, lunch, and dinner aren't the only things worth planning. Skinny chicks also plan their cheat days in advance, as we've seen in the previous chapter. Some cheat once a week, others just on weekends. Planning your cheat day will give you something to look forward to and you'll likely stay with your menu plans knowing that you are earning your cheat day—and your favorite foods will just taste all the better.

Checklist

☑ Take a real inventory of your refrigerator and pantry. Clean out any foods that have expired and other foods that you haven't planned for.

☑ Clean out foods you don't love. Otherwise you may find yourself eating things that aren't worth the calories just because they are there.

☑ Lock away or throw away foods you won't be able to resist.

☑ Don't deprive yourself. If you just can't bear throwing away your favorite sweet or tempting treat, plan it into your week.

☑ Find recipes to use up the rest of the food in your fridge and pantry.

☑ Starting with a clean slate, devise a weekly menu and write a shopping list.

☑ Shop to fit that menu as many times a week as you need to.

☑ Don't forget to factor in leftovers. Use those for lunch the next day and consider that when planning.

☑ When you are almost out of food, it's time to start again!

☑ Write down what you eat and how you feel afterward. Are you satisfied? Full? Are you hungry too soon after? Have you planned enough snacks?

☑ Plan cheat days. You'll feel more in control of your cravings and feel less guilty afterward.

Secret Number 11: Avoid Sugar and Refined Wheat

The "bad" carbohydrates, such as sugar and wheat, have been a hot topic for the last few years. A rash of high-protein diets have led to a new appreciation for the importance of protein and some much-needed information about which carbs are healthy and which are not. Many of these diets make use of something called the Glycemic Index (GI), which rates the speed at which the sugar in carbohydrate foods (your body turns the energy in carbs into sugar in order to use it) gets absorbed into your body. This is important because the faster the sugar is absorbed into your bloodstream, the faster you will be hungry again. In a nutshell, the whole-grain choices are preferable. They take longer for your body to digest and help you to feel full longer. You will notice that the skinny chicks in this book reserve all of their sugar—and most of their wheat-eating—for their days off. These gals usually choose the smarter carbohydrates, such as vegetables and fruit. You should too! For more information, see Chapter 7.

Make It Happen Now: The Real Chick Plan for #11

Give up your morning bagel, oh my! Don't think you can do it? Well, considering that many bagels have between 300 and 400 calories (and that's without the cream cheese!), it may be something to seriously consider. Why not replace your morning doughy delight with a serving of slow-cooked oatmeal sprinkled with some Splenda and/or cinnamon? (It's important to pick slow-cooked oatmeal because the packets of instant oatmeal typically have lots of sugar added.) Low-sugar cold cereal can be good if you pay attention and honor serving sizes. It's amazing the way these low-glycemic, whole-grain options stick to the ribs for the whole morning while making you feel like you've had something pretty substantial. What do you know? Grandma was right! You can even cook a big batch of regular oatmeal, spoon servings of it into plastic storage bags, and have them on hand in the refrigerator when you need a filling snack.

If you are a real carb addict, you can go through your cupboards and toss anything that isn't whole grain and is a temptation. (If you've got other people in the house, they can always have a separate little cupboard—perhaps even one that locks—

so they can indulge if they want to without tempting you.) Find healthier-carb options that won't put too much of a dent in your daily calorie count and stock up! Find lots of tasty whole-grain options and sugar substitutes and have them on hand.

But how can you tell if something is a healthier carbohydrate or a less-healthy carb? Well, for starters, the labels on the food packages provide lots of useful information. And if the carbohydrate doesn't even come in packaging, like fresh fruits and vegetables, then you *know* it's a good option. But for those foods that do have packaging, you want to look for words like *100 percent wheat, whole grain, whole rye flour, whole oats*, and *whole barley*. Beware of labels that say *multigrain*. What you are looking for is for the grain used to make the product to be in as close to its original state as possible, not smashed and refined. On the snacking front, you want to think about how each product was made. For instance, popcorn is a better option than pretzels because popcorn is whole kernels of corn while pretzels are made from refined white flour. And whole-grain alternatives are popping up for everything, from pasta to pizza dough, making it much easier for you to find those healthier-carb options.

Checklist

☑ Come to terms with the fact that bready, fluffy carbohydrates are not our friends.

☑ Treat these fluffy friends like condiments and relegate them to the position of occasional indulgence.

☑ Try to eat some protein and fat with every carbohydrate you eat so that you feel full longer. (Protein and fat take longer to digest and therefore keep you satiated longer than carbs alone.)

☑ Remove any temptations from your home. (If your partner and/or children are not going along with your low-carb move, help them create a special cupboard for those foods you don't want to see.)

Secret Number 12: Have a Cheat Day Once a Week to Eat What You Want

Broccoli. Chicken. Apples. Lettuce. Oatmeal. Eggs. All yummy, healthy foods that can help build a smart, low-calorie diet regimen, but can you live on these healthy choices forever? No way! Even skinny chicks need a break. In fact, many skinny chicks take one day off a week to allow themselves the things they can't eat every day. Pizza and cookie dough are Skinny Chick Kristia Knowles's secret pleasures. What are yours? As long as you make it a one-day-a-week indulgence, you can loosen the reins and eat what you want! It's what you do the majority of the time—the other six days—that will dictate what your body looks like. White-knuckling it with a healthy diet and thinking that you can never again eat your favorite bad foods will only end in binges and feelings of failure. So go ahead, have a cheat day, but plan for it!

Make It Happen Now: The Real Chick Plan for #12

This one should be easy. Chowing down on our favorite foods isn't usually something that takes any effort! What will take effort is sticking to your plan for the rest of the week. But you can do it. Just remember that banana split or pizza you've got coming to you at the end of the week. It's a good idea to save your day off for the weekend because that's when most of us entertain and dine out. But plan which day you will choose. You can easily get caught up in the "Well, I have a party Saturday night but a gals' brunch on Sunday, so I'll just split my day off into two sections" kind of thinking. You get one day. Stick to it.

It's important to remember, too, that eating everything in sight can pack on some pounds that may take all week to lose again. No all-out binges allowed. This is unhealthy and can lead to disordered eating. (Seriously, seek help if you think you may be sliding into a binge habit.) It's your day to eat the things that just won't fit into the calories limits of the rest of the week, but it's not license to become an eating machine. If you are unable to get back on the wagon after a cheat day, don't beat yourself up. This is natural and is likely to happen from time to time. Being hard on yourself may make it more difficult for you to get back on track. Also, you may begin to obsess about food, and that's not healthy. Instead, sit down and write a list of reasons why you want to get back to healthy eating. Then write a list of reasons why you can't keep up the unhealthy eating. Do some hard thinking about these reasons, then plan out what you are going to eat the next day. Plan a good, challenging workout for that day too. Just jump back on the wagon. A misstep does not spell disaster.

Checklist

- ✓ Pick your day and be smart about it!
- ✓ Resolve to be good with your eating every other day of the week, knowing that that beloved day off is coming fast!
- ✓ Think about what it is that you want to eat, so that you don't waste calories on things you don't really want and can instead really revel in your enjoyment of the things you do want.
- ✓ Think twice about filling up on tons of greasy foods, carbonated beverages, and other things that might make your tummy upset. You don't want to spend your glorious day off suffering from indigestion or possibly worse.
- ✓ Pace yourself and try to listen to your body. Eat when you are hungry, but eat what you want!
- ✓ Relax and enjoy. After six days of sticking to your healthy eating plan, it may feel strange and even guilt-provoking to dig in and chow down. But remember, you need this day to keep you going the rest of the week. So sit back, eat, and enjoy!

Secret Number 13: Adopt a "No Excuses" Mindset

Skinny chicks don't make excuses. When it comes to hitting the gym, they just do it. And when it comes to eating well, they stick to it. This is one of the most important secrets of skinny chicks. Over my years of helping other women get fit and fabulous, I have noticed that this ability to adopt a "no excuses" mindset is so critical to sticking to a healthy lifestyle. While the women I have coached will usually start off with all of the gusto and commitment I could ever hope them to have, they often start to lag after about two months. That's when I start to hear the excuses. "Oh, I couldn't go for a run, it was raining." "I didn't work out this week because I had a cold." "I had ate badly a lot these past two weeks because there were a lot of parties."

No matter what your situation is, sooner or later eating well and exercising regularly is going to become inconvenient a lot of the time. It's just a fact. It's easier and more convenient to eat badly and sit on your butt. That's the plain truth. But if you want to get your body and mind happy and healthy, you've really got to stop making excuses for why you can't stick to your plan. On most days most people can come up with a compelling reason to not work out or to eat unhealthy foods. So if you start down this road, soon enough you'll find yourself right back where you started.

Make It Happen Now: The Real Chick Plan for #13

How do you shake the making excuses habit? Well, for starters, you should set ground rules. For instance, how many days a week do you want to work out? You may want to start by making it a rule that by the time you get to Sunday night you will have done four one-hour cardio workouts in the preceding seven days. If that means you have to cram all four workouts into the last four days of the week, so be it. Otherwise, you may soon see your weekly workouts dwindle to far fewer than you'd like.

Set rules for when you are "allowed" to beg off a workout. For instance, fitness professionals often advise active people to not engage in hard cardio activity if they have any symptoms from the neck down. For instance, running nose and sore throat won't get you a day off, but an impressive chest cough will. Fever should always earn you a day off. So those can be your sickness rules. Perhaps you have asthma or other recurring ailments that may add to this short list of reasons not to work out.

Next—the weather. Outdoor workouts, like running, are so cheap and convenient but can give people a whole list of "reasons" why they can't exercise. My rule used to be that I didn't run on days when it was below −30°C with the wind chill, but after a group of beginning runners showed up to one of my clinics on a −33°C night, I decided I'd been a wimp. So now I run unless any body parts really seem to be in danger. I run in the rain, snow, sleet, wind, but I won't run in lightning or hail.

As for food, I stick to a set number of calories six days a week, then splurge on the seventh day. When a coworker brings in cookies to a meeting, my rule is to not eat any unless I count it into my daily calories. Those are my rules. You should make up your own. But make a set of relatively strict rules and then stick to them. Otherwise, you'll be drifting back to a sedentary, unhealthy life and wondering how you got there.

Checklist

☑ Decide on a weekly exercise plan and make rules that encourage you to stick to it.

☑ Make rules about what situations qualify you for a get-out-of-exercising-free card. Think about illness, weather, busier-than-usual schedules, and so on.

- ✓ Seriously consider whether being tired should be an excuse not to exercise. Keep in mind that you will probably find yourself feeling tired most days. Skinny chicks don't use this as an excuse; they know that exercise will invigorate them and give them more energy.
- ✓ Make rules about when you are allowed to cheat on your usual healthy diet. Can you eat bad things on any day of the week as long as you count the calories and stick to day-end goals? Can you eat what you want one day a week? Is a breakup with a boyfriend reason to hit a box of cookies, but not a bad day at work? These are some of the questions you should answer before you face these situations.

Secret Number 14: Eat Smaller Meals Throughout the Day

Notice that the women profiled here rarely eat more than about 500 calories at one time. They spread their calories out into three meals and a number of snacks throughout the day. Five hundred calories or less is all a meal really needs to be. In our culture, the idea of a *meal* now means enormous serving sizes and unbelievable amounts of unhealthy fats and sugars. Take, for instance, a McDonald's "meal." A Big Mac with large fries and a medium Coke comes to a whopping 1,358 calories! That's the total number of calories many skinny chicks eat in an entire day, not just one meal. While that may be an extreme case, it's amazing how many calories are packed into the super-sized meals you get in most restaurants. A plate of pasta with meat sauce can creep up into the 1,000-calorie range. It's crazy! Skinny chicks who have to work at it know this. They are well informed about the number of calories in restaurant meals and are careful to steer around them. Skinny Chick Susana Aguila, who is originally from Spain, says that the Spanish eat smaller meals several times a day. So, it's important to learn about the foods we eat, make healthy choices, and spread our food intake healthfully over a day. Remember, 2 heaping cups of broccoli have only 60 calories and will leave you feeling stuffed while giving your body much-needed nutrients. Education and careful selection are key to staying fit and fabulous! Read more about this in Chapter 7.

Make It Happen Now: The Real Chick Plan for #14

OK, so how do you spread out your calories throughout the day? Well, for starters, make sure that you eat first thing in the morning to jump-start your metabolism. Your body starts burning fuel when you start fueling up. You'll notice most of the skinny chicks do this—they start off with a good breakfast of 200 to 300 calories, followed by a 100- to 200-calorie snack, a 400-calorie or less lunch, then a 100- to 200-calorie snack in the afternoon, followed by a 400-calorie or more dinner, and then they finish off with another 100 to 200 calories after dinner. The idea is to keep feeding the body, but never overfeed it. You want to spread those calories across the full day the way these gals do.

To determine how much to eat at each sitting, the skinny chicks say eat slowly and listen to the cues from your body. I can't tell you how often I heard them say that they stop eating once they feel full, even if they haven't finished what's on their plate. So listen to your body and put that extra food away to eat later. Also, pay attention to when you typically like to eat more food. Some people don't like to eat much first thing in the day, so eat something but save those extra calories for later. Also, remember to always try to put some protein and healthy fat with everything you eat so you feel full longer and so that you are getting a well-rounded diet. Next, when you are planning your meals, start with sufficient protein for the day, add on plenty of fruits and vegetables, and you will soon see there is plenty of room left to add in some whole grains and other more caloric options. But don't try to start off with a large muffin or some other high-calorie option. If you take that route, you'll be up to your calorie limit by 2 P.M. and feeling panicked about how you'll ever make it through the rest of the day with nothing to eat. It's all about planning and making smart choices. But if you do make a bad choice that leaves you in a bit of a pinch, don't fret. You can always cozy up to an apple and a nice, healthy salad for dinner.

Checklist

- ☑ Think about the things you like to eat and plan daily and weekly menus built around these favorite things.
- ☑ Plan three meals of approximately 400 calories each and then add a few snacks containing approximately 100 calories each.
- ☑ Think about when you tend to eat more and when you tend to eat less and use that information when planning your menu.
- ☑ Really listen to your body as you eat and stop when you are full. Pack that extra food away to eat later.
- ☑ Beware of eating high-calorie foods early in the day; space out your calories.
- ☑ Don't forget low-calorie fruits and vegetables.
- ☑ Find some low-calorie, yummy snacks to spice up the day, such as sugar-free ice cream bars.
- ☑ Make sure your meals have lots of fibrous bulk. For instance, a heaping stir-fry full of veggies can make you burst at the seams, while keeping the calorie content quite low.

Secret Number 15: Concentrate on How Eating Well and Exercising Make You Feel

Most of the skinny chicks in this book mentioned how great eating well and exercising make them feel. This is something they focus on when they are tempted to not exercise or eat something bad. They really love having a body they love. They know that they created their bodies with hard work, will-power, and commitment. "It feels good to be healthy," says Skinny Chick Katie Katke. On the other hand, skinny chicks often talked about how eating badly or not exercising made them feel sick physically and made them depressed emotionally. Knowing this, they are inspired to stay on course. Whenever they are tempted, they think about how eating well and exercising make them feel strong, lean, healthy, and proud. Ultimately what they are doing is keeping their eye on the ball and reminding themselves of the payoff for all the sacrifices they make. If all they did was think about the things they aren't eating or how they could be sleeping in instead of running, they might be more inclined to get lazy. But they don't—they stay focused on the payoff.

Make It Happen Now: The Real Chick Plan for #15

This secret, like so many of them, is all in your head. It's about focus. It's about what you say to yourself when you are tempted to eat badly or not exercise. Whenever I really, really, really don't want to go out running, when it's raining or snowing or I'm feeling cold, I remind myself of how I feel like I'm flying when I get back. I always feel like a million bucks when I come back from a run. And that amazing feeling stays with me for the rest of the day. Studies have shown that aerobic exercise not only can reduce stress but also can enable you to better handle stress for hours afterward. So, when I don't want to go, I remind myself of this. It's a good idea, too, to not wait for temptation to strike—remind yourself all day long about how great you feel. Think about how strong you feel, how full of energy you are, how great you look. Think about how great your favorite jeans feel when you are sticking to your fit-and-fabulous plan. Then, think about how yucky you feel after you eat something bad. You feel lethargic, drowsy, depressed, and can even have an upset stomach. So, get started on making how great you feel your new focus.

Checklist

- ✔ Make a list of all the psychological benefits of eating well and exercising. (Do this before you start your program to help you get moving, and then do it again after you've started to keep yourself motivated.)
- ✔ Make a list of all the physical benefits of eating well and exercising. (Do this both before you start and after you've started for motivation to keep you moving.)
- ✔ Make a list of all the benefits you've already experienced, what that means to you, and what you had to do to get there.
- ✔ Make a list of how you feel, both physically and mentally, when you eat badly and don't exercise.
- ✔ Hang these lists on your refrigerator or someplace where you'll see them every day and read them often.
- ✔ Pick a trigger, such as every time you go to the bathroom, to remind yourself of how great you feel sticking to your healthy plans.
- ✔ Whenever you feel tempted to eat badly or skip a workout, grab your lists and read them or, if you aren't at home, remind yourself about what is on them. Remind yourself that the benefits of sticking to your plan far outweigh the short-lived enjoyment you get from eating badly or being lazy.

Secret Number 16: Work in the Yummy Stuff

Having made women's health and fitness the focus of my professional life for many years now, I didn't expect the women I interviewed to have too many surprises for me. One thing that did surprise me, though, is just how many of them make sure to eat the so-called "bad" stuff a little bit every day. Whether it's a few Oreo cookies or a small packet of chips, many of the gals in this book make sure they work a little bit of the yummy stuff they just gotta have into their daily diet. This, they say, is the best way to make sure they don't feel deprived, and therefore less likely to walk into the nearest doughnut shop in desperation. The skinny chicks know that totally depriving themselves of the yummy stuff is setting themselves up for failure. Skinny Chick Sazzy Varga says she "cheats smart" by working yummy stuff into her day. "If I want a chocolate chip cookie, I know I will have to cut back elsewhere to stay in my calorie zone, or else burn those calories." Skinny Chick Kristin Cheh agrees, saying she never deprives herself of the things she loves, namely vanilla Oreo cookies. So, if you just love cookies, it's impossible to commit to a life that involves no cookies except on rare occasions. That is simply not something that is maintainable over the long term. That said, if you want to be fit and fabulous, you shouldn't be adding cookies on top of your daily calorie count. Instead, work them into your daily calorie count.

Make It Happen Now: The Real Chick Plan for #16

So this is a fun one. You get to eat bad stuff! Potentially every day! Yeah! Now, before you get too excited, this is where you have to make some smart choices. If you decide to have a large chocolate éclair every day, that's 300 calories you don't get to eat elsewhere. That's a real big chunk of calories to lose to a food that's almost completely sugar. It's going to get absorbed into your bloodstream really fast, causing a spike in your blood sugar, followed by a sharp drop, which is going to make you hungry again prematurely and craving more sugar. That probably isn't the best choice for your daily cheat food. However, if you've just gotta have it, have it. But count it into your daily totals. On the other hand, a 50-calorie cookie (or even two or three of them) makes a lot more sense. If you shop around and keep your eye out for great lower-calorie versions or smaller portions of the things you love, you can eat that much more yummy stuff without reducing by very much the number of calories you get to spend on real food.

Checklist

☑ Rejoice in the fact that you can lose weight and eat some cheat foods every day.

☑ Go shopping and look for some smart daily cheat food choices (i.e., lower-calorie, lower-fat, or smaller-portion versions of your favorite food).

☑ Decide how much of various cheat foods you can squeeze into a day.

☑ Resolve to not allow yourself to go over your daily calorie allowance. If you do, consider revoking the cheat-a-day privilege.

☑ When it's time to dig into your treat, sit down, focus on eating, and really enjoy it

☑ When you are done, think about how great it is to be able to eat something like this and still lose or maintain weight.

☑ When you eat something that takes too many calories away from the rest of the day, reflect on this and resolve to make better choices in the future.

Secret Number 17: Get a Portion Size Wake-Up Call

The portion sizes in North American homes and restaurants are simply ridiculous and completely out of control. The average restaurant pasta serving is a whopping 480 percent larger than the portion size suggested by the USDA, according to a 2002 study published in the *American Journal of Public Health*. In 1955 a single order of fries weighed 2.4 ounces, while today it is 7.1 ounces, nearly a 200 percent increase. A medium serving of french fries at many take-out restaurants packs a 350-calorie punch. That's more calories than are in many of the skinny chicks' *meals* in this book. Getting portions this size while eating out has stretched our stomachs and warped our sense of what is an appropriate amount to eat in one sitting.

But we can't blame it all on the restaurant industry. We must take responsibility for how much food we put in our bodies. The problem is, however, that too many of us simply don't know how much is an appropriate amount to eat. Look at Skinny Chick Susana Aguila, for instance. When she has muesli cereal for breakfast, she has just ⅓ cup with ½ cup of milk. She doesn't fill the bowl right up as so many of us do. We need a portion size wake-up call. But it won't be easy. The truth about appropriate portion sizes can be a little shocking compared to what we are used to. Some people like to write off these much smaller, appropriately sized meals, but the truth is, it's the way human beings were designed to eat. It's the way we used to eat, and it's the way we should eat again.

Make It Happen Now: The Real Chick Plan for #17

So, the first step to getting this portion size wake-up call is to get educated. The USDA published the 2005 Food Pyramid to help make things clearer to people. The old pyramid talked about foods in terms of "servings," pointing out that one piece of fruit was one portion, for example, as was a piece of meat the size of a deck of cards. Ultimately, the pyramid told people how many servings of different foods they needed each day. To make things simpler and more exact, the new pyramid now tells you how much food each category of person needs in terms of measurements, like cups and ounces. I think this method gives people the hard numbers on how much of each thing to eat. It's a good idea to use the recommended amounts of each category of food to help you distribute your calories appropriately to ensure a balanced diet. So to lay the landscape of this portion size wake-up call, let's get caught up on what the USDA Food Pyramid recommends women nineteen years old and over eat each day.

FOOD CATEGORY	DAILY RECOMMENDED INTAKE	WHAT THAT TRANSLATES INTO IN REAL MEASUREMENTS
Grains (bread, cereal, rice, etc.)	3–6 ounces	One slice of bread or ½ cup of rice, pasta, or cereal equals 1 ounce of grains
Vegetables	2–2½ cups	1 cup (8 ounces) of vegetables equals a 1-cup serving
Fruits	1½–2 cups	1 cup (8 ounces) of juice or one small apple equals 1 cup of fruits
Milk (cheese, milk, etc.)	3 cups	1 cup of milk or 1½ ounces of processed cheese equals 1 cup in milk category
Meat and beans	5–5½ ounces	¼ cup of dry beans, 1 tablespoon of peanut butter, one egg, and ¼ cup of tofu equal 1 ounce in meat category
Oils	5–6 teaspoons	1 tablespoon of Canola oil equals 3 teaspoons, 4 olives equals 1 teaspoon, 2 tablespoons of peanut butter equal 4 teaspoons

Compiled from the USDA Food Pyramid, which can be found with very detailed recommendations at mypyramid.org.

Take a good, hard look at this summary of the recommendations and learn how much of each type of food you should be having each day. As you can see, it's a good idea to forget about these 8- or 12-ounce steaks you are served at restaurants. Five and a half ounces of protein is all you need in a day. Any more than that is going straight to your thighs unless you hit the treadmill big time! Now, looking down at a plate with so much less food on it may be a little upsetting and shocking at first. We are used to eating so much more. But this is how much you need to eat. This is not about dieting, this is about changing the way you look at food and your perception of how much you need. Skinny chicks know that portion control doesn't mean hunger; they can control their portions and still feel satiated.

Checklist

☑ Visit mypyramid.org to learn more about just how much of each category of food you need.

☑ Learn how much food you need daily from each category and keep that in mind as you plan your menus and as you eat.

☑ Revolutionize the way you look at how much food you need. Accept that larger portions are unhealthy and that smaller portions are healthy.

☑ Recognize that this is not a diet; you are changing the way you fuel your body for life.

☑ Think of your body as a machine that needs a certain amount of fuel and no more.

☑ Use smaller plates to make your meals appear larger.

☑ Use smaller spoons so that it takes longer to eat your meals.

☑ Put your utensils down between each bite.

☑ Have a glass of water with your meal and take several sips between bites.

☑ Eat slowly and chew each bite.

☑ While eating, focus on eating and not other things. The more distracted you are, the more you will eat.

☑ If you're still hungry right after you've finished your meal, wait 20 minutes. This is the length of time it takes for your brain to tell your body you are full.

Secret Number 18: When You Reach Your Goal, Keep It Going

This secret may be the most important of all the secrets of skinny chicks. Remember, these women don't diet; eating well and exercising is just a way of life for them, plain and simple. That's why we can learn so much from them. They have to look good all the time, so they do what it takes to look good all the time. Because skinny chicks don't "diet," there is no end to what they are doing, and so they make sure what they are doing is manageable over the long term. At no point do they go "back to normal"—eating well and exercising is normal for them.

When we diet, we tend to restrict our eating with short-term goals in mind. That is one of the things that is so wrong with dieting. You can't maintain such a restricted regimen, and so backsliding is inevitable. Once skinny chicks hit their body goals, they just keep on going. They don't stop. They may raise their calorie intake slightly to stop losing weight, but overall their lifestyle is a lifelong commitment, not a short-term mission.

Make It Happen Now: The Real Chick Plan for #18

So, how do you make this secret happen for you? Well, for starters, you have to recognize the fact that what you are doing is not a diet. It's a way of life. If you want to have tight buns and a body you are proud of, you've got to make a commitment to a healthy way of life over the long haul. You can't be looking at this as a short-term deal. It's great to have goals, even short-term ones, but it's the maintenance part that gets tricky. If what you are doing feels unmanageable over the long run, you need to loosen things up a bit.

Take a closer look at the choices you are making. Make sure you are not depriving yourself completely of the things you love. Make sure you are eating high-volume and high-nutrient, but low-calorie, foods. Make the changes needed to ensure you can do this over the long term. Write down your goals, do what you have to do to reach them, and as you cruise into the final stretch, don't stop! If you have to white-knuckle it that much to make it to your goals, perhaps you need to set a longer time frame so that it's not so hard on you. The key is to not feel like you desperately need a break from eating well and exercising, so constantly assess and reassess your menus and exercise plans according to your current needs. Make adjustments when your schedule changes, your stress levels rise or fall, or you are feeling more or less hungry. Studies have shown that when the end of a diet is celebrated with a binge, it's more likely that people will go back to their old habits because they have suddenly broken with the healthier lifestyle and gone back to their old ways, even if they think it will just be for a day. That's what we are trying to avoid here: a sense of this thing coming to an end. When you reach your goal, keep on going!

Checklist

- ✓ Do something nice for yourself to celebrate your success in achieving your goals.
- ✓ Take a hard look at what you did to reach those goals.
- ✓ Create a plan based on the calorie intake, water intake, menus, and exercise plans you used to get to your goal weight.
- ✓ If you continue to lose weight and don't want to/need to, add more food to your plan.
- ✓ Monitor your progress by weighing yourself regularly and assessing how you feel in your clothing.
- ✓ Be sure to maintain your healthy living and eating environments.

- ☑ Think about your new fitness regimen as a lifelong venture.
- ☑ Keep a journal and record your thoughts about your total lifestyle change.
- ☑ Monitor other things besides your weight, i.e., periodically checking your endurance during a certain exercise or having a physical and seeing that the changes are making you healthier, not just thinner.
- ☑ Think about how great it will be to feel strong and healthy and proud of your body and know you're responsible for it!
- ☑ Get excited about having laid the groundwork for a healthy, strong body for life.
- ☑ Periodically make sure you are still implementing the fifty secrets of skinny chicks in your life.

Secret Number 19: Live in Healthy Environments

Would you dare walk into a gym munching away on a box of doughnuts? Not a chance! Those hard bodies would drop their weight stacks to gawk at you as you walked by. You wouldn't do it because it's simply not a behavior that is suitable to that environment. Likewise, showing up to Christmas dinner at your in-laws' house with your own Lean Cuisine meal to pop in the microwave wouldn't be seen as appropriate either. The people you surround yourself with, the places you go, and the situations you enter into ultimately have a big effect on how likely it is that you will be able to stick to your healthy lifestyle. Whenever I am training for a marathon with a running club, we go out for bagels and coffee after the runs. Looking around you see people eating healthy, whole-grain bagels, asking for the cream cheese spread thin, and talking about the chicken salad they had for dinner the night before. I shopped for sporty clothes with these friends, felt inspired by them, and whenever I was with them I felt compelled to stick with my healthy choices. Living the healthy life is just easier when you surround yourself with people like that.

On the other hand, if I go out for dinner and drinks with my husband and some of his friends, I can expect round after round of beer to be served to the table, baskets of greasy fried foods to abound, and gluttony to be a theme of the evening. It can be very hard to stay on course and not be tempted to dig into those fries in an environment like that. Skinny chicks know this fact well. That's why they seek out healthy environments and limit their exposure to unhealthy situations.

Make It Happen Now: The Real Chick Plan for #19

Does this mean you can never go to the pub with your better half and his friends? No! It just means that you have to limit ventures like these and go into them with your eyes open. In the meantime, it's a very good idea to try to immerse yourself in as many healthy environments as possible. Joining a gym and hanging out there before and after workouts is a great idea. Look around and get inspiration from the people you see. Take your bottle of water and a book and kick back in the lounge area for a while. Make this space part of your world. Drink it in. Join a running club or sign up for dance classes. Go for coffee with your workout mates afterward. Be open to making new friends in environments like these. Official exercise environments are not the only healthy environments you can seek out. There are all sorts of mini-environments all around you. Where you spend your lunch break, the places you go to hang out with your friends, there are all sorts of environments you may be able to improve. Skinny Chick Danielle Gamba swears by this secret. "It makes staying on track a lot easier," she says. So open your eyes and embrace these healthier options.

Checklist

- ☑ Identify unhealthy environments in your life and limit exposure to them.
- ☑ Join a gym or find a workout partner.
- ☑ Sign up for a dance, Pilates, yoga, or other kind of class.
- ☑ Frequent places where healthy people like to spend time, such as fitness centers, health-focused restaurants, book club meetings that include women you met in an exercise class, and so forth.
- ☑ Make friends in these new environments.
- ☑ Seek out friends living healthy lifestyles.
- ☑ Inspire your mate, roommate, family, and so forth to live healthy, too.
- ☑ Start a healthy dinner club with friends.
- ☑ Buy subscriptions to fitness magazines.
- ☑ Avoid food courts or other temptation-rich scenarios.
- ☑ Shop in fitness stores.
- ☑ Shop in health food stores.
- ☑ Read new health books and learn about advances in diet and fitness.

Secret Number 20: Have a Holiday/Vacation Game Plan

OK, so you're cruising along, sticking to your healthy diet and exercise plans just fine, when up ahead you see a major road-block: the holidays. It could be Christmas or a cruise vacation or Hanukkah or even your birthday weekend. You may have the best of intentions, but deep down you know that this holiday will go down the same way it always has. You'll eat too much, you'll eat the wrong things, you'll become a lazy slouch on the couch, and you'll end up feeling like a heifer by the end of it all.

The National Institutes of Health (NIH) reports that the average person gains about one pound during the Christmas holidays. That may not sound like a lot, but experts say people tend to maintain that weight gain for the rest of the year and that over the course of ten years they will have gained fourteen pounds from holiday eating alone. For those of us who would rather not go down this road, this is a call for action. But those butter cookies and chocolate brownies will just be too much to resist, right? Even the skinny chicks face the same challenge. From playing in the snow with their nieces and nephews to burn off gingerbread cookies (Skinny Chick Sazzy Varga) to eating only their favorite things on the table (Skinny Chick Erin Kirk) to regifting chocolate they are given (Skinny Chick Danielle Gamba), all of the skinny chicks in this book have specific plans for how not to go off the rails around times of celebration.

Make It Happen Now: The Real Chick Plan for #20

The holidays are coming, so here's what you do. First, start a preholidays exercise and diet regimen to lose a couple of pounds. Two pounds equals 7,000 calories, which is a lot harder to lose than to take in, so you're going to have to start a few weeks ahead. It's safe to lose up to two pounds in one week, but that's a lot of extra exercise and a lot less food if you try to do it just the week before. So start about a month early and trim a little here and there and work out a bit more each day. I always run ten miles or so on Christmas Eve and then again on Christmas Day. I call it my "preemptive strike" against the calories that I may eat on those two days. (I try to limit my "go for it" food days to just these two, and, if I can't, I take a preemptive strike run on those days, too.)

Now, for many people, the holiday seasons consists of three or four weeks of parties, luncheons, treat tables at work, and get-togethers, which make it very hard to stay on a healthy diet track. Instead, what you need to do is plan ahead and decide what parties or events you are going to let loose at and which ones you won't. If you let loose at every event, you are going to gain several pounds by the end of it. If you don't want that to happen, don't do it. Make a plan. Some events are just too much fun to not eat what you want, so figure out which ones those are and plan for them. Then, exercise more before and/or after that event to help offset that extra eating. You can also make sure you eat for a little less than usual the rest of that day. Also, people tend to send and give other people indulgent foods at this time of year. Skinny Chick Danielle Gamba told me she regifts all of the chocolate she gets over the holidays so she doesn't eat it. In my own case, on Christmas morning I always go for a run and bring any chocolate bars and other indulgent foods I don't want lying around with me to hand to homeless people along the way. Danielle and I both know that that chocolate is going one of two places: on our butts or out the door!

Next, when the parties begin, eat smart. Look around at what's coming and what is already out on the tables and think about what you can't live without eating. Then, listen to your body. If your tummy is full, just stop. Just because things are there and look delicious, that doesn't mean you have to keep eating. After the event, head home and work out or hit the gym the next day. By going into these high-risk celebrations with the knowledge that you have a plan, you'll be able to sit back, eat, and enjoy yourself knowing that you've got it all under control.

Checklist

☑ Work out more and eat better to lose a pound or two in the weeks leading up to high-risk celebrations.

☑ Work out harder on the morning of any celebration.

- ☑ Assess the food at the event and decide what you are going to eat and what you can live without.
- ☑ Avoid foods and drinks that your heart isn't set on.
- ☑ Don't eat things just because you think you should (e.g., turkey on Thanksgiving), just eat what you have been really looking forward to.
- ☑ Don't linger at the buffet table or in kitchen. Focus on socializing.
- ☑ Educate yourself about calories and keep a running tally in your head as you go, so you know how much you are eating and feel more in control.
- ☑ Do a mini-workout when you get home.
- ☑ Assess the damage on the scale and set a goal and a plan for getting back on track.
- ☑ Give away any holiday treats you have left over or that you receive as gifts. (You could be facing weeks of temptation otherwise.)
- ☑ Don't turn Christmas into a four-day event. Don't wait until the New Year to get back into your groove.

Secret Number 21: Research Restaurants

When surveyed for this book, almost all of the skinny chicks said they stick to salads and chicken or fish dishes with vegetables when they eat out at a restaurant. They do this, they say, because these two meal selections provide the healthiest, most calorie-conscious options. Both of these meal choices usually have a lean protein base (salads often have chicken offered as a topping), which will make you full. You can also easily see how much chicken you are getting (unlike in a meat pie, for instance). Next, heaps of multicolored veggies surround that protein center in these two meal choices, which will also make you feel good and full while loading you up with vitamins. And finally, it's easy to ask that dressings, sauces, and oils be served on the side because the sauces and dressings don't have to be cooked into the meal. As a result, this truly is the safe way to go if you are watching your waistline.

But not everyone wants to eat the same meals every time they go out. Besides, sometimes even salads can pack a mean calorie punch, depending on their ingredients and how they're prepared. That's why it's a great idea to research the restaurants you like to go to and learn as much as you can about the foods you plan to eat there. Most of the fast-food restaurants these days, from McDonald's to Starbucks to Pizza Pizza, post the nutritional information about their meals and products on their websites. Some even have brochures outlining all the information you need. In smaller, nonfranchised restaurants, however, it can be much more difficult. But there are ways of finding out, or working out, what you are getting while eating out. The reality is, many people today like to, and in some cases have to, eat out. So, instead of allowing these meals on the go to become calorie traps, let's educate ourselves and get armed with the facts. Skinny Chick Sazzy Varga says she often researches restaurants' nutritional information. "I think if more people did, they'd pass up the Whopper and fries," she says.

Make It Happen Now: The Real Chick Plan for #21

Research the restaurants you love and see if they have online information or brochures on their nutritional information. You may be shocked to see just how many calories are in some of your favorite foods. Or you may find that some of the things you have been steering clear of are not that bad after all. But the important thing is to look things up. It can be very enlightening. Next, consider calling or walking into restaurants without posted nutritional information and asking a few questions about exactly what goes into the dish. Ask things like, how many ounces of chicken are in the dish, or how many cups of pasta come with that meal? Ask them how many tablespoons

The Skinny Chicks' Guide to Eating Out

WHILE DINING OUT, INSTEAD OF ORDERING THIS . . .	TRY THIS HEALTHIER CHOICE . . .
*McDonald's Big Mac meal (560 calorie burger) with medium fries (350 calories) and medium soda (210 calories) *Total: 1,120 calories* **OR** Sausage McMuffin with egg (450 calories) with hash browns (140 calories) and a large orange juice (250 calories) *Total: 840 calories*	Cobb Salad with Grilled Chicken (400 calories) with a Fruit 'n Yogurt Parfait (156 calories) and a large Diet Coke (0 calories) *Total: 556 calories* **OR** A Fruit and Walnut Salad (310 calories) with 1 percent milk (100 calories) *Total: 410 calories* **OR** Grilled chicken sandwich (410 calories) and a diet soda (0 calories) *Total: 410 calories* ***Beware of McDonald's high-calorie salads.***
*Wendy's Homestyle Chicken Strip Salad (680 calories) with a Broccoli and Cheese baked potato (340 calories) and a medium Coke (140 calories) *Total: 1,160 calories* **OR** Big Bacon Classic Burger (580 calories) with Biggie French Fries (490 calories) and a medium Sprite (130 calories) *Total: 1,200 calories*	Ultimate Chicken Grill Sandwich (225 calories) with a Mandarin Orange Cup (80 calories) and 2 percent reduced fat milk (120 calories) *Total: 425 calories* **OR** Sour Cream and Chives Baked Potato (320 calories) with a side salad (35 calories) with fat-free French dressing (80 calories). *Total: 435 calories* ***Beware of Wendy's high-calorie salads.***

WHILE DINING OUT, INSTEAD OF ORDERING THIS . . .	TRY THIS HEALTHIER CHOICE . . .
*Dominos Pizza Ultimate Deep Dish Pizza with pepperoni and sausage, 3 slices of 8-slice pie (921 calories) **OR** Ultimate Deep Dish Beef Pizza, 3 slices of 8-slice pie (830 calories)	Three slices of green pepper, onion, and mushroom Crunchy Thin Slice pizza (426 calories) **OR** Two slices of Classic Hand-tossed pepperoni pizza (446 calories) *Steer clear of the high-calorie Cinna Stix, Cheese Bread, and Chicken Kickers.*
*KFC Original Recipe chicken breast (380 calories), two drumsticks (280 calories), individual coleslaw (190 calories), potato wedges (430 calories), and a medium Pepsi (180 calories) *Total: 1,270 calories*	Tender Roast Filet Meal (360 calories). *Total: 360 calories* **OR** Roasted Caesar Salad (220 calories), pack of Baked Cheetos (120 calories), and a Diet Pepsi (0 calories) *Total: 340 calories*
*Dunkin' Donuts Apple Pie a la Mode (810 calories) **OR** Pumpkin Muffin (580 calories) **OR** Reduced carb croissant (370 calories) **OR** Apple Danish (330 calories) **OR** Vanilla Bean Coolatta, 16 ounces (440 calories)	Coconut coffee, 10 ounces (20 calories) with an English muffin (160 calories) *Total: 180 calories* **OR** One Chocolate Chunk cookie (110 calories) with a cup of Earl Grey Tea with milk (25 calories) *Total: 135 calories* **OR** A French Cruller (150 calories) and a 16-ounce Iced Latte with skimmed milk (70 calories) *Total: 220 calories* *Don't be fooled by muffins. Even Dunkin' Donuts' low-fat blueberry muffin has 400 calories*

WHILE DINING OUT, INSTEAD OF ORDERING THIS . . .	TRY THIS HEALTHIER CHOICE . . .
*Hardee's ½ Pound Six Dollar burger (1,060 calories), medium fries (520 calories), regular chocolate shake (550 calories) *Total: 2,130 calories* **OR** Big Country Breakfast chicken platter (1,140 calories) with a 20-ounce Minute Maid lemonade (250 calories) *Total: 1,390 calories* **OR** Big Chicken Filet Sandwich (770 calories) with small Crispy Curls (340 calories) and 20 ounces of Sprite (260 calories) *Total: 1,370 calories*	Tortilla Scrambler (230 calories) with a cup of tea with sweetener (0 calories) **OR** A croissant (210 calories) **OR** ⅓ Pound Low-Carb Thick Burger (420 calories) with a large Diet Coke (0 calories) **OR** Fried Chicken leg (170 calories), mashed potatoes (90 calories), 10 ounce Minute Maid orange juice (150 calories) *Total: 410 calories*
*Taco Bell Grilled Stuft Steak Burrito (680 calories) with Nachos BellGrande (790 calories) *Total: 1,470 calories* **OR** Cheese Quesadilla (490 calories) with Cinnamon Twists (160 calories) *Total: 750 calories* **OR** Beef Chalupa Supreme (400 calories) with Nachos (320 calories) *Total: 720 calories*	Nachos (320 calories) with a large diet soda (0 calories) **OR** One taco (170 calories) with rice (200 calories) and a diet soda (0 calories) *Total: 370 calories* **OR** Fiesta Taco Salad without shell or Red Strips (420 calories) and a large diet soda (0 calories) *Beware of high-calorie salads*

WHILE DINING OUT, INSTEAD OF ORDERING THIS . . .	TRY THIS HEALTHIER CHOICE . . .
*Subway 12-inch Chicken and Bacon Ranch sub sandwich (1,060 calories) **OR** 6-inch Meatball Marinara sub sandwich (560 calories) **OR** Twelve-inch Tuna sub sandwich (1,060 calories)	Grilled Chicken Breast Strips Salad (140 calories) with 2 oz. Honey Mustard Dressing (200 calories) and a diet soda (0 calories) *Total: 340 calories* **OR** 6-inch Ham Sub, no cheese (280 calories) with fat-free Honey Mustard dressing (30 calories), Vegetable Beef Soup (90 calories), diet soda (0 calories) *Total: 400 calories* **OR** Roast Beef Deli Sandwich (220 calories) with light mayonnaise (50 calories) and a small package of Baked Lays Potato Chips (130 calories) *Total: 400 calories* ***Beware of 200+ calorie single cookies***
*Dairy Queen Large Oreo Cookies Blizzard (1,010 calories) **OR** Large Dipped ice cream cone (710 calories) **OR** Large Chocolate Sundae (580 calories)	A small Lemon Misty (170 calories) **OR** DQ Fudge Bar (50 calories) **OR** Chocolate Dilly Bar (210 calories)

* Provides complete nutritional information about products online.

WHILE DINING OUT, INSTEAD OF ORDERING THIS . . .	TRY THIS HEALTHIER CHOICE . . .
Privately owned sit-down restaurant Spaghetti with meatballs (1,160 calories) **OR** Porterhouse steak, with no sides (1,000 calories) **OR** Hamburger and onion rings (1,500 calories)	Grilled chicken breast, 4 ounces (222 calories) two cups of steamed vegetables (100 calories), ½ cup of rice (100 calories), plus 1 table-spoon of oil in cooking (100 calories) *Total: 522 calories* **OR** Grilled salmon steak, 5 ounces (200 calories) on bed of lettuce (13 calories) with veggies (50 calories) and 3 tablespoons of oil vinaigrette (150 calories) *Total: 413 calories*

of oil are used to cook the vegetables and main dishes. Or, if you don't have the courage to do that, the next time you order the meal, take a good hard look at it. Arm yourself ahead of time with facts like how many calories are in an ounce of chicken and what an ounce of chicken looks like (see Chapter 7). Then, size up your entree choice. The calories in these restaurant meals can add up fast, so it's really important to know this nutritional information if you plan to eat out often. It is also a good idea to take the initiative and, when you are dining with others, suggest the restaurants that you know have healthful choices for you.

Size up the meal yourself, using calorie counts and portion sizes you know and can tell at a glance. Once you've figured out the numbers on your favorite dishes, make up a little cheat sheet with the calories noted and pop it into your purse. That way you are ready the next time you want to drop in for a meal.

Checklist

- ☑ Make a list of restaurants you like to visit.
- ☑ Check to see if they have online or published nutritional information. If so, check out your favorite foods and decide what to eat when you go there.
- ☑ At other restaurants, ask for nutritional information or try to make some rough estimates yourself.

Secret Number 22: Sort Out Your Emotional Problems

This may be the place where many of us differ from the skinny chicks. My survey of the gals in this book found that the majority actually find they lose their appetite when they get upset, worried, or stressed about something. This may be one of the key reasons why they are able to stay slim and many other women cannot. Speaking for myself and many of my friends, when things go wrong in my life, I'm heading for a bag of barbecue-flavored Fritos. I don't know whether my mother comforted me with food as a child or if I learned it some other way. But it's rather common that women deal with stress—and even much more severe emotional traumas—with the help of food. Sales of snack foods increased more than 12 percent in the month following September 11th according to a Nielson poll. Experts suspect people were comforting themselves. If you think you have emotional issues that make it hard for you to control how much or what you eat, it's important to address this issue. The secrets in this book are only going to help you if you are starting from a point of relatively good emotional health. Even if your emotional problems are mild, seeing a professional may help in many ways, including eliminating your need to use food as a healer.

Make It Happen Now: The Real Chick Plan for #22

If you are an emotional eater, you know it. And this is the first step. The next step is deciding whether you can deal with it on your own or whether it would be beneficial to get some professional help. There are techniques outlined in Secret Number 32 for replacing emotional eating. You also might read other books that focus on the emotional issues that seem close to home. But you may find that you need more help than that. If that's the case, you should consider talking to your doctor or making an appointment with a counselor, psychologist, or psychiatrist.

Also, if you are in the midst of a crisis or major life change such as a move, job change, divorce, marriage, or death of a loved one, then this might not be the right time for you to start a new eating and exercise regimen. That's OK. Just find the right time to get your head back into the game and you will be able to get back on the road to skinny chickdom—when you are ready.

Checklist

- ☑ Consider seeing a therapist to help you work out any emotional problems that you may have standing in your way of success on a healthy eating and exercise program.
- ☑ Find a support group.
- ☑ Keep a journal and write down how you are feeling about things going on in your life. Think about strategies for resolving any issues you uncover.
- ☑ Remember: One thing at a time. Focus on taking care of your emotional health first, and then go ahead and start your new eating plan.

Secret Number 23: Learn What Your Body's Metabolic Rate Will Allow

This secret is critical. If you compare the daily calorie intake and daily exercise of all of the skinny chicks, you will see some girls can get away with eating far more and exercising far less than others can. Some work out three hours a day and consume about 1,400 calories. Others work out an hour or so and consume about 2,000 calories. While most of the gals fall somewhere in between, the fact that some women have fast metabolisms (allowing more eating and requiring less exercise) and others have slower metabolisms is worth some serious discussion. Your metabolic rate is the rate at which your body converts energy stores into working energy. And everyone's metabolic rate, or metabolism, is different.

Scientists use complex methods, such as placing people in isolated chambers to measure the heat released from their bodies, to get a reading on their metabolic rates. (The reading they determine, called the Basal Metabolic Rate or BMR, is the amount of energy the body needs to maintain itself in its resting state. For activities and exercise, more energy needs to be added to that.) While people can use some basic calculations to determine how many calories their bodies need (adding 9 to 20 calories per pound depending on how active they are, then subtracting 100 calories for each year over the age of thirty), some women find these calculations leave them with calorie totals that would have them weighing considerably more than they would like to. Plus, there are so many factors affecting your metabolism that no one calculation can be right for everyone.

Your metabolic rate can be influenced by what you eat, your age (aging slows it), thyroid conditions (speeding it up or slowing it down), your activity level (starting an exercise regimen can speed it up), your muscle mass (more muscles speed it up), having had a baby recently (can slow it down or speed it up), being pregnant (speeds it up), going through menopause (slows it down), and severe dieting (slows it down). But ultimately, it's your genetic makeup that determines your metabolism—how much you can eat and how much you have to exercise to look the way you want to. In my case, I have fat genes. Many people in my family struggle with weight, and if I didn't exercise two hours a day I wouldn't fit into my size-6 jeans. I just don't seem to have a very fast metabolic rate, and it's become worse since I hit thirty. So, I know I have to keep my calories down and keep up with my cardio and weights. The women in this book are aware of their resting metabolisms and know what factors (age, genetics, etc.) affect their ability to lose weight and stay fit. Skinny Chick Erin Kirk says, "You really have to learn (about) your body to learn how you need to eat (and exercise) to not gain weight."

Make It Happen Now: The Real Chick Plan for #23

Learning your metabolic rate will help you find out just how hard you have to work at being active and eating well. To find out how many calories you need a day to be the weight you want to be, start with 1,600 (the number recommended by the USDA for the average woman). Then, set up your exercise program of at least one half hour of cardiovascular exercise three times a week. Add two weight-training workouts to that mix, and you are well on your way to getting the body you want. However, as you go along you may find, as I did, that you have to increase the exercise and drop the calories to get the body you want.

After a few weeks of your new diet and exercise regimen you should start to notice some weight loss. If you are losing more than two pounds a week, you need to slow down because that rate of weight loss is not healthy. One to two pounds lost each week is ideal. If you find you hit a plateau and are not losing weight for several weeks in a row (give yourself some time, sometimes things stall only to ramp up again on their own), you might want to consider cutting calories again and/or increasing your exercise. On the other hand, you may find you are losing weight too rapidly, are hungry all the time, or just don't have enough energy. If that's the case, you may need to add some calories. (But make sure they are healthy calories, no Snickers bars!) The bottom line is that no two bodies are the same. What works for one may not work for another. Find out what *your* body needs. If you've got obese parents or siblings or have struggled with weight in the past yourself, you may already know that you have to be more careful than other people. Most of us find that our metabolic rate just won't allow us to eat as much as we want to, nor will it allow us to be sedentary. For most of us, we have to work at it and work at it hard.

Checklist

✔ If you find you have hit a plateau and aren't losing more weight but would like to, cut back on the calories, 100 calories per day, and increase your cardio.

✔ Keep adjusting your calorie intake and calorie expenditure until you are losing again. But it's important that you don't go below 1,200 calories per day.

✔ If you hit a plateau with your weight loss, you may also want to check to make sure you are getting enough water, protein, and fiber and that you are being patient with your body.

Secret Number 24: Keep Weight Within a Set Range

One secret that all skinny chicks have in common is something known as a "weight buffer zone," or a range within which they will allow their weight to fluctuate. Skinny Chick Diana Bernier referred to two pounds above her ideal weight as an "orange light" alert and five pounds as a "red light" alert. At the orange-light level she needs to watch it and clamp down before it gets out of hand. At the red-light level, things are out of hand, and she needs to make changes immediately. Most people who are able to maintain a healthy weight over time report that there is a "magic number" that indicates to them they've gone too far in their indulgences. Monitoring your weight daily or weekly is one of the best ways to maintain weight loss, according to the National Weight Control Registry (an ongoing study of people who have successfully maintained weight loss of 30 pounds or more for more than a year), based at the Brown Medical School in Providence, Rhode Island.

So, if you want to be fit and fabulous and always feel in control of your body, it's important to figure out what your weight buffer zone is going to be. And it doesn't necessarily have to be a five-pound range. You may find that to be too restrictive. It may be ten pounds or eight pounds. Whatever you decide is right for you. Everyone will gain a few pounds at certain times of the year—it's inevitable. But what separates those who keep on gaining from those who keep it under control is setting a weight range and limit. Many of the skinny chicks, including Ann Currell, report they weigh themselves several times a week or at least once a week. Some people may prefer to use the way their clothing fits as a guide. While studies haven't shown this to be as effective as keeping an eye on the scales, for some women it's right for them. (Keep in mind clothing made with cotton or cotton blends can stretch, so use synthetic fabric clothing to keep an eye on your waistline.)

Make It Happen Now: The Real Chick Plan for #24

This, too, should be an easy one. Set a weight buffer zone and stick to it. But for many women it's just simply not that easy.

That's why the first step toward implementing this secret into your life is to really believe that this is an important new rule to live by. If you don't take your upper weight limit seriously and allow reaching it to signal alarm bells inside of you, then you're going to hit that limit and keep on going right back to where you started from . . . or worse. So let's get serious about this weight buffer zone. It's a way of life for the skinny chicks. I remember watching Cheryl Tiegs on the "Oprah Winfrey Show" in 2004 talking about how she keeps her figure so slim right into her fifties. She said that every morning she gets on a scale and if her weight has gone up even just one pound, she wears a pair of tight pants all day as a reminder that she has to watch it.

I tend to think weighing oneself every day is a little extreme, but women with fabulous bodies have to work to keep their figures in check. Realty means facing the music, and if we've done something to put a pound on and we don't stop doing it, over time the weight will just keep coming. That's why this weight buffer zone is so important. The range allows you to cut yourself a little slack, while the upper limit allows you to know when things have gone far enough.

Checklist

☑ Consult the body mass index to assess what is a healthy weight range for your height. (Use this BMI weight range, which can be up to a 40-pound healthy range, to help determine what particular weight range will work for you.)

☑ Get yourself down to that weight if you aren't there already. (This is a big step, but it must be achieved before this secret can be implemented.)

☑ Decide on what your weight buffer zone is going to be: five pounds, ten pounds?

☑ If you have decided to judge your weight by the way your clothing fits, pick a pair of bottoms (skirt, pants, or shorts) and a top to use consistently to judge how you are doing. Remember to choose garments that are form-fitted and made from synthetic fabrics that won't stretch to help you judge accurately.

- ✓ It's important not to set this weight buffer zone too low or make it too narrow. If staying in that zone is just not supported by your long-term lifestyle, it will only lead to frustration.
- ✓ Weigh yourself regularly, either once a day or once a week.
- ✓ Pat yourself on the back for staying in the low end of the zone and put your weight out of your mind until the next weigh-in.
- ✓ If you hit your "orange-light" zone, take action to rein things in: eat better, eat less, and do more cardiovascular exercise.
- ✓ Should you hit your "red-light" zone, action should be taken immediately. Cut out all cheat foods and cheat days, increase the cardio, drink plenty of water, and focus on lean, portion-appropriate servings of protein and fruits and vegetables.
- ✓ Check your weight every few days to monitor your progress. When you get back down in your preferred range, you can go back to your usual regimen.
- ✓ Continue to weigh yourself regularly (either daily or weekly).
- ✓ Don't let your weight buffer zone drive you crazy. If you start to get panicky about your weight or obsess about your weigh-ins, you may need to consult a health professional to ensure your relationship with food and weight is still healthy.

Secret Number 25: Learn Positive Self-Talk

Imagine walking around with this internal, personal dialogue: "I am hot. I have a strong, lean, healthy body. I work hard to be healthy. I love my body. I eat well to nourish my body. I am a good person. I am smart and happy and successful and fun. I rock." Now compare that internal self-dialogue with this: "I am a fat pig. Look at how wide my butt is. I am stupid and lazy and mess up everything I do. Why should I bother trying to eat well? I'll never look good anyway." If you say the same thing over and over again, it will become real in no time. Negative self-talk will cause a negative self-fulfilling prophecy.

The skinny chicks use positive self-talk, which reflects on their behavior and leads to positive results. When I asked the skinny chicks to talk to me about how they feel about their bodies, about a third of them admitted they have weak moments in which they are overly critical of themselves. But a remarkable majority said things like, "I love my body" and "I feel fit and strong." Reality exists in our minds—things are how you perceive them to be. Too many gorgeous women think they are ugly. They may be a size 6, with flawless features and long, blond hair (our culture's ideal), but if they truly think they are ugly, then, sadly, that's their reality. But the woman who thinks of herself as a "fat pig" can change her self-dialogue. For instance, if she embarks on a new exercise and healthy-diet regimen, her internal self-dialogue could change significantly. Her new self-dialogue might sound something like this: "I am a smart, funny, good person with many talents. I am committed to getting myself healthy both physically and mentally. I am taking the appropriate steps to make healthy changes in my life. I am going to reach my goals. I am excited about my future. I am beautiful." In fact, the very same woman who had those horrible initial self-thoughts could change her internal self dialogue within minutes, simply by deciding to think about herself and her worth differently. The things we say in our minds and hearts about how we feel about ourselves are very powerful. And we are in control of these thoughts. If we stop to really think about our strengths and inner beauty, we will see ourselves in a more positive and hopeful way and change our self-perception dramatically.

Note: For some women self-esteem issues can be quite severe. If you think this might be the case with you, it's important to seek professional help.

Make It Happen Now: The Real Chick Plan for #25

We are in control of what we say to ourselves. We need to make a conscious decision to think about all of our positive attributes and focus on these things instead of negative internal messages. Take a moment to think of as many positive things as you can about yourself. I think most of us, at the core of our being, really love ourselves. We need to get back in touch with that. Then, we need to use this positive outlook and create exciting plans to make our lives even better. To make a change in your life you have to truly believe you can do it. If someone hears a message repeated enough times, sooner or later, they'll start to believe it.

Checklist

✔ Make a point of writing down any messages you "say" to yourself over a period of three days.

✔ Sit down and think about those messages and, regarding the negative ones, ask yourself why you said those things to yourself. What has happened in your life to make you believe that? Do you really and truly believe it? How is this message affecting your life?

✔ Resolve to stop yourself each time you "say" something negative to yourself.

✔ Sit down and write out every single positive thing you can think of about yourself. Call it a love letter to yourself. Read that list as often as you need to.

✔ Use that "love letter" to create a list of affirmations that you can repeat to yourself, such as "I am a strong, intelligent woman who is taking control of her body, mind, and destiny." Resolve to repeat these affirmations to yourself every morning or as often as you think you need to.

✔ One trick I learned from motivational speaker and life coach Tony Robbins is to imagine you are wearing a cape, and it represents your superhuman strength. It's amazing how just doing this little, silly thing can totally transform not only the expression on your face (you start to smile and laugh, but you hold your head higher too) but the way you feel about yourself in that moment. Nothing is, it's only how you perceive it to be.

☑ Do something nurturing for yourself every day, like take a bath or listen to soothing music.

The Skinny Chick Plan for Real Women: Secrets 26 Through 50

6

NOW FOR A CLOSER look at the last half of the fifty secrets of skinny chicks. Just like in Chapter 5, this chapter will put each secret under the microscope and break it down so that real chicks can integrate these directions into their own lives. Each section starts off with a full explanation of each secret, followed by a real chick's plan for making it happen in your own life, and a checklist to follow to make sure you've got all your bases covered as you work to change your own lifestyle. So, let's take a closer look at Secrets 26 through 50.

Secret Number 26: Portion Foods Out

Digging your hand into the cereal box is really not a good idea. Neither is reaching into a big bag of peanuts. Eating "from the box" is the best way to blindly eat your way into huge portions because you feel like you're just nibbling. Portioning your foods in advance prevents you from eating mindlessly. In his book *The Ultimate Weight Loss Solution*, Dr. Phil McGraw estimates that he used to consume as much as 10,000 calories just by "grazing" through his kitchen while his wife was cooking during family get-togethers. After tallying up the damage, he decided to nip this behavior in the bud.

Most of us don't nibble to this excessive degree, but you can eat your way into hundreds of calories in just a few short minutes. That's why it's so important to only eat what you have placed out in front of yourself. Putting your head in the sand about your calorie intake by eating out of boxes is something skinny chicks avoid. By portioning foods out you also learn what a healthy-sized portion looks like so you can use "the eyeball method." As a result, you can estimate at a glance how many calories you are eating wherever you are. Portioning out your food also prevents you from unintentionally allowing your portions to grow. (Maybe you measured your cereal out the first time you had a bowl, but after some time, each time you pour it you may pour more and more.) Everything you eat should either be portioned out ahead of time or portioned out as you eat.

Make It Happen Now: The Real Chick Plan for #26

Your venture into portioning out your food should start with your favorite foods, those things you are most likely to go a little overboard with. The nutritional label on the side of the package, if there is one, will tell you the size of one serving.

Check out the calorie content and decide if that serving size will work as the amount you use as one portion, and package up that amount so it's ready to go. Snacks such as pretzels and peanuts and crackers can be a little tempting, and it can be easy to eat more than you planned on. If this is the case with you, again, read the label, then baggie them up, with ten crackers per baggie for instance. One example of portioning food that many of the skinny chicks use is putting 4- or 5-ounce pieces of chicken into baggies and popping them in the freezer. You can put them in raw or cooked. Either way, you know you've got one portion when you reach for one. Skinny Chick Diana Bernier says she loves almonds, but to keep her intake controlled, she puts a small amount into a bowl and eats from there.

Some cracker companies have begun selling their products in helpful 100-calorie packets. Go through all of the foods in your pantry and fridge that you love and portion them out ahead of time. With the rest, such as fluids, make sure you have measuring cups and spoons on hand to keep on top of how much you are getting. Without measuring the foods we eat, it can be too easy misjudge portion sizes and increase the number of calories we take in each day.

After you've eaten a meal of the appropriate size, it's important to sit back and listen to the signals your body is sending you. Do you feel full? Do you feel satisfied? You may have to wait a few minutes after finishing your meal to tell for sure if you do feel full, but once you assess your state of fullness, reflect on how much more you would have normally eaten and just how unnecessary that extra food really was.

Refer to Secret Number 17 for a rundown on exactly how much of each kind of food you need each day, which should be a guide for you on how much to have at each serving. But let's recap here what those amounts actually look like for when you need to use the eyeball method to determine how much to eat.

The recommended portions:

* 3–6 ounces of *grain product* each day = **3–6 slices of bread** or **1½–3 cups of pasta** or **1½–3 cups of cereal** or some combination of all three
* 2–2½ cups of *vegetables* each day = an actual measurement of **2–2½ cups of green beans, broccoli, carrots**, or other vegetables
* 1½–2 cups of *fruits* each day = **1½ cups of fruit juice** or **1½–2 small apples** or a combination of other fruits
* 3 cups of *milk product* each day = **3 cups of milk** or **4½ ounces of processed cheese** or some other combination of dairy products
* 5–5½ ounces of *meat and beans* each day = **approximately 1¼ cups of dry beans** or **5–5½ tablespoons of peanut butter** or **5–5½ eggs** or some other combination
* 5–6 teaspoons of *oils* each day = about **2 tablespoons of Canola oil** or **20 to 24 olives** or **2½–3 tablespoons of peanut butter** or another combination

Checklist

☑ Check the labels on your favorite foods, decide on a single portion, and package them up if you can.

☑ Go through other foods you are likely to eat too much of and portion these out, too.

☑ Look in your grocery store for preportioned packets of foods, such as crackers.

☑ Portion out fluids as you eat or drink.

☑ Keep measuring spoons and cups and a kitchen scale on hand.

☑ Once you've learned how much a portion of each food is, make sure you double-check every now and then to be sure you aren't "ramping up" your portion sizes.

☑ Use the eyeball method in restaurants to ensure you don't eat more than you need.

Secret Number 27: Get a Total Daily Intake Wake-Up Call

In 1971, American women ate 1,542 calories each day on average, according to the Centers for Disease Control (CDC). In 2000, women on average were up to 1,877 calories per day. Meanwhile, the average woman needs only 1,600 calories a day to feel full and energized. After just one year, that difference in calories (between what we ate thirty years ago versus what we ate in 2000) equates to twenty-eight pounds after just one year. Meanwhile, many women eat far, far more than 1,877 calories per day. It's no wonder, then, that so many women (and men) are dealing with weight issues. On the other hand, some of the women in this book work out for three or more hours a day. Most work out for at least an hour. Some compete in fitness competitions. Many work long, hard, physical days, yet the number of calories these skinny chicks eat is quite low—exactly where it should be.

Make It Happen Now: The Real Chick Plan for #27

Take stock of how many calories you consume each day. There's no point in lying to yourself about this. Write it all down: what you typically eat in a day and how much. Then either type it all into a computer program that will do the calorie counting for you or get yourself a calorie guide and add up the numbers yourself. Are you consuming more than the 1,600 calories recommended for the average woman? How far away from that number are you? You may think that this level of eating is crazy low, like being on a diet, but it's important to realize that eating less than 2,000 calories a day is what is normal and healthy for most women. The point of this secret is to really shake up your thinking about how much food is normal, healthy, and appropriate.

In an earlier secret we talked about the importance of burning all of the calories we consume each day. In fact, some women go below 1,600. (But no one should go below 1,200 calories a day.) Some people do have faster metabolisms and can therefore eat more. But likely it won't be much more than 2,000 calories. I believe many people think there's some magic formula; that some trick that will allow them to eat as much food as they want. "If I run I can eat as much as I want . . . or if I eat only protein and fat I can eat all I want . . . or if I eat only low-carb muffins I can eat all I want . . ." None of these things is true. You *will* pay for it in the end, weight-wise or health-wise. We need to radically change what we consider a healthy amount of food to eat in a day.

Checklist

☑ Write down everything you eat, with exact amounts, for three consecutive days. (Try to eat normally; don't make an effort to be "good.")

☑ Choose a method of calorie counting: an online program, a book, a homemade spreadsheet or notebook.

☑ Total up the calories for the three days you logged. Now compare that to the 1,600 calories the average woman needs. Then compare it to the 1,400 to 1,800 calories many of the skinny chicks take in daily.

☑ Set a goal for how many calories you will consume from now on and start cutting away at the things you eat each day that aren't necessary.

☑ Build yourself a series of daily menus made up of high-bulk, low-calorie foods and lots of snacks that are well within your daily calorie goal.

☑ Watch women with fabulous bodies in restaurants, on the street, and at work. Note what they are eating—you can even ask them! You'll probably notice many of them making healthy choices.

Secret Number 28: Think Ahead About Risky Outings

So you've got a yummy diet plan, your refrigerator is stocked with healthy snacks, and you're sticking to your exercise plan and loving every minute of it. Your weight is where you want it—or on its way—and you are feeling great. But your friends want to go out for lunch to that really great restaurant with the fabulous lasagna and your favorite banana daiquiris. How in the world are you going to venture into such tempting territory without ruining everything?

One strategy would be to make this lunch day your cheat day and give yourself permission to just go for it, as many skinny chicks do. Remember they said, "everything in moderation." They don't deprive themselves of food, a few drinks, or time with their friends, but they also do not allow their social outings to be an excuse to lose sight of their normal lifestyles. Skinny Chick Cathy Stanbrook says she often goes out to dinner but knows she can stick to a healthy plan and will not even entertain the idea of a hamburger or steak and fries; she goes in there knowing she's going to order a chicken or fish entree. Another approach is to keep close tabs on the calories you consume and make sure you hit the gym that night and the next few days to burn those extra calories. Or, even better, you could plan ahead: educate yourself about the number of calories in the various menu items and make healthy choices. Thinking ahead about risky outings is something most skinny chicks do. Experts call this "mental rehearsing" and say it's critical to preventing risky situations from sending you down the path to a binge. Many of the skinny chicks in this book, like Cathy, have a set plan for all such outings. As a result, they have fun like everyone else, but they leave feeling guilt-free—and wearing the same size jeans they came in with. And all of the skinny chicks say they make sure to count their alcohol calories into the mix, too.

Make It Happen Now: The Real Chick Plan for #28

The skinny chicks tend to stick to a pretty strict risky-outings plan. If your goal is to maintain a healthy body weight, you need to do the same. Before your outing, devise a game plan ahead of time. Think about what meals you may be eating there, what kinds of foods will likely be available, and what kinds of foods you may be unable to resist. If it's a restaurant, you may be able to go to the restaurant's website ahead of time and find the number of calories in the menu items as we've mentioned in a previous secret. Many of the fast-food restaurants now have this option. My husband loves eating at McDonald's, so their website became critical to me. I learned I can eat the Cobb Salad with Grilled Chicken with a Fruit 'n Yogurt Parfait and a Diet Coke and keep it around 500 calories. Smaller restaurants may not provide this option, but if you stick to salads with lean meats on top and ask for your dressing on the side, you can keep your calorie intake at a healthy level. Chicken dishes with vegetables are also often a good choice, although you may want to ask how the vegetables are cooked and ask them to limit the oils. If you're heading to Mom's house, find out what she's making ahead of time and research the calorie contents in different amounts. Work out how much of each thing you will have ahead of time. That way you go in prepared.

Skinny Chick Katie Katke says that during "risky outings" she always starts with sparkling water and a dark green salad to fill herself up. For Skinny Chick Diana Bernier, planning ahead means making sure she doesn't walk into these situations hungry. Skinny Chick Sherry Boudreau fills herself up with water before walking into high-risk food situations, plus she makes sure she does a cardio workout either before or after.

However, be sure to allow yourself at least one yummy thing so you don't feel like you are denying yourself all the joys of life. But in general make the healthiest choices you can on the menu. Serve yourself appropriate-sized portions (and don't go back for seconds!), fill up on veggies but steer clear of bread baskets and high-calorie extras, and ask for dressings on the side so you can control how much you are getting. When she goes to the movies, Skinny Chick Danielle Gamba says she often orders nothing at all, but when she does she opts for the kids' tray to keep the portions of snack food small.

Checklist

- ✓ Don't be afraid to go on risky outings.
- ✓ Try to limit the number of risky outings you take. The planning requires a lot of effort, and even with good planning they put you at risk for consuming more calories than you need. More than two per week might be difficult to manage unless you are really good at "being good."
- ✓ Find out what food choices will be available and either research the calorie contents of the menu items or familiarize yourself with the number of calories in the ingredients so you know exactly how much you can have.
- ✓ Find good substitutions or eliminate. If you really want that steak, forgo the accompanying potato, especially if it's "loaded." If you really can't deny yourself pasta, order a marinara sauce rather than one with cream.
- ✓ Decide what you are going to eat while out and stick to the plan.
- ✓ If you think you will be going over your desired calorie intake for the day, make a preemptive strike against those calories by doing an extra cardio workout earlier in the day. After the event, hit the stationary bicycle or take a walk.

Secret Number 29: Accept and Act Upon the Fact That Your Body Is Unique

The goal of this book is to demystify the fitness and diet lives of women with fabulous bodies. It's about learning the truth about what it takes to be fit and fabulous when it doesn't come naturally. We can either use this information to get a body like these women, or, more likely, use the information to pick a point along the fitness continuum that is right for *us* and to finally make peace with that place because it is an informed decision. As part of that, it's important to remember that even if you do exactly what one of the women in this book does, down to the very last ounce of food or minute of cardio, your body will likely never look exactly like hers.

Every body in the world is unique. If you don't have long legs now, you never will, no matter how closely you follow the diets of the skinny chicks. Learning their secrets will help you become your fit and fabulous best, but ultimately it will be *your* best, with all of the little imperfections that are part of *you*. You can get lean and strong and healthy, but ultimately you will still be you. So you need to learn to love your body and accept it for what it is. If you get yourself into a healthy range, loving your body will be much easier. But if you've always had bigger thighs, chances are even at your fit and fabulous best, your thighs will still be bigger than the rest of you. That's the place where your body stores fat; that's the way your body was meant to be. So keep all of this information in healthy perspective and remember that your body is unique and you need to learn to love what you've got. Skinny Chick and former Ford Supermodel of the Year Monika Schnarre, who is almost 6'2" tall, says you need to "learn to love your body, flaws and all." Skinny Chick Julia Beatty, says having an honest, loving, and accepting view of your unique body is crucial to feeling great in your own skin. "It is necessary to consider your genetics," she says. "This will help identify your body structure but also (help with) workout patterns."

Make It Happen Now: The Real Chick Plan for #29

Cindy Crawford's legs go on forever. Short of having a leg bone–extending operation, you aren't going to have long legs like that unless you are born with them. The reality is that although you can get your body fitter and healthier, ultimately your body is still your body. But remember that those imperfections and unique features are what make you special. They are part of the essence of you. So, if you are just about to get on the fitness bandwagon, it's a good idea to take a good hard look at yourself naked in the mirror first. That's a hard thing to do when you don't like what you see. But you really should take a good "before" look at yourself. It will help you gauge your progress later, but, more important, this inventory of what you've got can help you be more realistic about where you are going. If you are short-waisted, you will still be short-waisted no matter how fit you get. Take a good hard look and make realistic goals about how you would ultimately like to look for your body type. Then, as you see improvements, embrace those differences that are uniquely yours.

Maybe you are petite and flat-chested. That is such a sporty, sexy look! Or maybe you are tall with wide shoulders and a really sturdy frame. You are an athletic beauty! Or maybe you've got a big butt. Well, once you tone it up a little, shake that asset and make it your favorite body part! You can target specific body parts for improvements, such as doing lots of step work for a toned behind. *But ultimately spot reducing doesn't work.* To lose fat anywhere on your body you simply have to burn extra calories. That fat will come off, but you have no control of where it will come from. Targeting an area with strength training is helpful in terms of tightening the area up and making it look more cut, but if there is still a bunch of fat sitting on top of it, you won't see much of a difference. Women often tell me they want to lose their butts or thighs or hips. Ultimately with a good cardio program, supplemented with weights and a calorie-controlled diet, they will lose weight from all over, including the area of concern. But there is no real way to target that one area. You can sculpt your body so far, but in the end you are what you are. So embrace it. Don't compare yourself to others. But *do* compare your old body to the new one you're creating in order to see how far you've come.

Checklist

☑ Stand in front of a mirror while naked and take note of your unique body parts. Decide what changes you can realistically expect to see after committing to a healthier life.

☑ Aim for a long and lean body to help target those trouble spots.

☑ Reframe your view of your unique body. Focus on your best asset.

☑ Stop comparing yourself to other women, especially ones with different body types.

Secret Number 30: Keep Pregnancy Weight Gain Under Control

There is perhaps no more significant turning point in a woman's life when it comes to weight than a pregnancy. For many women, this is the time when their weight truly becomes unmanageable. They may have been ten or fifteen pounds overweight before the pregnancy, but once that pregnancy weight is added on, many women can find they weigh thirty or forty pounds more than they'd like to. While ten or fifteen pounds may have seemed manageable, many women are overwhelmed by larger amounts to lose and slip into obesity with no idea how to pull themselves out of it. This is one of the reasons why the American College of Obstetricians and Gynecologists recommends that every pregnant woman, with the permission of her health-care provider, exercise on most, if not all days.

Experts also recommend that women gain no more than twenty-five to thirty-five pounds during pregnancy, and even less if they eat a well-balanced diet and are already overweight. Skinny Chick Alex Barker gained more than the recommended amount, but she was not overweight to begin with, has a large frame at 5' 10", worked out right until the very end of her pregnancy—and lost all of her pregnancy weight in four months. She and the other skinny chick moms know the importance of keeping weight gain under control and losing it after the baby is born. Gaining too much weight in pregnancy is associated with such serious pregnancy complications as gestational diabetes and preeclampsia. It's also associated with obesity for Mom later in life, along with low self-esteem, poor body image, and depression. So it's important to keep things under control.

Make It Happen Now: The Real Chick Plan for #30

While this secret may seem only to apply to those gals planning a pregnancy or who are already pregnant, think again. Your ability to remain fit and active during pregnancy is very much tied to your level of fitness and activity prior to pregnancy. If you plan to one day have a baby, it's important to get to a healthy weight now and learn how to maintain it. That not only gives you a healthy starting point, but it also increases the range of exercises you will be able to do during pregnancy. Meanwhile, the American College of Obstetricians and Gynecologists recommends every pregnant woman, who doesn't have medical reasons not to, should do cardiovascular exercise most days.

Pregnant women are also encouraged to do resistance training two days a week or more and to stretch as often as possible. Note: If you have not been active prior to pregnancy you must wait until the second trimester to begin, because your body is not conditioned for exercise. It is advised that these women wait until the highest miscarriage risk has passed. Keeping their activity to a moderate to somewhat-hard exertion level, women can work out four or more days a week for an hour at a time. For more information on this, refer to my book *Nine Months Strong: Shaping Up for Labor and Delivery and the Toughest Physical Day of Your Life.*

As for calorie intake, pregnant women really only need 300 more calories each day starting in the SECOND trimester (the baby isn't requiring much before then), so the idea of eating for two really needs to be thrown out the window. And if you are a pregnant woman who is already overweight, you may not need any extra calories as long as you are getting sufficient nutrients. The bottom line is to keep as active as you can and eat as well as you can to get through your pregnancy with as little excess weight gain as possible. As long as you are gaining what the baby needs to be healthy, you are doing fine. There is no need to make huge gains. It's just more for you to lose afterward.

Checklist

✓ If you plan to have a child one day, get active now so you will go into it with an ideal weight and also so that you can continue to exercise in the first trimester.

✓ If you are already pregnant, continue to work out as much as you have been (after getting permission from your health-care provider), but reduce effort to moderate to somewhat-hard level. (Note: This is a subjective measurement of your exertion. It's recommended that pregnant women work out to a level that feels to them to be a moderate to somewhat-hard level.)

✓ Listen to your body during prenatal exercise; stop if you experience pain, bleeding, fluid leakage, light-headedness, or other symptoms that worry you. Contact your health-care provider.

- ✓ During the first trimester, try to consume the same number of calories as you did before the pregnancy, but make sure that you are choosing healthy foods from all of the food groups.
- ✓ If you are not already overweight, increase your calorie intake after the first trimester by up to 300 calories; continue to eat a balanced diet, focusing on healthy protein and fiber.
- ✓ In the second trimester, increase the duration and intensity of exercise by 10 percent if you desire; continue to listen to your body.
- ✓ Get regular checkups to ensure that it is safe for you to continue exercising during pregnancy; your situation can change from one day to the next.
- ✓ Resist the impulse to eat for two or binge on bad foods. You will pay for it down the road with more exercise.

Secret Number 31: Read Labels

All packaged foods are required to have nutritional labeling. This is usually a label on the side of the package that outlines such things as calorie content; the percentages of protein, carbohydrates, fat, fiber, and sodium in the product; and often what percentage of recommended daily intake each serving provides of different nutrients. If you learn about what to look for, these nutritional labels can be golden. Without them, you would really be stabbing in the dark in terms of knowing exactly what you are consuming. It would be particularly difficult to estimate how many calories you are getting with processed foods. Educating yourself about the food you are eating is critical to taking control of your body, and you can't do that without good information. Some labels can be tricky to read if you don't look at them carefully. So look carefully and do the math.

Make It Happen Now: The Real Chick Plan for #31

Before you even buy a product, you should be taking a good look at the label. The label will tell you the size of a single serving and also the number of servings in the package. The serving size on the label is usually smaller than what we would normally serve ourselves, but it's critical because it's the basis of all the nutritional information—including the calories. And from a weight loss or maintenance perspective the important thing is the calories.

If the product is high in fat, that will show itself in the final calorie count. Fat can't hide. Keep in mind that monounsaturated (like olive oil) and polyunsaturated fats (like corn oil) are good fats, while saturated and trans fats are not good for you.

A good solid protein percentage is also good. Your body really needs protein, plus it helps you feel full longer. Protein can also be a significant factor in the calorie content, so selecting lean protein choices such as chicken or fish is important.

As for carbohydrates, carbs get a bad rap. They are the nutrient we use to fuel our bodies and we shouldn't be afraid of them. Ultimately fat, protein, and carbohydrates contribute to the number of calories in a food.

Checklist

✓ While shopping, look for the nutritional information label on the package. If the product doesn't have a nutritional label, or if you are confused by the information provided, one option is to simply not buy it.

✓ When selecting a food, notice the serving size and the number of servings in the package. If the servings you eat are a different size, do the math and figure out how many calories would be in the serving that you would be eating.

✓ Consider the number of calories in another way. Do you really want to spend 300 calories on a small breakfast bar when you could

have egg whites on two pieces of whole-wheat toast and a small
yogurt for about the same amount of calories?

✓ Note whether the product has any trans or saturated fats. If so, you
may want to make a different choice, particularly looking for the
"good" polyunsaturated fats.

✓ Note the protein content of the product. If more than 10 percent of
the product's total calories come from protein, it will help you feel
full and may be a good choice.

✓ If you're looking at a high-carbohydrate food, look on the
ingredients panel and look for words like *whole-grain* and *whole-
wheat*. Don't be fooled by phrases like *100 percent wheat*,
multigrain, or *stone-ground*. These products have had much more
processing and so will be absorbed into your bloodstream faster
and cause you to be hungry sooner.

✓ Also, limit sodium (salt) intake to 2,400 milligrams per day.

Secret Number 32: Replace Emotional Eating

So you just had a big fight with your significant other and
you're thinking of heading out to the corner store to get a
chocolate bar and big bottle of Coke. That sugar and caffeine
ritual always lifts your spirits, right? Well, it might for a short
period of time, but afterward you'll probably feel worse than
you did before.

Many of us turn to food when something goes wrong.
(Many of the skinny chicks in this book told me they don't
like to eat when they are upset. Well, that's so nice for them,
but that's just not my reality—or the reality of most women
I know.) To find out if this is your pattern, too, start making
note of what's going on in your life whenever you fall off the
wagon. You may find that it's when things are going badly in
other parts of your life. By recognizing this, you can head this
self-destructive behavior off at the pass. You need to try to

replace the behavior with a new, healthier behavior; you need to replace your emotional eating with something else

Make It Happen Now: The Real Chick Plan for #32

It can be hard to break a habit. If you like to put food in your mouth when you are stressed, upset, nervous, or emotional in some other way, this habit will be hard to break. You may simply need to put something in your mouth, so try changing what it is that you put in your mouth. Having lots of healthy snacks on hand is essential. Head for the carrots, celery, and fruit instead of the bad treats. If that doesn't do the trick, try sugar-free cola or a few sticks of sugar-free chewing gum. Make a cup of tea, hold that warm cup in your hands, and savor every sip. Do something, anything, with your hands and mouth, but try not to head for that bag of chips!

Another way to replace your emotional eating is to exercise. When my nephew was born with a serious heart condition, once I'd left the hospital because there was nothing more I could do to help there, I immediately went for a run. There is nothing better for helping you cool off, calm down, perk up, or stop worrying than a good workout. Even a brisk walk can help. Getting your endorphins flowing can help you get your mind off your problems and on the road to feeling better.

When upset strikes, you can do many things instead of eating. Call a friend, pick up a good novel, clean the house—something, anything. The key here is to *realize* that you head for food when you are upset and to *plan* to do something else the next time it happens. Then, when upsets strike, direct yourself to your new form of comfort.

Checklist

☑ Which foods do you tend to comfort yourself with? Lock those foods up or get them out of the house.

☑ Think about some new ways you can comfort yourself. Consider snacking on veggies, fruits, or sugar-free snacks.

☑ Consider exercise as an outlet.

☑ Make a list of other things you can do that may give you comfort, such as calling a friend, reading a book, going for a walk, or cleaning the house.

Secret Number 33: Try the Healthy, Safe Weight-Loss Support Products

This can be dangerous territory. Once you start looking, you'll be amazed by how many weight-loss supplements are on the market and how many of them are downright unsafe. Do not blindly experiment with every product that you find in the health food stores or advertised in fitness magazines. For one reason, there are still a lot of products on the market that contain ephedra or "ephedrine alkaloids," despite the fact that the FDA has restricted the way this controversial and potentially harmful product can be sold and some countries have banned the substance.

A number of products supposedly suppress appetite. I am no fan of these products, either. On the other hand, some natural, healthy supplements have shown success in supporting weight loss. These are not the scary products we see at the back of fitness magazines that come with promises that they will speed up your metabolism and burn fat faster. Instead these products provide much subtler benefits, supporting the natural processes inside your body to help optimize your body's use of energy. Skinny chicks know the health effects of these healthy supplements and know they won't do them any harm. However, it is important to talk to your doctor about trying any supplements to make sure you have no medication conflicts or underlying medical conditions that might cause problems.

Skinny Chicks Don'ts and Do-with-Cautions

Don'ts

* Don't use artificial growth hormones (steroids) for any reason. You may hear that they will help you stay energized and help your body recover more quickly from exercise, but don't be tempted.
* Don't use pills to overstimulate your thyroid. This is unnatural and can do harm to your body and metabolism.
* Refrain from a diet approach called "peaking." This would have you, several days before a big event, cutting out all carbohydrates and taking diuretics that drain all the water from your muscles. This leads to the formation of ketones, which can lead to damage to your liver and kidneys.
* Don't use supplements with ephedra. Possible side effects of this drug include nervousness, dizziness, tremors, alteration in blood pressure or heart rate, headache, gastrointestinal distress, chest pain, myocardial infection, hepatitis, stroke, seizures, psychosis, and death.
* Don't smoke cigarettes to curb cravings or suppress hunger.

Do with Cautions

* Only occasionally and with caution should you do cleanses. These are periods of one to fourteen days during which you eat little to no solid food and take supplements to help flush out your system. This is risky behavior that can lead to disordered eating, says Dr. Virginia Dodd, assistant professor in the Department of Health and Behavior at the University of Florida.
* If you choose to have a "day off" to eat what you want, while eating "clean" on other days, beware of descending into binge behavior. For a detailed list of warning signs about bingeing, see the sections dealing with binge eating disorder and bulimia in Chapter 1.
* Use so-called "starch-blockers" or "carbohydrate blockers" at your own risk. Minimal research has been done on them, and so they have not been shown to be safe or effective.

Make It Happen Now: The Real Chick Plan for #33

Using diet supplements may be a little foreign to you at first. It may even feel wrong. With so many unhealthy and useless products on the market, it's easy to come away with a sense that this is dangerous territory you should avoid.

A few products on the market may help support your weight-loss efforts in a safe way. While none of these weight-loss support nutrients is being touted as a miracle drug, enough studies have shown they can play a role in maintaining a healthy weight. The first is Conjugated Linoleic Acid, or CLA. While experts are still waiting for a definitive study on this, some studies have shown that this enzyme, when taken with food, can interfere with the body's fat storage process. I use it myself, and it seems to keep me at a weight that's two or three pounds lower than when I'm not taking it. Another supplement that has shown some promise is green tea. While, again, experts are still not in agreement on the efficacy of green tea, some studies have shown that this age-old brew can help to speed up your metabolism, increasing the rate at which you burn calories; can slow down the rise in blood sugar (keeping you fuller longer); and can lower your HDL or "bad" cholesterol levels. You can simply drink green tea or you can find concentrated tablets of it in health food stores. Other supplements worth investigation include magnesium, L-carnitine, and omega-3 fatty acids.

Checklist

☑ Do some research on products and vitamin and nutrient supplements at wholehealthmd.com.

☑ Talk to your health practitioner to make sure there is no medical reason you shouldn't try them (and to ensure you have the latest medical information).

☑ Give them a try. Take them for at least a month to see if you notice any benefits.

☑ Stop taking them if you find they are causing any serious negative side effects. Some supplements may cause nausea and gastrointestinal upset, or even body odor (L-carnitine), but no major side effects are reported with the supplements listed.

Secret Number 34: If You Fall off the Horse, Get Right Back On

We all do it, even the skinny chicks. We all fall off the wagon and eat too much of the things we shouldn't or go for long periods without getting to the gym. It could start with an upsetting life event or it may just sneak up on you a little at a time. But before you know it, you haven't been eating the way you should or exercising regularly, and the numbers on the scale are starting to show it. We are all human. It's going to happen. But what we do once we realize it's happened is what's critical. Do we hop right back on that horse, or do we continue down the road to an unhealthy body? Experts say any diet will work if you can stick to it. The skinny chicks always get right back on that horse. People who have struggled with weight without success often report that one small slipup can cause them to go back to their old ways. So what does this tell us? We can really learn something from those who are successful at maintaining a healthy weight. It's how they handle it when they fall off the wagon that separates the skinny chicks from the rest of us.

Make It Happen Now: The Real Chick Plan for #34

The first step in fixing a problem is recognizing that you have one. Being self-aware, writing down what you eat, and weighing yourself regularly prevent you from living in denial. You need to take these steps to be able to recognize when you are going off course. You will also probably notice your clothes not fitting quite as well, you won't feel as energetic, and you may even have intestinal problems. Watch for these signs. This may sound a little silly because you would think that most people realize it when they have been "bad." But if you've had success and are feeling good, it can be easy to start slipping back down into unhealthy living. Many people have spent so much of their lives in unhealthy ways that it feels quite natural to go back to old habits. So recognize the changes when they happen.

Next, have a plan in place for what you are going to do about it. So many women figure that once they've had a day or two or seven of endless chocolate-fests and cupboard raids, that all of their previous hard work is for nothing. At some point we've all allowed ourselves to wallow in defeat and guilt and simply give up. But you need to stop this way of thinking and feeling now! One bad meal—a week of bad meals (and the desserts that go with them)—is still not enough to bring down the whole ship. It's over, forget it. It's in the past, and you can't change it. Move on. Don't get stuck in the rut of negative thinking and defeatism. If you do, you do it at the expense of your new size jeans and the renewed energy you've been feeling. There is a way out.

Think: Is there a number of calories each day that makes you feel like you are getting things under control but not depriving yourself? Can you increase your cardio workouts for a few weeks? What will it take to make you feel like you are back on track? You need to identify these things, even before you fall off the wagon, and even write them down in a journal for reference. Then, you need to just do it. Start as soon as you feel you have lost your way. Go for a run, drink extra water, have a salad for dinner. Get cracking right away. Then monitor your progress and congratulate yourself for getting back on track rather than wallowing in defeatism and guilt. Finally, it's a good idea to recognize the triggers or habits that lead you in the wrong direction in the first place. How can you avoid these in the future? Can you remind yourself of how crummy and lethargic you feel when you fall off the wagon? Can you hang a picture of yourself somewhere that shows how great you look when you're on track to use as a reminder? Figure out what it's going to take, then take action. It goes without saying that it's easier if you can prevent yourself from falling off the wagon in the first place.

Checklist

- ☑ Weigh yourself regularly. (Remember, this is one thing that people who have successfully lost weight all report doing in order to stay on track.)
- ☑ Keep a food journal, even when you're off the wagon.
- ☑ Stay in touch with how your body feels and how you feel emotionally and take note of any changes as a result of changes in diet and exercise.
- ☑ Don't live in denial.
- ☑ Stop beating yourself up and try to drop the defeatist attitude. All your previous hard work has NOT been negated by a slipup.
- ☑ Set up a plan for getting back on track should you fall off the wagon.
- ☑ Execute that plan as soon as you realize you've gone off course. Don't wait for another meal or another day for you to get started.
- ☑ If you think you're close to slipping, visualize yourself reaching your health goals, with detailed scenarios, or remember how terrible you felt the last time you went off track.
- ☑ Know that it's not a lost cause—everyone has their moments—but be sure to make it just that: a moment.
- ☑ Monitor your progress.
- ☑ Do something nice for yourself when you get yourself back on track.
- ☑ Note the triggers that put you off course in the first place and plan how to avoid these in the future.

Secret Number 35: Have Healthy Snacks on Hand

What do skinny chicks keep in their fridge? Well, if you look at their daily diet you'll know that they keep them stocked with healthy snacks. Carrots, celery, apples, oranges, strawberries and other berries, cut-up veggies ready for low-cal dipping. Keeping your cupboards and fridge well stocked with healthy, low-calorie options can be an integral part of staying on course with a healthy diet. Between meals it's likely that you'll get the munchies, and the easiest cure for that is munching. But if there's nothing healthy and low calorie at hand, you will be tempted to start grazing among the higher-calorie, less-healthy options. If there are some crunchy, sweet carrots right in front of you, you'll be more likely to eat them. If there's nothing left but your high-calorie, salt-and-oil-covered chips (that can be as much as 30 or 40 calories *each*), then you'll eat them. Those can add up fast if you are grabbing a handful. And one or two often just don't seem to cut it. Once you get nibbling on something that's high in salt or sugar or fat (or all three), you will start to want more and more of it. So, make sure you've got some healthy choices at hand at all times.

Make It Happen Now: The Real Chick Plan for #35

If something is healthy but you don't like it, there's no point in stocking your refrigerator with it—it will never be the food you grab when you have the munchies. You may have the best of intentions, but that may not be enough. Set yourself up for success by stocking the foods that you really like. I may love broccoli, but if it's not your thing, it doesn't matter how healthy and low-calorie it is—you won't grab it at the critical moment when you need to fend off a craving. And be creative. Maybe you love beets. I sure do. I love to open up a jar of pickled beets and pop a few into my mouth. Those prepeeled and prewashed baby carrots are great, too, because they're so convenient when you've got the munchies—you're more likely to grab them because they are ready to go. Cutting up different fruits and putting them all together in a big, covered bowl in the fridge is another great idea. You can just dig into the bowl whenever you need something sweet. I also love to snack on snow peas. There are so many vegetables and fruits that you can have ready to go in your fridge.

You may also want to stock up on some great low-calorie crackers and other snacks as well. Many times, we crave the act of nibbling more than we do the food itself. Maybe you need something sweet. A small box of raisins can deliver the sugar punch you might get from a chocolate bar. Crunchy veggies or a healthy spreadable snack can keep your mouth or hands happy while watching a movie. Buy some low-fat, low-calorie sour cream (almost no calories) and mix with onion soup or other mix to make a yummy dip for veggies. Also, shop around for some low-calorie, whole-grain cracker, pita, and bread options that you can use to create a healthy snack.

Checklist

☑ Take a tour of the produce section of your grocery store and refamiliarize yourself with all the fruits and vegetables you love.

☑ Try some new fruits and vegetables—even ones you can't pronounce or you've never heard of before.

☑ Resolve to keep some crunchy fruit and vegetable snacks in your fridge at all times.

☑ Stay on top of your shopping so you don't run out of healthy options.

☑ Take some healthy snacks with you on the go so you aren't tempted to stop for an unhealthy snack. The difference to your health and your momentum between a bag of carrots and a 400-calorie muffin dripping in oil, salt, and sugar is dramatic.

Secret Number 36: Keep a "Clean" Food Environment

I don't keep potato chips where I can reach them. I can't be trusted with them. As a result, my husband has a locked cupboard in the kitchen where he keeps all the things I don't want to have access to, including chips. That's one way to put this secret into action. Do whatever you have to do to keep a clean food environment. Healthy eating over the long term means creating a home environment where there aren't constant temptations.

Skinny chicks know this trick. They keep their refrigerator stocked with healthy snack foods and make sure their favorite healthy choices are on hand. They shop on the outer edges of the supermarket to stay clear of the highly processed, prepackaged foods that tend to carry the highest calorie contents and the lowest nutritional values. You won't find a big bag of potato chips on top of an FHM model's refrigerator. But you will find strawberries and apples and whole-grain breads inside her refrigerator. The way I see it, you only have to have willpower when you go grocery shopping. If you don't bring those nasty foods home, you won't have temptation the entire rest of the week. That way you will be *forced* to eat well most of the time.

Make It Happen Now: The Real Chick Plan for #36

My under-lock-and-key cupboard trick may sound extreme, but it's not. If you are one of those people who seriously—and let's get real here—cannot resist cookies or chips or whatever else, then this idea is for you. You must have a clean food environment at home if you want to stick to a healthy, low-calorie eating regimen. Just a couple of handfuls of potato chips a day could put a pound on you every other week. It's just simple math. On the other hand, a handful of grapes or a couple of bread sticks can probably fill that void—and keep you on track. But most of the time you won't reach for those healthier choices if a cookie or a bag of chips is sitting right in front of you. So go through your kitchen, clean out all the unhealthy choices, and lock up the ones your family members insist on keeping.

Next, keep your kitchen full of healthy choices, such as baby carrots, cut-up celery, strawberries, grapes, bread sticks, cut-up melon, apples, oranges, and peaches. It's important to extend your healthy food environment beyond your home as well. Having healthy choices on hand will ensure that you pack healthy lunches and snacks for work so you won't be as tempted by the muffin cart or the doughnut shop. Next, identify other unhealthy food environments and find a way to make them healthy. Stay away from the vending machine or food kiosks at work and ask coworkers to keep boxes of chocolates or dough-nuts out of your path. If you find you get hungry in your car and tend to stop for snacks, keep healthy snacks in your car. Also, if you notice triggers at work that cause you to think about food, plan replacement activities such as going for a walk or drinking a can of diet cola. Skinny Chick Diana Bernier has another tip: because she doesn't want to deprive her kids of yummy treats, she selects things for them that she doesn't particularly like her-self. These treats are easier for her to resist. Skinny Chick Sazzy Varga says she simply keeps the less-healthy options in a sepa-rate cupboard so that she "doesn't have to stare at them" every time she selects something to eat.

Checklist

☑ Clear out unhealthy foods from your fridge and pantry.

☑ Lock up any unhealthy foods other family members insist on keeping.

☑ Think about what you are craving. Is it the need to occupy yourself? Something crunchy to eat while watching a suspenseful movie? Or just plain old comfort food? Make sure you keep your fridge stocked with healthy snack foods such as carrots, apples, and anything else you think will satisfy your cravings.

☑ Buy ready-made snacks or cut-up foods that are ready to eat and portioned.

☑ Restock these healthy choices often so you don't find yourself with nothing healthy to nibble.

☑ Pack a healthy lunch and snacks to take to work.

☑ Change your routines to avoid going into high-risk environments, such as walking past your favorite doughnut shop.

Secret Number 37: Make Salad Your Friend

It's true—salad is a staple of my skinny chicks' diets. And before you huff, roll your eyes, and stop reading, take a moment to see why this can be a very important secret. For one thing, salads don't have to be tasteless, uninteresting wannabe meals that leave you hungry for more. On the contrary, salads can be thoroughly enjoyable and satisfying. Did you know that the women on the TV sitcom "Friends" ate Cobb salads every day for lunch for most of the years they filmed the show? And Cobb salads are delicious. They have eggs, cheese, bacon, avocado . . . think about all the wonderful flavors in that list!

The thing about salads is that the bed of lettuce provides a very low-calorie and bulky base to a meal that is often water and nutrient rich. Those leafy greens take up lots of space in your stomach and take a long time to eat, making you feel like you are eating lots. But in addition, that bed of lettuce is often topped with some filling, lean protein such as chicken, salmon, or shrimp, and some tasty, healthy fats in the form of cheeses and oils. In a sense, the greens replace the pasta or rice that you would otherwise be piling your chicken and sauces onto! Because the base is so low calorie, it gives you the freedom to enjoy tastier choices on top of the salad. Skinny chicks know this. Now you do too.

Make It Happen Now: The Real Chick Plan for Secret #37

Salads aren't just lettuce anymore. So, how do you make salad your new best friend? Easy, just start shopping around for the most delicious selections. Or, you can even invent some of your own. After visiting New Zealand where I was served a salad with banana, chicken, and crunchy noodles sprinkled on top, I came home and invented my own version and added shredded carrots and cabbage and raspberry vinaigrette to the mix. It's divine, very filling, and only about 300 calories. I eat it all the time.

The Cobb salad at McDonald's with grilled chicken, with just 400 calories, is also a great find. Be aware, however, that not all salads are created equal. Some salads have as many as 800 calories. That's usually the case when they are heaped with high-fat dressings and crazy things like chili. So, research the nutritional information for the salads in the restaurants you frequent and invent or recreate a few of your favorites at home. Be creative and don't be afraid to try new things. Sass up your salads with beans (there are so many kinds of beans!), chickpeas, mushrooms, beats, artichoke hearts, hearts of palm, roasted peppers, or even a touch of Parmesan cheese. Try a cucumber and tomato salad with fresh basil or find a recipe for a beautiful spinach salad. You'll never get bored! When you can, choose dark leafy greens over paler greens because they have more nutrients.

Remember that salad can become our enemy if we don't watch what dressings—and how much of them—we douse on. And, thankfully, many kinds of dressings are available in supermarkets and restaurants that will leave you feeling guilt free. A squeeze of lemon or a spoonful of salsa are great alternatives. Skinny Chick Kristin Cheh says, "Once you begin to train yourself to eat better, you will start to crave the healthier foods instead of the junk. Trust me, it's true . . . then you will get that smokin' bod!" And there's no better way to get a truly good meal that makes you feel full than with salads.

Checklist

- ☑ Sass up your salads with exotic vegetables and fruits.
- ☑ Try out some new salads at restaurants and research the nutritional contents.
- ☑ Try inventing your own salads. There are no rules!
- ☑ Buy bags of prewashed, precut lettuce to increase the likelihood of your making salads regularly.
- ☑ Try out new, tasty no-fat or low-fat dressings.

Secret Number 38: Learn How to Have Just One Cookie

That infamous line from the potato chip commercial, "I betcha can't eat just one," is so true, isn't it? I remember watching Susanna Hoffs, the lead singer of The Bangles, on TV talking about how she kept her body in such great shape by never eating more than three bites of something bad. At the time I thought, "How can she do that?" Take three bites of chocolate cake and then put it down? That's nuts! But if you look closely at the diet habits of women with fabulous bodies, you'll see that they often practice moderation and self-control techniques just like that. How great is it to be able to eat some chocolate cake, even while losing weight? I know I often keep 210-calorie Chapman's ice cream sugar cones in my freezer and plan them into my total daily calorie intake as an afternoon snack. Having a treat like that really makes me feel like I am free to eat whatever I want. In truth, I am free to eat whatever I want—and so are you. But it's all about moderation. The key is to learn how to stop at that one portion so you don't go overboard.

Make It Happen Now: The Real Chick Plan for #38

So how do you stop at just one cookie or just one handful of potato chips? Well, it's not easy, but recognizing that you are only able to have these treats because you are having a small portion is the first step. Take a look at your daily calorie allowance and think about one or two things that you'd really like to squeeze into your day. Maybe it's a couple of Oreos or a small bag of pretzels or an ice cream bar. Decide exactly how much of that thing you can allow and divide it into one-serving containers or bags. Then, when it's time to dig into your treat, take just one serving, sit down, eat slowly, and enjoy. But you do have to stop eating when it's all gone. You can't go back for more. You've had your treat; be glad you were able to have it and don't wreck a good thing. Again, the only reason you can have these treats is because you are putting a limit on how much.

There's no reason why you can't have delicious, high-calorie, high-fat treats if you account for them in your overall calorie intake. In fact, this may help you to not feel deprived or focus overmuch on these foods. Becoming obsessed with foods on your no-no list can become unhealthy and lead to bingeing when you can't white-knuckle it any longer. So figure out what you need to have and fit them into some or even all of your days.

Checklist

☑ Work out how large a portion of some of your favorite cheat foods you can work into your overall calorie intake on some or even all days.

☑ Divide these treats into portion-sized containers to help you avoid eating more than you planned.

☑ Don't allow yourself to eat straight out of the box or bag.

☑ Focus on your treat and eat it slowly. Think about how great it is to have a treat like this and still have a butt the size you want!

- ✓ When you have eaten your portion, STOP! Don't go back for more. It's critical to learn this kind of control.
- ✓ Look forward to tomorrow's treat.

Secret Number 39: Learn to Really Listen to Your Body

This is a trick that my favorite skinny chick, my best friend Lisa, has perfected. She has always had this amazing ability to simply stop eating when she feels full or when the food stops tasting good. I marvel at this because I have always been a clean-your-plate kind of person. But I have never seen Lisa finish a restaurant meal. She usually puts her fork down long before the cake she ordered is finished. Or when she's eating a slice of her delicious banana bread, she stops eating it when her stomach says no more. It's because she *listens to her body*. This is a critical secret of skinny chicks. We often get so caught up in the act of eating, the comfort it brings us on an emotional level, or the fact that it tastes delicious, that we lose touch with the signals our brain is sending us. We may actually be full, but out of habit we are still eating anyway.

Make It Happen Now: The Real Chick Plan for #39

This secret is a tough one. Most of us don't eat because we are hungry. We eat because it's lunchtime, or something to eat is right there, or we're stressed or sad or celebrating something. But the only good reason to eat is because we are hungry. We have got to learn how to get back in touch with our bodies and let them direct us. First thing in the morning, if you've got the time, give your body a chance to get a little hungry before you eat your breakfast. Then, only eat as much as you need to feel full. Stop when you do. Really make a point of listening to those signs coming from your stomach. Then, don't eat again until your stomach says you are hungry. This will work best if you have eaten a balanced meal that includes fat, protein, and whole-grain or whole-food carbohydrates, because the combination will make you feel full longer. As you go through your day, make a point of stopping and putting your food away when you feel full. Just because something tastes good doesn't mean you have to finish it. Try, even for just one day, to let your body tell you when to start and stop eating rather than your head.

Checklist

☑ Decide on a day to set aside to "listen" to your body.

☑ On that day, don't eat until your body says "go."

☑ Next, don't eat again until you feel hungry.

☑ Stop eating once your stomach feels full. (You have to pay close attention to notice when you get there.) This doesn't mean once your stomach feels too full—stop before that sensation.

☑ Eat your other snacks and meals only when your body gives you signals, not your brain. Beware of your brain telling you to snack because it's got a craving or because it's the time of the day when "everyone" eats.

☑ Pay attention to your food choices. A combination of fat, protein, and carbohydrates will help you feel full.

☑ At the end of the day, look back on how much you ate. Compare that to how much you usually eat.

Secret Number 40: Get Addicted to Exercise

Many of the skinny chicks in this book were surprised by my questions about how they stick to their exercise schedules. "That's like asking me how I manage to brush my teeth every day," they'd say. For these women, regular, concentrated, purposeful exercise is just a way of life. It's critical to keeping their bodies in great shape and, more importantly, keeping their minds healthy. The skinny chicks know that working out isn't just great for their bodies, it's fantastic for their mental and emotional health too, just as numerous scientific studies have shown. For these women, exercise has quite simply become an addiction. For those who are not regular exercisers, this may sound bizarre. But it's really not. First, psychologically you do become addicted to exercise over time (a very healthy addiction, in my estimation), learning to depend on it for a stress release and the other effects it has on your body. You also develop the belief that your physical and emotional well-being depend on continued exercise.

But you also can become physically addicted to exercise. While some of the science on this is still a little sketchy, experts believe that people do become addicted to the adrenalin released during exercise. People can also become addicted to the auto-hypnotic effect it can have on you. In addition, studies have shown that aerobic exercise can have as much of a beneficial effect on depression as conventional drug therapies. Ultimately, regular exercisers report they have withdrawal symptoms when they suddenly stop exercising, such as irritability, depression, anxiety, and headaches.

So this skinny chick secret is all about allowing yourself, even encouraging yourself, to become an exercise addict. Now, a word of caution: there is such a thing as a negative exercise addiction, which I mentioned in Chapter 1. Some people take it too far, and their relationships, work, and so forth suffer because exercise becomes number one in their lives. This is not healthy. Should you experience this, please seek professional help. You should control your exercise, exercise should not control you. And while it's important to not consume more calories than your body needs each day, it's also important that you don't fall into the unhealthy pattern of exercising excessively to burn off every last calorie. This, too, is unhealthy, and not the positive, healthy addiction I'm talking about with this secret. Exercise should be fun, not something you feel you have to do.

Make It Happen Now: The Real Chick Plan for #40

Get addicted to exercise. Many women may look at this secret and wonder how the heck they will ever make this happen in their lives. Maybe you dread exercise. Maybe you find it just plain boring. But once you get started, these feelings and fears will just go away. Once the benefits of exercise start mounting (and who doesn't want improved self-esteem, improved confidence, and a more fit body), those benefits will soon outweigh the fears and negative associations. But to get started, you may simply have to force yourself—use your drive, will, and determination to force yourself. There may be no other way.

Those things won't keep you at it in the long run, though. That's where healthy addiction comes in. You've got to get yourself to the point where you need and look forward to those exercise sessions. You need to get to the point where you fight for them and always squeeze them into your day and you guard that time as if it were precious—because it is. If you don't reach this level with it, it will be easy to fall back into a sedentary lifestyle. Skinny Chick Diana Bernier says, "I never avoid a workout; it's not something I would ever consider."

To get to the place were Diana is, all you have to do is get started. You need to pick a cardiovascular fitness exercise to do at least three times a week, then decide on what form of resistance training you want to do for two additional workouts each week (free weights, weight machines, exercise bands). Then, as the old Nike ad goes, you Just Do It. You just start. There's no magic here. The healthy addiction that will keep you going with your fitness regimen over the long haul will come in time, but first you have to force yourself to make the first move.

Checklist

☑ Choose a cardiovascular activity, or a few, that you will participate in most days of the week.

☑ Choose a weight or strength training routine to do once or twice a week.

☑ Throw yourself into your workouts, using sheer determination to make a change and get you started.

☑ While exercising, notice how the first ten minutes is the hardest, then something happens and it seems to get easier.

☑ Work up to at least a 45-minute cardio session each time to get the full effect of the adrenalin.

☑ Take notice of how great you feel during your workout and remind yourself of it whenever you can.

☑ Take notice of how great you feel after your workout and remind yourself of that feeling whenever you hesitate to head to the gym.

☑ Track your results—weight loss, clothing size changes, etc.—and revel in your successes.

☑ Allow exercise to become your new, healthy addiction.

Secret Number 41: Find Fun, Yummy Replacements for the "Bad" Stuff

From sprinkling water on your popcorn to fool your tongue into thinking there's butter to dipping your strawberries into fat-free whipped cream for a low-calorie treat that tastes like strawberry shortcake, the skinny chicks have lots of great ideas for low-calorie replacements for favorite foods. So much of what we love about "bad" foods is really about their sweetness or texture or the way they look. Because of this, it can be quite easy to trick your mind and your tongue with creative substitutes. This is a terrific way to have it both ways.

The What-to-Eat-When-You-Have-to-Cheat Sheet

Let's face it. There are days and circumstances that sneak up on us that have the words *double super-fudge chunk* written all over them. There's certainly nothing wrong with a craving or two and, even better, there's nothing wrong with giving in to them—once in a while. Here is the official Skinny Girls Cheating Substitution Guide, for when you want to cheat but still have some powers of resistance against it. These items will help satisfy cravings and offer comfort with less fat and fewer calories. Here's to better days!

WHEN YOU ARE CRAVING THIS . . .	TRY THIS INSTEAD
Half a large bag of potato chips (800 calories)	A small bag of Baked Lays potato chips (130 calories)
A medium chocolate ice cream cone (340 calories)	A Skinny Cow chocolate ice cream bar (100 calories)
A medium-sized buttered popcorn at the movie theater (910 calories)	6 cups of air-popped popcorn (186 calories) topped with two tablespoons of melted Becel (25 calories)
Chocolate chip cookies (200 calories for 4)	Miss Meringue Mini Cookies, Very Chocolate flavor, 13 cookies (80 calories)
Pepperoni pizza, 2 slices (1,000 calories)	Kraft's South Beach Diet Pizza, Deluxe (310 calories per package)
Strawberry shortcake dessert (450 calories)	10 strawberries (36 calories) topped with 4 tablespoons of fat-free whipped topping (30 calories) *Total: 66 calories*
Two slices of toast (140 calories) with 2 tablespoons of peanut butter (190 calories) *Total: 330 calories*	Two slices of lite bread, toasted (90 calories) topped with 1 tablespoon of reduced-fat peanut butter (94 calories) *Total: 184 calories*

WHEN YOU ARE CRAVING THIS . . .	TRY THIS INSTEAD
A slice of apple pie (356 calories)	One apple cut up and baked (80 calories), topped with 1 tablespoon of Splenda (0 calories) and 1 crumbled graham cracker (60 calories)
One large chocolate bar (300 calories)	Chocolate chip Kudos bar (124 calories)
A serving of tiramisu (410 calories)	Jell-O's Swiss Mocha Tiramisu (100 calories)
Two handfuls of crackers (270 calories for 18)	Two bread sticks (60 calories)
A large turkey sandwich made from six slices of turkey (173 calories), 2 tablespoons of mayonnaise (200 calories), and Italian bread (163 calories) *Total: 536 calories*	An open-faced turkey sandwich made from two slices of light Wasa slices (60 calories), two slices of turkey (58 calories), tomato slices (8 calories), and 2 tablespoons of light mayonnaise (72 calories) *Total: 198 calories*

Make It Happen Now: The Real Chick Plan for #41

Create your own low-calorie versions of your favorite foods and learn how to improvise as you go. Ask yourself what things you wish you could eat on a regular basis but that have calorie counts that are just too high. Are there certain components of the treat that are low calorie, such as strawberries? Is a major component of the food available in low-fat, low-calorie, or even calorie-free versions? Science has made exciting advances on the no-calorie sugar substitute front, with such choices as Splenda. You can actually bake with Splenda, and it really tastes just like sugar. Slices of bread that can have more than 100 calories each can be replaced with crunchy snackbread slices;

creamy, high-caloric ice cream can be replaced with low-fat frozen yogurt made with Splenda; and many recipes for baked goods have been reworked into low-calorie versions in low-calorie cookbooks. Do some research, get creative, and you will find all sorts of delicious replacements for your favorite foods.

Checklist

☑ Make a list of your top ten favorite high-calorie foods.

☑ Break down each treat into healthy components and components in need of substitution.

☑ Look for low-fat, low-calorie versions of those "bad" components. If you can't find any, consider new ways to create a dish that is close to your favorite, but without the calories.

☑ Surf the Internet for low-calorie recipes for your favorite dishes.

☑ Buy a copy of a low-calorie cookbook that appeals to you.

Secret Number 42: Focus on the Good Things You Do Get to Eat

The skinny chicks don't seem to feel deprived when it comes to food. Some of them even seemed surprised at my questions about how they manage to not eat tempting foods. They focus on the wonderful foods they do get to eat—including the "cheat" foods they work into their diets—and are not so focused on what they don't get to eat. One day not long ago I was out for a run and wished I could have my favorite corn muffin. I was thinking about how crunchy the top of it was, how much I love the texture of cornmeal in my mouth . . . then another thought hit me. I remembered that I could have a chocolate ice cream cone bar (my 210-calorie find) later that day. Then I thought about all the other delicious things I had already eaten that day and the other things I could still eat. This is what the skinny chicks do. They don't mess with their minds by focusing on the things they don't get to eat. They make sure they have lots of yummy choices and focus on those instead. If you can make this change in mental focus, staying on track with your healthy diet will be significantly easier.

Make It Happen Now: The Real Chick Plan for #42

This is one of those steps in which most of the work is really done in your head. It's a matter of mental focus. But don't underestimate it—it's a very powerful step. Think how powerful a thing focus can be. Have you ever ridden a horse? Driven a car? Do you remember being told that you should look in the direction you want to go because that horse or that car will *go* in the direction you're looking, whether you want to or not? Well, the same principle applies here. If you focus on the foods you can't have, you are already heading straight for them. By thinking about them, you are making them a part of your life and increasing the likelihood that you'll break down and binge. But by focusing instead on all the wonderful foods you do get to eat, and making sure that you have found some options that you really enjoy, you are instead steering toward success.

Checklist

☑ Think about what you had for breakfast. Wasn't it wonderful? If you don't like what you eat, the first step is to find healthy things that you do enjoy. Then throughout the day when you think about what you've eaten—or will be eating later—you can focus on how much you enjoyed every bite. Do the same for every meal and snack you eat.

☑ When you see or start to think about something you wish you could eat, think instead about all the yummy stuff you *do* get to eat each day, then go eat some!

☑ Keep a watchful eye out for healthy, low-cal snacks and treats and make a point of sharing these finds with friends—sort of like a recipe exchange!

Secret Number 43: Integrate a Few Meal Replacements into Your Diet

You'll notice that many of the skinny chicks use protein shakes and protein bars to supplement their diets. A thorough review of the literature on using meal replacements published in the *International Journal on Obesity* in 2003 revealed that the use of meal replacements can help people lose weight and keep it off. You can use them as the core of certain meals, adding a salad or piece of fruit to it, or you can use them as healthy, nutrient-dense snacks. Most of these bars and shakes have 150 to 250 calories per serving. They can be quite tasty and come in a wide variety of flavors. One of the biggest benefits of using meal replacements is that you know exactly how many calories you are getting. Additionally, they are usually nutrient rich, nutrient balanced, and quite filling. They are also convenient and can be eaten on the go. One of the drawbacks, however, is that when you eat them you tend not to slow down and focus on the food. That's why it's a good idea to use them just once a day or a few times a week. Shakes and bars help you to remember that eating is about fueling up your body.

Make It Happen Now: The Real Chick Plan for #43

This one is an easy one. It's time to go shopping! Check out the meal replacement aisle in your grocery store or head to your nearest health food store and take a look at the options. Read the labels and see what you are getting. Cookies and cream, chocolate chunk, carrot muffin . . . these are just some of the flavors you can choose from. However, avoid eating more than one meal a day using a replacement. Using more may be something you could do for the short term, but not the long term. You'll gulp your shake in a matter of minutes and then feel like you haven't eaten at all. Also, these products can be expensive. They are usually at least $2 each. There is usually some savings if you buy a whole box, but make sure you like the flavor first. And don't give up if the first few you try taste like chalk. Some of these replacements are really just like eating chocolate bars. Take a look at the labels to make sure they aren't 99 percent sugar. Preferably look for something with a substantial protein component, 15 percent or more, and at least a little healthy fat.

Checklist

☑ Research what kinds of meal replacements are available, including protein bars and ready-to-drink shakes.

☑ Take a few flavors home and try them out. Don't stop if you don't like the first few you try; keep looking for a flavor you like.

☑ Be careful not to fall into the mindset of these bars and shakes being "diet" products that you can go wild on. They are usually quite caloric. Remember, they are quite concentrated (they usually have 200 to 300 calories) and are actually meant to be either meal replacements (rather than snacks) or used to recover from serious two-hour or more workouts.

Secret Number 44: Keep a Food Diary

Denial is a funny thing. We are very good at keeping our head in the sand when we want to. But when the facts are laid out before us, in black and white, it is much harder to deny the truth. That's why keeping a food diary is a critical step for those wanting to stick to a healthy diet. Several of the skinny chicks in this book keep daily food diaries, especially when they see their weight slowly going up. When they want to crack down and "eat clean," they make sure to pick up a pen and keep careful notes about what they eat each day and exactly how much. That way, they can see what they are doing and know when it's time to stop eating for the day.

It can be hard to remember everything you've eaten, so keeping track as you go is important. Also, keeping a food diary is a great way to create a body of information to refer to when you want to look back on your progress. Perhaps you think you've been working quite hard at "being good," but it seems that your weight is inching up anyway. You can look back on your diaries of the last several weeks and see what's been going on. Maybe you've slipped back into a habit of having a muffin every morning at work. Referring to the diary will help you see exactly what got you where you are. Skinny Chick Sherry Boudreau says writing down everything she eats in a journal helps her stay on track. It can be motivational, too—you can look back on really successful periods of time in your journal and remind yourself of how you did it.

Make It Happen Now: The Real Chick Plan for #44

One of the best ways to keep a food diary is to use an online diet and exercise computer system. They cost as little as $20 and are terrific at calculating the calories in the foods you eat as well as the amount of protein and other energy sources you are getting. They also provide instant charts showing you where you are headed if you keep going the way you are going (exciting when you're being good!). Or, you can simply go the pen and paper route. Buy yourself a nice journal, one that you will enjoy using. (If you have taken up running or another activity, there are planners specifically for people who run, and it will have the added bonus of making you feel like a part of a greater fitness community.)

Write down everything, even if it's just a nibble here or there. Those tiny bites can really add up by the end of the day or week. So, don't lie to yourself. Write it all down. You don't have to look at it every day if you don't want to. If you feel like you aren't making the kind of progress you'd like to make, it can be a good idea to look at it every day. You can also refer to it throughout the day as you are making your food choices. As you are considering something that takes up a lot of calories, you could look back to see what food choices you made for the rest of the day the last time you enjoyed this particular indulgence. (It may be as easy as having a light salad for dinner!) This secret is all about empowering yourself with information.

Checklist

☑ Research Web-based food diaries and use one.

☑ Buy yourself a nice journal to use as a food diary or a journal created specifically for people who are working on their bodies. (These journals can make you feel like you are really on top of things and as though you are an athlete working toward an event—very inspiring.)

☑ Write down everything you eat, even if it's just for a short period of time. Don't forget to include the "free" stuff like veggies and caffeine-free beverages.

☑ Refer to your diary to see if you need to make any adjustments. You may realize you are doing some things you shouldn't be.

☑ Review your diary for ideas and inspiration—particularly look at stretches of time when you had success at losing or maintaining your weight.

☑ Write in your dairy notes about your week on a personal level. Look back and see if weight gain for the week can be attributed to a special circumstance, such as extra stress or anxiety or an overly scheduled week.

Secret Number 45: Set a Goal, Create a Plan

One of the best ways to inspire yourself and move into action is to set yourself a goal and create a plan of action to make it happen. The skinny chicks treat their bodies like projects and put a lot of time and thought into how they want them to look and how to make that a reality. Knowing where you are going is really half the battle. Maybe you have forty pounds to lose, or just ten. Or maybe you want to actually gain weight in the form of muscle. Perhaps what you want to do is get in good enough shape to run a half-marathon. Whatever your goals are, you can achieve them if you have a plan. But first you have to sit down and decide what it is you want. Once that's done, you can start implementing all of the secrets in this book into your life to make your goal a reality. It is important, however, to have realistic goals. If you set the bar too high too soon you may find yourself really disheartened when it begins to feel like you aren't making any progress or that your goal is too far away. Getting a health-care practitioner involved in the goal-setting process may be a good idea, too, especially if you've got more than twenty pounds you want to lose. Skinny Chick Sherry Boudreau says making a plan on paper and setting goals is critical to her staying on track. Setting both short-term and long-range goals is also a good idea. That way you can start meeting goals right way.

Make It Happen Now: The Real Chick Plan for #45

The first thing you want to do is think about what changes you would ultimately like to see in your body, health, and mental outlook. Think of "dream goals" or things you'd love to accomplish but you think are probably beyond your reach. Then think of at least one big goal that is attainable in the next six months or year, such as losing thirty pounds or working up to a running program of thirty minutes three times a week.

Then decide on some smaller, more immediate goals, like feeling less bloated or having more energy.

Write all of these goals down, either in your fitness diary or on a piece of paper placed somewhere you'll see it often. Under each goal write down what you need to do to make these things happen. If you want to be able to run three times a week for thirty minutes, write out a plan in which you start with running as many minutes as you can, followed by a walk break as long as you need, followed by another few minutes of running. This is a great way to extend your runs. You should write out a schedule for the weeks or months preceding your goal date, outlining what you need to do each week or even each day to make it happen. Once your plan is set, write it all out in your journal or on a chart and place it on your fridge. Check off your workouts and "clean" eating days as you go and write down your progress, such as pounds lost or duration of exercise. As you meet your immediate goals, the longer-range goals will seem that much more attainable. Then, once you've met those longer-range goals, you may just find those dream goals are not out of reach after all. I once wrote down that I'd love to run a marathon. I never, ever, thought it would happen. I've now run five a year.

Checklist

- ✓ Decide on dream goals, whether you think they are realistic or not.
- ✓ Decide on some attainable, long-range goals.
- ✓ Set immediate goals.
- ✓ Set out a plan, and create a schedule, for making these things happen, starting with the short-term goals.
- ✓ Start taking action, checking off each workout, "clean" eating day, new exercise conquered, etc. as you achieve it.
- ✓ Write down indicators of progress, such as pounds lost, improvements in how you feel, etc.
- ✓ Celebrate each goal as you achieve it.

Secret Number 46: Focus on Your Successes and How They Make You Feel

Once the skinny chicks achieve the body they want, they don't want to let it go. This is true of the big picture in terms of reaching their ultimate goals, but it is also true on a more immediate level with the smaller goals they achieve. A key element in their ability to do this, to not lose ground and go back to old habits, is to always keep their eye on the ball. What this means is they focus on their successes and how those successes make them feel. If eating a healthy, high-fiber breakfast makes these women feel energized, well nourished, and in control of their diet, they note those great feelings. If eating "clean" for the past week has meant they've dropped the two pounds that crept up on them, they celebrate that, think about how it feels to wear their favorite jeans, and pat themselves on the back for making it happen. If they slip up, they don't focus on that. They focus on what they are doing right. By focusing on your successes and how they make you feel, you will be more motivated to stay on track.

Make It Happen Now: The Real Chick Plan for #46

When you get up in the morning, look at yourself in the mirror. Run your hands over your abs, squeeze your buns, and really take stock of the state of your body. If you've been eating well and exercising, even for just a short time, the changes should be evident. Look for them, note them, celebrate them. And continue to do this throughout your day. You may notice as you are working out that your belly isn't jiggling quite so much anymore. Note how much easier it is to get up off of the floor. Check out your reflection in store windows and see how your posture is changing. Ask yourself, "Do I feel better now?" after your workouts. Note all of the changes and successes and remind yourself of them often. This is all, of course, in addition to jumping up and down every time you lose another pound or dress size. Create a mental space that is inspiring and all about how fit and healthy and happy you are. By focusing on your successes, no matter how small, you will be inspired to stay on the course of a healthy life.

Checklist

- ✓ Do a first-thing-in-the-morning body check. What's looking and feeling good?
- ✓ Think about the changes in your body as you exercise. Feeling stronger?
- ✓ Note the difference in how you feel getting up from chairs and the floor.
- ✓ Do you feel like you have more energy? Note this and celebrate it.

Secret Number 47: If Man Made It, Avoid It

I keep hearing the saying, "If man made it, don't eat it," and I think it's a really good rule to live by. Looking at the daily diets of many of the skinny chicks in this book, you'll see that many of the girls live by this rule. What it means is that it's healthier to stick to whole foods or foods that are as unprocessed as possible. For instance, it's better to eat a whole, fresh apple than to eat an apple that has been diced, peeled, sprinkled with sugar, and baked into a shell of refined, sugared dough. Another example of an even more refined, processed food would be a slice of white, fluffy bread. The wheat used to make the bread has been ground into its absolute finest form (and is no longer anything like its grainy, flaky, chunky original self) and has been mixed with sugar and salt and all sorts of chemicals before being baked into a loaf. The more refined a food is, the faster it is absorbed into your bloodstream and the faster you are hungry again, even if you don't really need more calories. Processed and prepared foods also tend to have a lot of sugar, salt, and fat, which means they pack a higher-calorie punch per ounce and are generally less healthy than foods that are more natural. For these reasons, it's a good idea to stay away from these foods as much as possible. You'll be able to eat a lot more food if you do!

Make It Happen Now: The Real Chick Plan for #47

The best way to make sure you are eating whole foods is to shop around the outer edges of your grocery store. However, keep in mind that whole foods don't have any preservatives in them, so they go bad much more quickly than processed foods. Choose whole foods, such as vegetables, fruits, fresh and whole-grain bread products, low-fat soy and milk products, eggs (ideally with omega-3 fatty acids), lean cuts of meat (chicken, fish, light cuts of pork and beef, and cold cuts that are low fat, low calorie, and low salt), brown rice, and lots of beans, such as red kidney beans and black beans. You'll know you are eating lots of whole foods when your composter (please compost!) is overflowing and you don't seem to be making much garbage. Those highly processed foods always come in lots of packaging. But whole foods make lots of organic waste—eggshells, apple cores, broccoli stalks, and so on. By eating this way you will be automatically making the lower-calorie, nutrient-rich, smarter food choices.

Checklist

☑ Take a look at the nutritional labels on the side of all of the processed, boxed foods in your pantry and fridge. Note the calorie content per serving.

☑ Compare the calorie content of processed foods to more natural, whole versions of the same foods.

- ☑ Replace some of your processed favorites with whole-food choices.
- ☑ Shop in the outer edges of your grocery store.
- ☑ Make regular stops to corner markets and health food stores for fresh, whole options.

Secret Number 48: Adopt a "Skinny Chicks" Mindset

If you read the profiles of the skinny chicks in this book, you'll probably come to a realization: these women simply think about food and exercise differently than the average person. They have what I call a "thin mindset." They don't see being overweight as an option. They don't see not exercising as an option. And they don't see eating badly or too much as an option, either. They have created worlds for themselves where exercising more days than not is sacrosanct. Junk food is not a part of their worlds, at least not much of it. They live daily with a mindset that supports a thin life. Without this, it can be very hard to get down to a size you are happy with.

If you are still thinking that it's acceptable to not work out at all for weeks on end, or that having half a big bag of chips after dinner every night is probably a reasonable "dessert" at the end of a hard day, you will find it more difficult to get into a "thin" mindset. It may not be your goal to be a size 2, but even the women who are size 10 in this book work out more days than not. Being fit and fabulous requires a fit and fabulous mindset. Remember: skinny is a state of mind. The way you look at your world and the way you live your life need to be in line with the kind of body you want. If you are living in an unhealthy mindset, you can't have a healthy body. Skinny Chick Diana Bernier says eating well and exercising is as natural to her now as anything else she does in her life. Skinny Chick Shelley Michelle cuts to the chase: "A lot of women are in total denial about how much they should be eating and they don't do the things needed to lose weight."

Make It Happen Now: The Real Chick Plan for #48

This secret, like many of the others in this book, requires a perspective shift. I'm not implying that you go to bed one night and wake up with a "thin mindset." But it may help to fake it a bit until you do. Start living a fit and fabulous life. Start exercising more days than not, start eating the number of calories each day that your body needs and no more. Start living that fit and fabulous life. Watch those changes come to your body and your mind. And as you wade your way deeper and deeper into the waters of this new world, keep in mind that remaining here will require this mental shift. Like anything else, it takes practice, but the longer you live this healthy life, the more you enjoy being healthier and happier, the more this "thin mindset" will come to you. Here's the trick, however: you've got to embrace it and really push away that old, unhealthy mindset that will at times try to rear its ugly head. When you've done things one way for so long, you will often drift back to those old ways. It can be terribly hard to venture off onto a new path. But it can be done. And making the mental shift is an important part of it. Too many people will make these lifestyle changes but inside they will think that at some point they will be able to go back to their old ways. And if your mind focuses on the old groove, sooner or later your body will follow it back.

Checklist

☑ Take note of your current mindset in terms of diet. Do you think you should be able to eat large meals and junk food every day? Even if your thinking is not that extreme, does your mindset about diet need to change? What ideas about diet do you need to change?

☑ Take note of your mindset on exercise. Do you think that you shouldn't have to work out most days of the week? Do you think it's possible to be fit and fabulous without working out regularly, for a lifetime? Do you think this sounds like torture? Create some new ideas about exercise.

☑ Write a list of beliefs you think you need to change to get the body you want. Then write a list of new beliefs that can support you in that transition. Read these lists often.

Secret Number 49: Create a Support Network

Going it alone can be hard. Sticking to a new plan of healthy eating and exercise is much easier when you've got someone doing it with you or a team of people supporting you. The skinny chicks know this. Most of them have been fit and fabulous for so long they no longer need that active support, but they know having it in the beginning can be critical. If it's just you, all alone, slipping back into those old habits can be easy. But if you've got the inspiration and support of others, you'll be much more likely to do it for the long haul. Skinny Chick Ann Currell credits the support of her teammates on her rowing team with helping her stick to a healthy lifestyle. "It is so much easier to get to all the workouts when you know everyone else is going to be there too," she says. "If I was always on my own and had to be totally self-motivated, I would find it much harder to stick to the program."

Make It Happen Now: The Real Chick Plan for #49

Find someone who wants to get healthy along with you. You can work out together, send encouraging e-mails to one another throughout the day, and generally support one another. Or, if that's not feasible, set up a team of people that you think can help you stay on track. Perhaps your partner is willing to sign up as the official "encouraging word" helper, who speaks up (with permission, of course) when he sees you going off course. Maybe you've got a fit and fabulous friend who inspires you. Can you e-mail her or call her when you need a bit of inspiration? Maybe your sister can be on call in case you feel like you are going to fall off the wagon and just need someone to talk to. The idea is to have a support group of people, who you have talked to ahead of time, who have signed on to help you make this happen in your life.

Designate a different "go-to" friend for each issue that you face. Maybe your college roommate loves to exercise, so make her your drill sergeant. And if your sister is a great listener, ask her to talk through the stressful times with you and help keep your anxiety level low. Your best friend may know a lot about food; ask her to help make suggestions for tasty, exotic ingredients. Technology has also made this easier, with online support systems such as Ediets (ediets.com), WeightWatchers (weightwatchers.com), and diets.com offering message boards, recipe swaps, and other support. These online supports can give you someone to talk to, inspiration, motivation, and some terrific new recipes.

Checklist

☑ Talk to your friends and family and see if anyone wants to get on a health kick with you.

☑ Look into fitness clubs, running clubs, dance classes, online recipe swaps, cyber exercise parties, online emotional support programs, etc., where other women may be looking for fitness partners.

☑ Think about the people in your life who may want to help keep you on track. Set up a team of five people. Ask them what they think they can do and "assign" them their official tasks.

☑ If there are any nonsupporting people in your life, try to stay clear of them or at least beware of their negative behavior.

Secret Number 50: Have a Plan for When Weight Goes Up

Chances are, despite your best intentions, you are going to gain a pound or two at some point. Maybe it's around the holidays, your birthday, a vacation, or the summer barbecuing season. Or, perhaps you haven't met your goal weight yet and you've just backslid a couple of pounds. All of this is OK, *if* you have a game plan for how to turn it around again. Even the skinny chicks admit to gaining a few pounds here and there. But what all of these gals have in common is that they have a plan of action for when that happens. If you plan ahead and do the same, you can indulge when you want to, relaxed in the knowledge that you can get it all back under control in just a couple of weeks.

Make It Happen Now: The Real Chick Plan for #50

If you want to be bad at some times, you've got to be particularly good at others. And right after a "bingefest" is a good time to be especially good. This means ramping up your cardio, perhaps even working out more than once a day. You can increase your duration, your intensity, and your frequency during the week. Throwing in an additional weight-training workout may be helpful too. And eating "clean" is essential. You may even want to decrease your calories a bit. But don't skip meals or lower your intake of the nutrients you need. Drink lots of water and steer clear of any risky outings.

Once you develop a plan for taking back control of your body after your weight goes up, write it down in your fitness journal, perhaps on a special page near the front, and refer to it when needed. Next, put your plan into action and chart your success. Skinny Chick Kristia Knowles says her plan of action usually involves a journal. "I write down what I eat when I feel I have to make myself more accountable," she says. Skinny Chick Cathy Stanbrook says going over her 125- to 130-pound range is a call for "immediate action." When that happens she knows what her game plan is: no more eating late at night, no more snacking, less wine, and she can't miss any visits to the gym until she's back on track. Skinny Chick Katie Katke says, "If you stop (eating well and exercising), start again and remember how good you feel when you exercise and eat well."

Checklist

☑ Write down your game plan for losing the weight again. Your plan should include increased cardio and weights workouts and lowered calorie intake.

☑ Make a list of other things you can do to help with weight loss, including steering clear of risky outings, drinking lots of water, and taking the stairs at work.

☑ Put your weight-loss game plan in a place where you can find it should you need it, such as in the front of your fitness journal.

☑ Don't punish yourself for going off track. It's bound to happen and it's okay, as long as you know when to stop.

PART 3

Putting the Plan into Action

The Lowdown on Food

I SOMETIMES WISH THAT HUMAN beings could simply walk into fuel stations once every few days to fill up with the nutrients they need, just the way we do with our cars. In this scenario, the "food" would be pumped right into our blood-streams, without any taste, satisfaction, or enjoyment at all. It wouldn't be fun to go to these fuel stations either; it would be just another chore in our day. Separating food from all of its attached enjoyments would be useful because it would strip the process of eating down to its basic function: fueling the body.

For most of us, food is often not about fueling up. It's about the ritual of sitting down to enjoy ourselves with family and friends. It's about making ourselves

> **Genetically I'm not a skinny girl, so if I don't consciously mind it, yeah, I get unskinny.**
>
> —Model Danielle Gamba on keeping the body she loves

feel better when something goes wrong. It's about rewarding ourselves when something goes right. It's about tasting something good. It's about a lot of things, but, least of all, it's about giving our bodies energy. And it's because we use food for so many things other than fueling our bodies that we can find it so hard to stay on track and eat the things we should in appropriate quantities.

While it would be extremely difficult for most people to ever really stop using food for these other functions, a good, solid understanding of how food works in our bodies can help us make the best choices possible along the way, just like the skinny chicks do.

Calories Demystified

When it comes down to it, the size of your body is determined by two factors: how much you move and what you eat. It's really that simple. Calories in, calories out. Energy in, energy out. More specifically, one pound of fat is equivalent to 3,500 calories of food. Each time your body finds itself with 3,500 calories worth of unused food, it creates a pound of fat. So, if you were to suddenly start eating a 500-calorie muffin every day without increasing the amount you exercise to offset it, you would gain a pound a week. By the end of the year, you would have gained 52 pounds of fat. (Again, this is assuming your other intake and amount of exercise remain the same.) Staggering, isn't it?

On the other hand, if you suddenly stop eating a 500-calorie muffin each day, by the end of the year you will have lost 52 pounds, if you've got it to lose. (Again, this is assuming your calorie intake and exercise remain unchanged.) Or, you could keep eating that muffin each day and start running for fifty minutes every day. Or stop eating the muffin (saving 500 calories a day) *and* start running fifty minutes (burning 500 calories on top of that) every day and you'll have lost 104 pounds by the end of the year, if you've got it to lose. Most people, however, choose a mix of trimming back some calories and increasing exercise moderately to achieve fat loss. This is the best method. I am just using these extreme examples to emphasize the basic point here: it really does come down to simple math. Energy in, energy out.

How Many Calories Do *You* Need?

I have found that many medical resources indicate that, at my activity level, I should be consuming far more than I actually do. Most of the skinny chicks in this book have also found this to be true. I was shocked by how few calories, usually fewer than 1,500, I need to stay at a size 6. I do two hours of cardio each day and, according to the experts, I should be able to eat well over 2,000 calories. That intake puts me well over a size 10, which is also healthy, but I much prefer my butt the way it is now. That said, I have all the energy I need. That's proven by my ability to chase after my three-year-old son while working from home.

So, as I researched the skinny chicks, I found that many of them keep their calorie intakes below the average 1,600 recommended for the typical woman by the Centers for Disease Control and Prevention (CDC) for weight maintenance. The USDA recommends between 1,800 and 2,400 calories for women aged nineteen to fifty, depending on whether they are sedentary or active, to maintain their weight. (Most women find they need to go below this to lose weight.) Now, in my case, I believe a big part of why I need to keep my calorie intake relatively low is that I come from a family that is very prone to fat. Scientists have isolated the so-called fat gene, and I believe I have it. Many other people have it, too.

While other factors such as health issues could have played a role in slowing the metabolisms of some of the women in this book, ultimately I think the difference in metabolic rate and genetic makeup are the major reasons why they need to eat the amount they do and exercise to the extent they do to stay the size they are. This is certainly true in my case. I have never dieted. Diets like the Zone have most women, like Jennifer Aniston, eating eleven or twelve "blocks" each day, which equates to 1,100 or 1,200 calories. And she runs the better part of an hour a day several days a week. Some studies have actually shown that people experience improved health by staying on the low end of calorie intake. (Animal studies have actually shown being 20 percent underweight is associated with longevity, although that is not recommended for humans.) However, this can be hard to do over a lifetime.

The CDC recommends 1,600 calories daily for the average woman, so this is a good place to start. I suggest you begin eating at this level and see where that gets you. You may want to trim back or you may want to add more, depending on what your goals are. But do not go below 1,200 calories, the minimum required for your body to get the nutrients it needs. The bottom line is that your own body will tell you what it needs. Every body is different. Have no doubt that keeping your calorie intake at the level you want can be a challenge. Your best chance of achieving your goal will be by making the best food choices possible, which we will discuss throughout the rest of this chapter.

What You Need to Know About Protein

As I am writing this, the high-protein, low-carb bandwagon is finally slowing down. The Atkins company just filed for bankruptcy protection and is currently restructuring. According to Productscan Online, a service that tracks consumer trends, many of the four thousand low-carb products that flooded the market following the low-carb boom are now collecting dust on store shelves. The NPD Group research firm noted a peak in interest in these products at the start of 2004, followed by a steady decline. However, given the amount of weight people have lost on these diets, it's unlikely that bagels will be embraced again the way they were in the low-fat craze of the 1980s. And that's a good thing, because they are incredibly high in calories!

One crucial lesson people learned from the low-carb craze was the importance of getting enough protein. Your body needs three nutrients to function—carbohydrates, protein, and fat. According to the USDA, between 10 and 35 percent of your daily food intake should come from protein in the form of meat, cheese, dairy, and other protein sources, like soy. Protein builds muscle. But, in terms of sticking to a healthy diet, remember that protein helps you to feel full longer because it takes much longer for your body to digest it. This is a big part of why people on the Atkins diet were losing weight. They felt full sooner and longer because they were eating mostly protein and therefore ate fewer calories at the end of the day. According to nutritionist Rosie Swartz, author of *The Enlightened Eater's Whole Foods Guide*, as soon as companies found a way to make low-carb bread, pasta, and muffins, people started gaining back the weight because they started eating more food again. So always remember that you need to get enough protein, and you should have some with every meal or snack so that you feel satiated sooner and for longer.

What You Need to Know About Carbohydrates

Carbs are really the fuel of your body. You need them, period. First of all, it's important to know that apples, lettuce, half of the ingredients in cheese, half of the ingredients in milk, kidney beans, pasta, and most of peanut butter are carbohydrates. Every food that is not a pure protein or a pure fat is a carbohydrate. They are everywhere, and that's a good thing. But not all carbs are created equal. As we've discussed in previous chapters, when you are trying to keep your calorie count down, it's best to choose the high-bulk, lower-calorie carbohydrates. Vegetables are the best example.

You could have five crackers or 2 cups of broccoli for 60 calories—but the crackers will rev your appetite, while the broccoli will stuff your belly. Those crackers will be absorbed into your bloodstream quickly, giving you a quick blast of sugar, then a quick drop again as the sugar suddenly leaves your bloodstream. This will leave you with low blood sugar, which will make you crave more carbohydrates because your body will want another boost of sugar. But broccoli, because it is so fibrous and bulky, will take much longer to break down in your stomach, giving you a much more steady injection of blood sugar, keeping you full longer and avoiding that sudden blood sugar drop.

The speed at which foods are absorbed into your blood is the essence of the Glycemic Index (GI), upon which most of the low-carb diets (the Zone, Atkins, the Mediterranean Diet) are based. These diets use this index to recommend certain foods over others for maximum satiation and weight loss. The problem with the GI is that it doesn't take into account the fact that carrots, for example, may get absorbed into your body faster than many other foods, but they are low in calories, fibrous, full of vitamins, and should therefore not be avoided just because they have a high GI value. Also, if eaten with protein and healthy fat, the rate at which those carrots are absorbed slows down, thereby making you feel full longer, which is the goal of assigning foods these numbers on the index.

It's important to stay away from highly processed foods, such as white fluffy bread and crackers, which the GI helps you to do, but there's something very wrong with putting the sweet potato on the hit list! Some people believe it is actually the perfect food. Mind you, even among the healthier carbohydrates, there are some that get absorbed faster than others. This is where a relatively new method of assessing carbohydrate absorption comes in, called the Glycemic Load (GL). The old GI value tells you only how rapidly a particular carbohydrate turns into sugar, but it doesn't tell you how much of that carbo-hydrate is in a serving of a particular food. You need to know both things to understand a food's effect on blood sugar.

There are plenty of books and Internet sites on GI and GL if you are interested in finding out more about them in relation to the foods you enjoy. But generally speaking, you are doing well if you stick to whole grains and whole foods (unprocessed foods such as apples and eggs). Remember, according to the USDA, a total of 45 to 65 percent of your diet should come from carbohydrates.

What You Need to Know About Fat

The important things to know about fat are (1) it's an essential nutrient, (2) there are good fats and bad fats, and (3) they are all high in calories. The USDA's 2005 Food Pyramid recom-mends that 10 to 35 percent of your diet come from fats, prefer-ably healthy fats. Saturated fats are bad. Saturated fats solidify at room temperature, like the beef fat that you see in your roast-ing pan when it cools. You want to stay away from these fats as much as possible because they solidify inside your arteries much the same way, putting you at risk of heart attacks if you eat too much of them.

The better fats are the monounsaturated fats, such as olive oil, canola oil, and polyunsaturated fats, such as fats found in fish and soybean oil. These fats help your body to function in a number of ways, including helping to improve heart health. They also take longer for your body to break down in the stomach and help your body to feel full longer. Additionally, they tend to taste really good. But they are high in calories—

even the good fats. So the calorie content should be considered. Eating too many fatty foods is going to make it pretty hard to keep you calorie intake low. The good thing, however, is that fats can't hide. If something is high in fat, the calorie content on the box will show it. So it's easy to keep fat under control if you pay attention to calories and read food labels carefully.

Spreads like margarine can be a problem. To make these products solid, so they resemble butter, the companies put them through a process called *hydrogenation*. This process takes a healthy fat and actually makes it worse for your body than the saturated fat in butter. As a result, you'd be better off eating butter, in terms of heart health, than eating most margarines. Therefore, it's a good idea to choose nonhydrogenated margarines, such as Becel.

Food Pyramid Recap

As we've learned about the secrets of skinny chicks, we've discussed the USDA's Food Pyramid dietary recommendations in some detail. But now that we've taken a closer look at the three main nutrients our bodies need—protein, fat, and carbohydrates—and the total number of calories our bodies really need, it's important to put that information into context by reexamining the way those calories and nutrients should be spread out across your day in real food terms.

You know that you need approximately 1,600 calories each day and you know you need those three nutrients in balance, but what would a day eating that way really be like? Well, following are some of the USDA's 2005 Dietary Guidelines. Use these recommendations as a guide for how to eat, but remember that ultimately the size of your body comes down to the number of calories you consume versus the number you burn. You can make lower-calorie choices or higher-calorie choices, all while sticking to these recommendations. An example of this would be to choose low-fat or no-fat milk instead of full-fat milk or choosing fish as your protein source instead of peanut butter. Refer back to the dietary guidelines found in Chapter 5 for women over the age of nineteen.

Check It Out

This chart will help you on your way to tracking the calorie content in the foods you eat. Listed here are some of the basic staples many of us eat, so this should get you started. Use online systems or a calorie book to start to build your own chart with the calorie contents of the foods you eat most often. This will give you an easy, quick-reference guide to help keep you on track.

Food	Calories
Apple	80
Slice of bread	About 100
One serving of cereal with skim milk	150 to 400
1 egg	80
1 ounce of chicken breast	55
1 ounce of cheddar cheese	100
1 cup of pasta (cooked)	196
1 cup of rice (cooked)	203
1 cup of 1 percent milk	102
Bagel (large)	245
Mayonnaise, 1 tablespoon	99
Pizza, 15″ with meat and veggies	2,900
Lasagna with meat (⅙ of 8″ square)	328
Butter, 1 tablespoon	102

Reality Check

Now this should be more than a little enlightening for most people. The following chart outlines the truth about just how much exercise you would have to do to burn off a variety of our favorite "bad" foods. Take a good hard look at this chart and then consider whether it's really worth it. Maybe it is, and maybe you're willing to work it off. In that case, enjoy! On the other hand, you may find those goodies go straight to your behind. Remember, this is all about being informed and making educated decisions. Don't put your head in the sand about what you are eating.

Food	Activity Needed to Burn It
Half of a large meat and cheese pizza	2½ hours of running
Two chocolate doughnuts	1 hour, 10 minutes of stationary cycling
Snickers bar	25 minutes of swimming
Movie theater–buttered popcorn, cooked in oil, 10 cups	3 hours, 45 minutes moderate walking
Pizzaburger	45 minutes on elliptical machine
Chocolate cake with frosting, 1 slice	30 minutes of running
Potato chips, 2 cups	1 hour of stationary cycling
French fries, medium serving	40 minutes of swimming

With all of the fad diets captivating popular attention in recent years, it has been easy to lose touch with the basic science of weight gain and loss when it comes to the consumption of food. This chapter has been about clarifying exactly what goes on inside the body to make it gain or lose weight. It's important that you familiarize yourself with the basics on calories, protein, fat, and carbohydrates. You also need to learn how many calories your body needs.

But as we learned in this chapter, this is not all that complicated. By learning some basic principles of how to fuel your body and keep it feeling full, you will be armed with all the information you need to navigate your way through the murky and often rough waters of eating in this world. Now, let's take a look at the other half of the equation: burning those calories once we've consumed them.

The Best Ways to Burn the Fat

CARDIO. CARDIO. CARDIO. NO fitness regimen is complete without a good strong core of cardiovascular activity. That's the kind of exercise that gets your heart pumping and your limbs moving continuously in a repetitive, rhythmic way, and begins to make you out of breath. Weight lifting is not cardio. Most forms of yoga are not cardio. Pilates is not considered cardio. Running, cycling, swimming, elliptical trainer workouts, step classes, aerobics classes, tennis, soccer, and walking are all forms of cardiovascular exercise. The reason why cardiovascular exercise is so important to skinny chicks is that it burns far, far more calories than any other kind of exercise. Even at a vigorous effort, weight lifting only

I was skinny in high school and could eat anything I wanted. After age seventeen, the pounds started creeping on. I eventually weighed twenty-five pounds more than I do now. I hated myself and did the yo-yo diet thing for years. I finally lost the weight and kept it off once I had been exercising for a solid year. I joined a gym and finally stuck with exercise.

—Skinny Chick Diana Bernier

burns about 360 calories an hour. But one hour of running, even at just a moderate pace, burns almost twice that amount—600 calories per hour. Strength training and stretching exercises are also critical forms of exercise, which we'll talk about in the next chapter. But it's really cardio that you want to make your best friend. It's the best way to kick-start fat burning.

How Often, How Long, How Hard?

The U.S. Surgeon General recommends people engage in at least moderate physical activity on most days of the week for at least thirty minutes. However, up to ninety minutes of exercise a day may be needed for weight loss. Most of the skinny chicks in this book do at least one hour of exercise, mainly cardiovascular exercise, on most days of the week, if not every day. Engaging in cardiovascular exercise for an hour, three to four times a week is probably a good way to start if you want your exercise regimen to have a strong impact on your physical conditioning. But, again, it's up to you to decide what is right for you. Working out three times a week is the minimum for maintaining good cardiovascular health. Each workout should be at least twenty minutes long. For cardiovascular activity to truly have an impact on your cardiovascular system, that's the length of time you need to spend. Ideally you'll be spending at least thirty minutes or longer on each cardio workout.

As for intensity, there are two schools of thought on this. One side says to keep your intensity relatively low to optimize fat-burning processes by staying in a range known as the "aerobic zone." Others say the harder you work out, the more calories you burn, and therefore the more fat you will ultimately burn. Staying in the aerobic zone basically means keeping the activity below an intense level, but still challenging. (Your aerobic zone is the workout level at which your heart is beating at a rate that is between 50 percent to 85 percent of its maximum, or Maximum Heart Rate, MHR.) The easiest way to determine if you are staying within the lower, fat-burning end of the aerobic zone is to do something called the *talk test*. Simply make sure you can talk throughout your workout. Now, if you want to make sure you are working out hard enough, or simply want a more complicated approach than the talk test, you can do a simple calculation. To find the range of your aerobic zone, calculate you MHR by taking 226 and subtracting your age. Then multiply this number by 50 percent to 60 percent. That will tell you the number of times per minute your heart should beat if you want to stay at the lower end of the aerobic zone. Use 70 and 80 percent calculations to find the upper end of your aerobic zone, should you want to move up to that for more intensity. Don't go beyond 85 percent of your MHR, however, unless you are training for speed and don't mind fizzling out after just a few minutes of effort.

It's up to you to decide if you want to just keep to the low end of the aerobic zone for the fat-burning effect or to move up your intensity to burn more calories. Both are very effective. Beginners would probably prefer to take it easy in the beginning. Also, with aerobic exercise, remember to warm up for at least five minutes before you start and cool down afterward for the same amount of time.

Top Five Forms of Cardio Chosen by Skinny Chicks

Skinny chicks know which forms of cardiovascular exercise pay off the fastest. They also know which cardio workout gives them the biggest effect in the least amount of time. And, finally, they know which cardio workout is fun! So, the following will give you all you need to know about the five most popular forms of cardio done by the skinny chicks. This is critical information. Too many women spend too much time doing exercises that just aren't burning the fat very quickly at all. Some take a mat class, such as Pilates or yoga, and spend an hour three times a week in these classes but wonder why it's taking so long to lose weight. These exercises are really not that high on the fat-burning scale. That's not the case with the five cardio options outlined here. These exercises will help you get lean and strong in short order. Just remember, you've got to do these cardio sessions at least three times a week for a minimum of thirty minutes at a time.

Running

Running is the godfather of all cardio. If you look through the profiles of the women in this book, you'll see that the vast majority have made running a part of their life. Burning 600 calories per hour (that's 100 calories every ten minutes!) by running packs a calorie-kicking punch in comparison to most other forms of cardiovascular activity. Some forms of intense dance are in the same league, but few workouts are as convenient, easy, cheap, and potentially enjoyable as running.

Now, I know that a lot of people are afraid of running. I hear you. I remember when the twelve-minute fitness test in high school gym class was the bane of my existence. But, trust me, by starting off with just a few minutes of running at a time, mixed in with walk breaks of a few minutes, you can slowly work your way up to being a runner. I have seen so many women at the beginning of my beginner running clinics tell me that they just didn't think they could do it. And I can't tell you how many times I've seen those same women cross the finish line of our celebratory 5K races just ten weeks later with tears in their eyes in disbelief as they finish and have, in fact, done it. For busy women running is ideal. You just lace up your shoes and your workout starts the second your foot hits the sidewalk. You can even bring your kids with you in a stroller. (Secondhand strollers are often readily available, too.)

Running Tips

* Buy a good pair of shoes with the help of a sport shoe professional.
* Dress for the weather in layers of moisture-wicking fabric.
* Drink a cup of water two hours before running, a cup an hour before running, and drink regularly along the way. Drink more water when you get back.
* Focus on keeping control of your breath. It's not about physical power in distance running; it's about developing your cardiovascular system.
* Don't try to go too far, too fast, too soon. This is the route of rookies who burn out because they hate it so much. Take it slow and easy.
* Relax into your runs and let your mind wander. Enjoy.

For more information on how to get started running, refer to my book *Run for It: A Woman's Guide to Running for Emotional and Physical Health* (Burford Books, 2002).

Elliptical Trainer

These machines are terrific. They give you the same calorie-burning workout as running (about 600 calories an hour), only without the potentially damaging results of impact with the ground. You can find elliptical machines in virtually all gyms and can even purchase cheap, yet effective, versions for home use. The elliptical trainers usually allow you to monitor calorie burning, heart rate, time elapsed, and intensity as you go.

Most machines have bars that get your arms in on the action too, so you are moving in a way that's a cross between running and cross-country skiing. You can also pedal in reverse. Different parts of the body are targeted, depending on whether you go forward or reverse; choose a particular incline; or use the bars for developing biceps, triceps, back, and chest. Most machines give you a variety of programs you can follow, allowing warm-up and cooldown periods. These machines can give you a terrific workout, but you do have to be careful on them to avoid injury from losing your balance or falling. If you are using a machine at home, you may want to aim a fan at yourself to avoid overheating.

Elliptical Training Tips

* Dress in light clothing to avoid overheating.
* Drink a cup of water two hours before the workout, another cup an hour before the workout, and drink regularly during the workout. Drink more water after the workout.
* Wear supportive sports shoes, but don't fret about which kind.
* Stand tall with shoulders back, pull in your abdominals and buttocks, and try to remain symmetrical throughout exercise (i.e., don't lean to one side).
* Breathe in through your nose and out through your mouth.
* For a good cardiovascular workout, choose exercise programs that are challenging but allow you to carry on a conversation the entire time. (This optimizes fat burning.)
* Try working out while watching TV. (While some studies suggest that watching TV may slow you down a little, my theory is that it will make you much more likely to show up for your *next* workout!)

Stationary/Street Cycling

Stationary cycling is terrific. You can sit back and read a book or watch TV and get a terrific workout while you are at it. Cycling can burn 360 calories or more each hour. I hop on my stationary bike each night after I tuck my son into bed, and I click on my favorite TV shows. It's a great way to indulge in some guilty TV pleasures without feeling like a lump on the couch. Although cycling is not a weight-bearing exercise (weight-bearing activities involve feet hitting the ground and are beneficial for women because they build bone density), cycling can actually be a good choice for people who have injuries from other activities or want to avoid developing impact-related injuries, such as shin splints or knee and hip problems. Spinning classes, intense group-stationary cycling, is very hot right now and packs a huge calorie-burning punch. Another great benefit of these machines is that you can get inexpensive versions for home and watch your children while working out.

Street cycling is a great workout also, but for some it is less convenient. If it's the real McCoy you prefer, though, you can bring your kids with you in one of those terrific cycling trailers. My son has a blast in his. Or, riding to and from work is a terrific option for some people.

Cycling Tips

* Adjust the pedals so that your knees are only slightly bent at the bottom of the rotation.
* Try to find a comfortable seat or wear padded bicycle shorts to improve comfort.
* Drink a cup of water two hours before the workout, another cup an hour before the workout, and drink regularly during your ride. Drink more water after the workout.
* Wear lightweight clothing and, if you are indoors, aim a fan at yourself.
* For a good cardiovascular workout, choose exercise programs that are challenging but allow you to carry on a conversation the entire time. (This optimizes fat burning.)
* Keep arms and wrists in line with shoulders, spine in a neutral position, chest open, neck in line with spine, and shoulders blades down and back.
* Adjust the handlebars so that you are sitting slightly forward in a relaxed position.
* Consider a recumbent bike. (On these, you sit back and pedal in front of yourself.)

Walking/Hiking

While not one of the top calorie-burning options, walking can be a very safe, effective, and convenient form of exercise. Burning up to 400 calories an hour, or more if you are hiking on rocky and uphill terrain, walking is a great workout. It's also a terrific way to get things done while exercising. However, I recommend that you drive your route ahead of time so that you know in advance how long your walk will be.

Walking to work, walking on your lunch break, or even walking after dinner with your family or friends are great ways to squeeze in a little exercise. You can burn more calories by adding weights to your hands and feet and/or picking uphill or more challenging routes. Be sure to stick to safe, populated areas, however. You can also multitask and make your workout harder by taking your kids in single or double strollers. Bike trailers, which have the children sitting side-by-side, can convert easily to strollers and even kids as old as six or seven probably won't mind sitting in these cool "tents on wheels," as I've billed them to my friend's five-year-old. You can also wear babies in carriers on your front or back, which makes the workout much more challenging.

Walking/Hiking Tips

* Drink lots of water before, during, and after your walks.
* Wear lightweight clothing in layers because you will heat up when you get moving and may want to strip down.
* Keep your head high and tucked back, shoulder blades back and down, arms at sides, chest open, and abdominal muscles and buttocks in. With each step, plant your feet hip-distance apart. (Don't allow your legs to cross over an imaginary center line in front of you.)
* Breathe deeply through your nose and out through your mouth.
* Swing your arms.

* Stay aware of your surroundings.
* Wear reflective clothing.

Dance Classes

Skinny chicks have a passion for dance classes. With funky music, fun routines, and the possibility of burning 500 to 650 calories an hour, it's no wonder. There are lots of different styles of dance classes to choose from, with the more up-tempo varieties obviously burning the highest number of calories. Classes like hip-hop dance, striptease, and even 1980s-style (learning *Flashdance* and *Dirty Dancing* routines) are very popular choices these days. More traditional choices, like jazz, tap, and folk dancing are also available in many community centers, gyms, and dance studios. You don't ever have to perform in front of anyone; these classes can just be about getting an awesome workout and burning lots of fat along the way.

Some of these moves also build lots of muscle, which is surprisingly not always the case with such cardiovascular exercises as running. But in dance, moves like squatting, lunging, and reaching challenge the body in a way that's more like strength training. Also, for those who are too shy to show up to a class with a wall of mirrors in workout wear, there are hundreds of fantastic videos you can purchase so you can practice your moves in the comfort of your own home.

Dancing Tips

* Drink a cup of water two hours before the workout, another cup an hour before the workout, and drink regularly during the workout. Drink more water after the workout.
* Dress in lightweight, moisture-wicking clothing that allows free range of motion.
* Wear the footwear appropriate to the kind of dance, i.e., tap shoes for tap class, jazz shoes for jazz.

* To avoid injuries, closely follow all instructions provided by the dance coach on proper form and body alignment.
* Keep your shoulders back and your belly button pulled into your spine, and remember to breathe.
* Listen to your body and stop if anything hurts, even just a little bit. Assess the injury and take appropriate steps.

Workouts by the Numbers

The following chart shows you just how many calories are burned by various forms of cardiovascular exercise. Use this to help you decide what forms of cardio are right for you and add to this list as you research other forms of exercise you enjoy. You can also use this guide when you are trying to decide what kind of workout to do each day.

Activity	Calories Burned
Baseball	151 per hour
Weight training	181 per hour at light effort, 362 per hour at vigorous effort
Walking	200 per hour at moderate pace, 300 per hour at brisk pace
Yoga	230 per hour breaking a sweat
Pilates	260 per hour for general mat class
Dancing	275 calories and up, depending on style and effort
Aerobics class	300 per hour at low impact, 422 per hour at high impact
Tennis	422 per hour for general effort
Soccer	422 per hour for noncompetitive, 603 per hour for competitive
Cycling	422 per hour at moderate effort, 634 per hour at vigorous effort
Elliptical	483 per hour at moderate effort, 543 per hour at brisk effort

| Running | 483 per hour at 12-minute miles, 600 per hour at 10-minute miles |
| Swimming | 483 per hour at moderate pace, 664 per hour at vigorous effort |

Learning how to get your cardiovascular system clicked into high gear is an absolutely critical element in losing weight and maintaining a fit and fabulous body. If weight is an issue for you, you simply can't get around this. Getting your heart rate up for as long as you can several times each week is the fastest way to make sure you don't end up with unused calories at the end of each day and week. If those calories are left unburned, they turn to fat. Plain and simple. Also, it's critical to your overall physical and emotional health and well-being. So, pick your cardio workout, and get moving!

Now, keeping your body's fat content within healthy levels is critical, but building muscle is also fundamental to your health. It helps you have a nice long, lean form, but also speeds up your metabolism and makes you stronger overall. So, let's learn more about how to build a strong body.

9

Getting Long and Strong

CARDIO MAY BE KING when it comes to burning calories, but stretching and strength training provide some pretty fabulous benefits as well, including the creation of long, strong, visible muscles. While a few of the women profiled in this book are fitness models and work very hard to bulk up their bodies as much as possible, big muscles are not what most women want. Many women would, however, like to have nicely sculpted arms; some definition in their legs; and a soft, feminine set of six-pack abs. Most of the women in this book have at least these.

A well-toned body is the best feeling in the world.

—Skinny Chick
Amanda Williams

Strength training alone cannot give you a sculpted body. Cardiovascular activity is required to shed layers of fat so that you can actually see the muscle you've built beneath. Otherwise you'll just seem bigger all around—stronger, yes, but not really defined. So, once you've got your cardio plans in place, it's time to add some stretching and strength training to sculpt long, lean muscles.

Some women avoid strength training because they believe it will give them big, hulking muscles. But this simply is not true. For starters, women just don't have the hormones to build the muscles men have. Also, muscle takes up less space than fat. So, five pounds of muscle looks about half the size of five pounds of fat. For those who take up weight training, keep this in mind when you get on the scales. Using a tape measure or paying attention to how your clothing fits will actually be a better way to track your progress in this arena.

So, there's no need to worry about bulk. Building muscles helps to boost your metabolic rate (the rate at which you burn calories), because muscle takes more energy to maintain than fat. Strength training is also a great complement to cardiovascular exercise because it can prevent injury by correcting muscle imbalances that may lead to overuse injuries.

On the other hand, stretching exercises help to ensure you have a large range of motion (so you're not all tight and unable to move freely) and that your muscles are long and not short and pumped up. It's the long, strong look most of us are looking for. Also, stretching exercise increases blood flow to the muscles, which may help to prevent injuries. So, there's no good reason not to stretch and strengthen and lots of great reasons to get started. This chapter will introduce you to strength-training techniques, including weight and resistance training and circuit training, and stretching and strengthening exercises such as Pilates and yoga. It's a good idea to pick one practice from each of the two categories to make sure your cardio-stretch-strengthen exercise combo is rounded out.

Strengthening Practices

Let's take a closer look at the strength-training techniques, weight and resistance training, and circuit training. Pick one of these two practices to work into your regime at least two times a week.

Weight and Resistance Training

Weight and resistance training involves putting stress on your muscle (in the form of a weight or a system of tension) while it goes through its range of motion. This stress causes microscopic tears in the muscle, which get filled in later when you eat protein, ultimately making your muscle larger. It is important to take the muscle through the full range of motion while doing strength training, to make long muscles. (If, for instance, you do mini bicep curls but don't bring your fist all the way up to your shoulder level, then you will be defeating your purpose and building short, bulky muscles.) This can be done with free weights (handheld weights), with weight machines (targeting most major muscles with a system of stacked weight bars and pulleys), or on resistance machines like the Bowflex system or home resistance products like the Thera-Band rubber strips that cost next to nothing. There are lots of options for you to consider. I use an exercise band and a set of two 15-pound hand weights to do my workouts.

You want your weight workouts to target as many of the major muscle groups as possible. If venturing off to the gym isn't something that's compatible with your lifestyle, you can get close to the same effect using home equipment. You can hit every major muscle group with just a simple set of hand weights and a rubber exercise band. Start with 2- or 5-pound hand weights. (But you do want to be challenged, so make sure that you are fatigued by twelve repetitions. If you are not, then you need more weight).

Obviously, these weights will allow you to work on all the major muscles in your arms, but they can also workout your legs. Squats, lunges, and going up on your toes with the weights in your hands can target all the major muscles. The rubber exercise band can hit the muscles of the inner and outer thighs. With each exercise you do, be sure to do two sets of eight to twelve repetitions. You want to be fatigued by the end of each exercise to ensure that you are pushing your muscles into new territory. Also, you should start by working on your largest muscles first and then move on to the smaller ones. Don't forget to warm up and cool down. Suddenly working out cold muscles can lead to injury, and not stretching and slowly easing out of exercise afterward can lead to unnecessary muscle soreness later.

Five Essential Home Gym Skinny Chicks Weight Moves. The following require 2-, 5-, 8-, or 15-pound free weights. For best results isolate the body part that you are working on, keeping the rest of your body as still as possible. You don't want to rely on momentum to get the weight lifted, just the muscle.

① Bicep Curl

1. Sit tall in a chair with your abs pulled in and shoulders down and back. Hold the free weight in your right hand and allow your arm to hang relaxed at your side.
2. On the exhale, slowly bend your elbow upward, bringing the weight up toward your shoulder. To bring your forearm into the action, begin with your palm facing your leg; turn your palm toward your face as you bring your hand up.
3. Return to starting position slowly. Repeat 8–12 times for two sets on each arm.

② Triceps Extension

1. Sit tall in a chair with your abs pulled in and shoulders down and back. Holding the free weight in your right hand, extend your right arm toward the ceiling and straight above your head, keeping your arm in line with your shoulder.

2. Slowly, on the inhale, bend your right elbow to bring the free weight down toward your shoulder blades.

3. On the exhale, slowly straighten that arm again. Note: You do not have to touch the weight to your back. Allow for 2–3 inches of space between your weight and your back for best results. Repeat 8–12 times for two sets on each arm.

③ Lateral Raises

1. Sit on a chair with your abs pulled in and shoulders down and back, and hold a free weight in each hand.

2. On the exhale, slowly raise both arms up to the side, with palms facing down, as if you were a bird flapping her wings. Raise your arms as far as you can without shrugging your shoulders. Do not use momentum to help you. This exercise is designed to isolate the shoulders, so if you cannot lift your arms without pulling with the rest of your body, decrease the amount of weight you are using.

3. Slowly return to starting position on the inhale. Repeat 8–12 times for two sets. Note: The muscles you are developing in this exercise are tiny, so you do not need to use a lot of weight; 5 pounds or less is sufficient.

④ Squats

1. Stand with your feet shoulder-distance apart, your abs in, and your shoulders down and back. Hold a free weight in each hand.

2. On the inhale, slowly lower yourself, bending your knees and moving your butt into a sitting position. Be sure to keep your body back, not allowing your knees to come past your toes.
3. On the exhale, straighten your legs again and come to a standing position, but don't bounce up or lock your knees. You want to keep your joints relaxed. Repeat 12 times for two sets. Note: If you have a bad back, try this with a stability ball propped between your lower back and a wall.

⑤ Lunges

1. Stand with your feet shoulder-distance apart. Grasp a free weight in each hand. Drop your arms down to your sides with your abs pulled in tight and shoulders back.
2. On the inhale, take a step out about 2 feet in front of you with your right leg. (Adjust this distance so that both legs are bent at right angles.) Bend your left leg (the leg supporting your weight) so that your left knee comes as close to the ground as possible, and your right leg forms a right angle.
3. On the exhale, shift your weight to the right leg. Then use it to push yourself back up to a standing position.
4. Repeat, remembering to watch your breath, beginning this time with your left leg. Repeat on each side 12 times for two sets.

Circuit Training

This is one of the hottest forms of exercise around today because it offers a variety, calorie burning, and muscle building all in one workout. Circuit training includes a mix of traditional weight- and resistance-training exercises with popular forms of cardiovascular exercise. Circuits usually involve eight to ten exercises completed one after another with very little rest in between. They optimize fat-burning potential and provide a full-body workout by pairing cardiovascular exercise with strength training, and the mix of activities keeps it fun and interesting. Here's an example of a circuit-training workout: warm-up, squats for one minute, jumping rope for one minute, static lunges for one minute, running for five minutes, push-ups for one minute, and then kickboxing for one minute. You would then repeat the circuit one to three times, or more. Do not rest for more than thirty seconds between each exercise.

You can join gyms specifically focused on circuit training, hire a trainer to set up a program for you at your gym, buy a circuit-training video, or set up a program of your own at home or in the park. What's great about circuit training is that you never get bored and you're always working your muscles in new ways.

Sample Skinny Chick Home Circuit
1. Brisk walking for two minutes
2. Squats for one minute
3. Jumping jacks for one minute
4. Running for three minutes
5. Standing lunges for one minute
6. Jumping rope for one minute
7. Push-ups for one minute
8. Kickboxing for one minute
9. Squats for one minute
10. Brisk walking for one minute

Repeat one to three times, depending on your endurance level.

Stretching and Strengthening Practices

Now, let's take a closer look at the stretching and strengthening practices of Pilates and yoga. Pick one of these practices to integrate into your program at least once a week. It's also a good idea to do a few Pilates or yoga moves every day to keep your body long and limber.

Pilates

Pilates was developed in the 1920s by legendary physical trainer Joseph H. Pilates. He developed more than five hundred different exercises aimed at developing the body uniformly, with a specific focus on what he called the Powerhouse, comprising the back, abdominals, and buttocks. His idea was that you could get a lot more value out of doing a few good exercises correctly at each workout than you can doing less-productive exercises many, many times. Pilates was partially inspired by yoga, but he mainly created the method on his own. This form of exercise has remained in practice, and has seen a recent resurgence, because it works! In terms of strengthening your core, particularly your abdominals, few workouts are better. The exercises also help to elongate your body; stretch out your spine; create long, lean muscle; and develop a full range of motion at all major joints. Just like running, Pilates gives you a big bang for your time buck. You can get tremendous results in a short time and can spend a short time doing each workout.

Now, there are a great number of submethods of Pilates, from Winsor to Stott. All of these approaches are based on the same Pilates moves, with a few changes. You can choose from organized classes at gyms and community centers or purchase a DVD for private use at home. You'll need a Pilates mat to protect your back, but other Pilates tools aren't necessary for the beginner. Pilates is a great addition to any workout regime! Here are the top-five Pilates moves for rock-hard abs.

The Hundred

1. Lie on the ground (or mat) on your back and pull your powerhouse in, belly button to the spine, to achieve a neutral spine. (Lying flat on the floor is not natural, neither is arching too much.)

2. Lift your head and raise both legs to a 90-degree angle to your body. Hold your arms straight at your sides, lifted a few inches from the ground. Palms should be facing the ground. Keep your neck long and shoulder blades down. You can reduce the angle of your legs to the ground to 45 degrees or less to make it more difficult or bend your knees to make it easier.

3. As you continue to inhale and exhale normally, pump your palms at your sides as though you are pretending to pound nails into the ground.

4. Pump 100 times as you continue to breathe, hold your legs in position, and suck your belly button in to your spine.

The Can-Can

1. Sit up, placing your hands on the ground behind you with your fingers pointing out and back and arms straight. Keep your shoulder blades down and back.

2. Using your abs, pull your knees together into your chest with your toes pointed.

3. Hold your knees together and, on the inhale, tilt your knees to the right, then the left, then the right again. On the exhale, kick your feet out.

4. On the inhale, pull your knees in again and move them to the left, to the right, and to the left this time. Kick your feet out on the exhale.

5. Repeat on each side six times.

The Crossover
1. Lie with your back on the floor.
2. Bend your elbows and place your fingertips behind the back of your head.
3. Bend your knees and lift your feet until your shins are parallel with the floor.
4. Exhale as you crunch your right knee in toward your left shoulder as you simultaneously lift your shoulders. Do this slowly, with your belly button pulled into your spine the entire time.
5. On the inhale, slowly twist your body the other way so that your left elbow and right knee move toward one another. Knee and elbow never meet, they are simply moving in the direction of one another. In fact, it's just a twist of the spine that makes this exercise challenging.
6. Continue to alternate sides six times slowly.

The Sailboat
1. Lie on your back, with your spine in a neutral position (lying flat on the floor is not natural; neither is arching too much) and your belly button pulled into your spine. Place your fingertips loosely on the back of your head, with elbows bent. Keep elbows behind your ears. Keep neck long and shoulder blades down and back.
2. Lift your head as you bend your knees up. Note: Use your abdominal muscles to lift your head; do not use your neck.
3. Extend your right leg straight along the floor, keeping the left knee bent. (From the side, it will look like your body is positioned in the shape of a sailboat.)

4. Hold your body in this position for ten seconds, breathing as normally as you can before slowly switching legs.
5. Alternate sides six times.

Double Leg Pull-Ups

1. Lie on your back, with your spine in a neutral position and belly button pulled into your spine. Place your hands behind your head and lift your head up.
2. Pull your legs up to 90 degrees and keep them straight.
3. Hold your legs together and, on the inhale, slowly allow your legs to drop toward the floor until they are only a few inches from it.
4. On the exhale, pull them back up to 90 degrees. Be sure to use your abdominal muscles to lower and raise your legs and not your quadriceps or hip flexors. To make it more difficult, lower your legs closer to the ground.
5. Repeat this exercise ten times at a drop-level you find challenging. Note: If you have a back problem, place your hands between your lower back and the floor.

Yoga

This ancient form of exercise is practiced by people all around the world and is a favorite among skinny chicks. This form of exercise can not only make you long and strong, but it can also help you to relax and combat stress. There are many different forms of yoga to choose from, including more aerobic versions and gentler, more meditative approaches. Yoga involves stretching your body into different positions, called *poses*, and holding yourself there for (in most forms of yoga) at least thirty seconds at a time. Hence, the stereotype of a yogi twisted into a pretzel. In yoga, you can move into each pose to whatever degree you feel comfortable. Pushing yourself too far is not encouraged. With each exercise session, your body will slowly open up and allow you to move further into each pose.

A great deal of strength is involved in holding your body in these various positions for several seconds or minutes at a time. It requires, in particular, lots of core strength. While beginners may only be able to hold a pose for a few seconds at a time, as they progress, their bodies will get stronger and stronger and their posture improves. It's amazing the body strength that yoga can develop. Just look at Madonna! Did you know she can stand on her head? The abdominal strength involved in that is remarkable. Anyway, you can investigate classes at yoga studios, gyms, or community centers, or purchase a DVD to help you become a yogi in the privacy of your own home.

A Little Taste of Yoga: The Sun Salutation

Sun Salutation consists of twelve postures. It is usually done in one flowing movement, although you may want to hold each pose briefly in the beginning so you have a chance to notice how your body feels in each position.

1. Stand tall, with your arms at your sides, abdominals pulled in, and feet hip-width apart.
2. As you inhale, raise both arms up in front of you and over your head in a slow sweeping motion. When you come to rest, your back should be arched to whatever degree is comfortable for you.
3. On the exhale, bend forward with your arms and body in one fluid motion as you touch your palms down to the ground near your feet. You may want to bend your knees slightly to prevent straining your back—this is fine.

4. Inhaling again, take a big step back with your right foot, placing your toes firmly on the floor. Your left knee should be bent and aligned over your left foot. Place your hands on the floor at either side of your left foot for balance. You are in a *lunge* position.

5. As you exhale, step your left foot back to meet your right foot (staying on your toes) and hold yourself flat just above the floor with your hands, so now you are in a *plank pose*.

6. While exhaling, gently lower your knees and chest to the ground. (This isn't an opportunity to collapse. Position your body purposefully.)

7. Inhale again, and press your palms into the ground and arch your head and shoulders up and back for a nice chest stretch. If you can, lift your legs so that only your tops of your feet and your hands touch the floor.

8. As you exhale, turn your toes into the ground and pull your hips up to make an inverted **V** with your body, keeping your shoulders relaxed. Do not hunch or arch your back—try to keep it flat.

9. As you exhale, lower your hips toward the floor and step your left foot forward into a lunge position, as you did with your right leg in pose 4.

10. Step the right foot up to meet the front foot and bend over, head tucked, hugging your knees. Again, it is OK to bend your knees slightly to prevent straining your back.

11. On the inhale, slowly rise and swing both arms up and back over your head, arching your back as much as is comfortable.

12. Exhale as you lower your arms so that your hands stop in front of your chest in a prayer position. Repeat 3 to 12 times, alternating which foot you step out with first.

In this chapter, we learned about two forms of strengthening exercise and two forms of strengthening and stretching exercise. Remember, in addition to burning calories with cardio workouts, you need to add some exercise that focuses on building muscle and some exercise that focuses on stretching your muscles. These two elements round out a complete exercise program.

You only need to add in two or so strength-training sessions each week, and they don't have to be that long. You can probably get two sets of ten to twelve reps done on your arms in fifteen minutes or so. Couple that with fifteen minutes one other time each week focused on lunges and squats for your lower body, and you have your strength training covered. Next, you need to add some stretching. Why not add in one thirty-minute yoga class a week? Or simply learn some yoga and Pilates moves or do a twenty-minute session in front of the TV on your own? It can be very easy to work these critical exercise elements into your life.

Now, let's change gears and move to a discussion of the most important "muscle" of all: your brain.

10

Food and Thought

WHAT IS IT ABOUT women and food? Why do we have a love-hate relationship with something that should be nothing more than fuel for our bodies? It's a complex question, and one that needs to be asked by any woman who wants to successfully change her eating habits. That's because the way we think about food is the linchpin in our ability to truly be in control of what we eat. So many of us eat to cheer ourselves up, to celebrate, to destress, to wake ourselves up, to congratulate ourselves . . . the list goes on and on. We use food for so many things, but least of all, it seems, for nourishment.

But we are not exposed to just the necessities as our ancient ancestors were—nuts, leg-

> Just being aware of the fact that emotions influence my desire to eat certain foods has helped. I sometimes have to remind myself that I'm really not hungry, and I just try to get through the next hour without eating.
>
> —Marathon runner and mom,
> Diana Bernier

umes, and fruit—and with variety comes sugary, doughy, salty, and fatty "comfort" foods that we find it hard to resist and that make it possible to eat for so many other reasons than to satisfy hunger. While many of us do reserve the truly bad stuff for serious comfort sessions (a carton of Häagen Dazs after a breakup) and other special occasions, many highly caloric foods have made it into our daily lives and onto our daily menus.

Over the past one hundred years, we have allowed a complete mental shift in terms of what is considered food for regular consumption, how much should be eaten at each sitting, and how much is an acceptable amount to consume each day. This mental shift, coupled with our propensity for turning to food when our hearts or minds say so, rather than our tummies, has created a very unhealthy approach to food for many women today. While our waistlines may tell us that we must be eating too much of the wrong things, our ability to break the cycle and stop doing that is impeded by complex psychological barriers. This chapter hopes to start you down the road to changing that for good. Many of the skinny chicks have faced these same problems in their lives but have found ways out of this trap. Let's learn more about how they did it.

Turning to Food

When I have a really bad fight with my husband, I head right to the doughnut shop around the corner and grab a big, crunchy 500-calorie corn muffin. I fight this urge most of the time and tend to make it through the minor bumps in life, but if I am really freaking out, I gotta have that muffin. It just plain makes me feel better. Now, I've decided that it's OK for me to turn to food in serious situations. That's all a part of my plan. But I have stopped turning to food when I hit little bumps in life—that's part of my plan, too.

Linda Craighead, Ph.D., professor of psychology at the University of Colorado and author of *The Appetite Awareness Workbook: How to Listen to Your Body and Overcome Bingeing, Overeating and Obsession with Food*, says it's very common for women to turn to food for reasons other than hunger. "Usually it's for emotional reasons, to self-soothe, to tolerate doing something they don't want to do, to procrastinate, to celebrate," she says. "Food is a natural, primary positive reinforcer. You don't have to learn to like it and often it tastes good so it gives pleasure. It's not just that it gets rid of hunger, so we eat for many reasons."

While it's OK to do this on occasion, giving in to it regularly can be a recipe for obesity. In this regard, our biology actually works against us in our efforts to keep things under control. "In a plentiful and tasty food environment, it is natural to eat more than you need to maintain a healthy weight," says Craighead. "Our biology is set up to protect us from starvation but not from obesity. It is tough to lose weight because your biology is set up to fight it. The more extremely you diet the harder your body makes it for you. So you need to lose weight slowly. But then it's hard to maintain motivation and you tend to get frustrated and give up." But it is possible, despite this, to regain control of your mind when it comes to food. "Yes, many women do shift their mindset and find a way to enjoy food in moderation and to eat healthfully most of the time," she says.

Making That Change

It's OK to eat for pleasure, but it's important not to get stuffed or eat mindlessly, says Craighead. With this in mind, the first step toward taking control of your mind when it comes to food is to take note of when you are eating for reasons other than hunger. "Pay attention to why you are eating to see if there are places you are willing to make other choices," advises Craighead. "I recommend appetite monitoring. You have to recognize what you are doing and be willing to try alternatives, not just wish the problem would go away," she adds.

So, to begin to take control, you need to start eating mindfully, which means checking in every time you are going to eat and asking yourself if you are really hungry and if so what do you really want to eat, suggests Craighead. This will prevent you from mindlessly eating food that you don't even really want and that doesn't give you much pleasure. "All eating needs to be a quite conscious and deliberate choice so you get the most benefit from whatever you do eat."

Even though you want to lose weight, or at least prevent weight gain, the worst dieting strategy is to wait until you are very hungry before you eat. "When you try to save calories that way, you get so hungry that it's hard to maintain control," says Craighead. "When you do eat, you tend to eat more than you need. Eating starts to feel dangerous. The better strategy is to eat fairly frequently and focus more on when to stop—not overeating or getting stuffed.

Ultimately, Craighead suggests women find a positive reason to eat healthfully. "If you focus on how unfair it is and how much you want to eat other foods, it is punitive, and either you can't maintain it or you do but are miserable and preoccupied with food." Model Danielle Gamba says she's an emotional eater but has learned to work around her tendencies. "When I'm upset, yes, I like to eat," she says. "But I also lose my energy when I am upset or depressed so I find a cup of coffee helps me. I take the energy and try to keep myself busy doing something else to get my mind off of it."

The Breakdown Plan

* **Step one: Begin eating mindfully.** Every time you eat, write down what you eat. Make note of how you are feel-

ing, why you are eating, and, most important, what triggered you to want to eat. Finding that emotional trigger is the most important step in eating mindfully.

* **Step two: Assess your choices.** Are you often eating to soothe yourself or for other emotional reasons other than for hunger? Are you often choosing the worst foods in these situations? Are you feeling better or worse after you have eaten?

* **Step three: Decide to make better choices.** If you find you've been eating too often for emotional reasons, decide on some new things to do instead, such as chewing sugar-free gum, drinking diet soda, buying an outrageous tabloid magazine, working out, or calling a friend. If you find you are turning to bad foods when you are hungry, find healthier favorites and always have them on hand.

* **Step four: Implement the plan.** Start making those healthier choices. Keep track of these choices and how you feel after you've made them. Or do as I do and designate certain situations for your comfort foods. Perhaps it's the first day of your period or when your mother-in-law comes into town. But with this plan, there must be a plan set for when you won't allow yourself to give in, like a bad day at the office or a difficult day at home with the kids.

* **Step five: When you fall off the wagon, just get right back on.** It's OK to turn to food on occasion, when you really just need to let loose, but don't make it a regular pattern.

Emotional Situation	Healthy Comfort Food Suggestion
Fight with significant other	A bowl of fat-free chocolate pudding with low-fat whipped topping

Boss flips out on you at the office	English muffin pizza (these make you feel like a kid again!) made with fat-free mozzarella cheese, low-calorie sauce (such as Healthy Choice),and low-fat, whole-wheat English muffins
In-laws coming to town	Glass of cabernet sauvignon and small handful of mixed nuts
Children driving you mad	A cup of chamomile tea (to calm nerves) with 1 tablespoon of peanut butter spread onto two slices of crispbread
Money troubles	Chop up the fruit that's starting to go bad in your refrigerator and enjoy with a scoop of ice cream or yogurt

This chapter may well be the most important part of this book. We all know we should eat less and eat better. We all know we should exercise more. But when it comes down to it, all the best-laid plans can fall apart when our emotions take over. That's why it's so important to take a good, hard look at how emotions are affecting how and what we eat. By being aware of what we are doing and, more critically, what we are likely to do the next time we get upset, we can arm ourselves with plans, resolutions, and strategies to help us stay on track as much as possible.

We need to stop putting our heads in the sand and ignoring the fact that we've got to get a hold of our emotions and what we do about them if we're ever going to stay on a healthy track and not lose ground to emotion-induced binges. This chapter gives you a start down this road. Use the following resources to help you deal with this issue further.

Recommended Reading

* *The Appetite Awareness Workbook: How to Listen to Your Body and Overcome Bingeing, Overeating and Obsession with Food*, Dr. Linda Craighead, New Harbinger Publications, Inc., 2006.

* *The Ultimate Weight Loss Solution*, Dr. Phil McGraw, Free Press, 2003, Chapter 7.

11

Making That Change for Life

SO YOU'VE MET ALL the skinny chicks, seen the reality of what it is they do to look the way they look, and learned the details about the fifty secrets that could help you make that happen in your own life. My hope is that these women and these secrets have inspired you. I want you to feel excited about what all of this can mean in your own life. I want you to use all of this information to make an informed choice about how far you want to go down this fitness road. You now have the information to get that absolutely perfect body, should you decide you want it.

But given the time commitment and mental focus required, that may not be realistic for you. In any case, I'm hoping all of you will pick the

> **You won't fit into those $140 jeans.**
>
> —Skinny Chick Naomi Jay, on what she says to herself when she's tempted to eat badly or skip a workout

> **Women are in total denial. They know in the back of their minds that they want to shed that weight but they don't do what they need to do to make it happen.**
>
> —Julia Roberts's *Pretty Woman* body double, Shelley Michelle

point along the healthy-body spectrum that is right for you and use these secrets to once and for all make it happen. This is how the skinny chicks do it. By following all of these secrets you will be doing exactly what the skinny chicks do, it's just up to you to decide how much of each thing you do and how far you go. But let their commitment, their energy, and their focus inspire you.

Get excited about the fact that you are finally on the "inside"; you finally know what the skinny chicks do and you now have the information to make the changes needed in your life to remain a healthy, happy weight over the long term. Whether you have a good chunk of weight to lose, are just looking to trim off those last few pounds, or are trying to maintain a healthy weight, you now have the facts needed to make that happen. Psychologists say one of the key components of a successful weight-loss plan is self-efficacy, or believing that you can do it. So, what you need now is to harness the excitement this book has inspired and let it move you into action, setting you on a healthy track for life.

Getting Inspired

Even though I was already an avid exerciser who was obsessed with healthy lifestyles, I have to admit that, while I was doing the research, even I was inspired by the women in this book. These women are amazing, and it's exciting to immerse yourself in their way of life, if only to get a taste of the things you have to do to get yourself into a healthy zone.

Feeling a sense of excitement and exhilaration is critical to embarking on a new healthy chapter in your life. So it's important to capture this initial excitement on paper so that you can rekindle it later when you need it. Start by writing down on a piece of paper what exactly it is that you want. Do you want to feel sexy and strong and healthy? Great, but be more specific. Do you just want to be able to walk around feeling stronger and healthier? Terrific, but if you can, be even more specific than that. Is there a certain size of jeans you'd love to fit into? Whatever it is that you want from a healthy new lifestyle, write it down with as much detail as you can.

Next, write down a long list of all of the positive things that will likely come as a result of your achieving this goal. Feeling more confident, feeling healthier, getting your doctor off of your back, fitting into your "skinny jeans" again, being able to get up off the floor more easily, being able to play with your kids longer, improved self-esteem, getting sick less . . . Make this list as long as you can.

Then, make another list. Write down all of the things that will happen if you don't make this change in your life. Be thorough here as well. Diminished health, possible depression, diminished self-esteem, feeling uncomfortable, having to buy clothes you don't like, feeling ashamed, feeling embarrassed, worrying about special outings where you think people will judge you, and so forth. This list needs to be exhaustive, too.

Now, look at all of these lists and really think hard about the things you've written down. Close your eyes and imagine yourself as this person who has allowed herself to continue down a less-than-healthy road. What do you see? How do you feel? Now, close your eyes and imagine yourself as this woman who has moved into action to get those things on the other list. Imagine yourself having achieved your goals. What do you see? How do you feel? Now, use those emotions to propel yourself into action. You now have the leverage needed to finally, once and for all, make that change. Whenever you feel your drive waning, read your lists again and remind yourself of why you are committed to changing your life. Remind yourself, too, of other times in your life when you have successfully made changes for the better.

Other Tips for Getting Inspired

* Buy a subscription to a fitness magazine.
* Read about or watch/listen to the work of someone you find inspiring. (Madonna's *Truth or Dare* documentary has me so ready to hop off the couch and get moving that I can barely watch the whole thing through.)
* Build a "Wall of Inspiration" on your fridge. Place photos, words of encouragement, and anything else you feel helps you stay focused on your wall.
* Join a running club, dance class, or other exercise social club and get to see these other people as teammates working toward a common goal.
* Get a friend to join you in your new fitness regime.

Overcoming the Obstacles

According to a study of inactive women done by the Melpomene Institute, a women's health research and education organization in St. Paul, Minnesota, a lack of discipline and feeling tired and low on energy were the top two reasons for not starting an exercise program.

Fortunately, these two obstacles can be overcome. In fact, in the case of a lack of energy, exercise and healthy eating will actually help with that a great deal. And, ultimately, when you start to reap the rewards of exercise, the discipline will come too. According to an article written by Diane E. Whaley, Ph.D., and Tiffany Redding, in the *Melpomene Journal* in 2001, titled "Turning Want into Will Do: The Role of Future-Oriented Plans in Exercise Behavior," once women start to change their actions, they see their personalities change too. "Most individuals have multiple possible selves, representing a range of desires and dreams for the future," the authors say. "Some possible selves are quite likely to be realized, while others, such as winning the lottery, are quite unlikely to occur. Possible selves that are well-conceived, complex and accessible to the individual are most likely to result in behavior."

These possible, hoped-for selves are significant motivators for future behavior, they say. It's important to test out these desired roles. "As a person feels more comfortable in the new role, she will take on this new identity and further focus behavior by making plans for continuing her activity, even when other activities come up that might interfere with exercise," the authors say.

When comedian and Skinny Chick Carla Collins feels like she wants to fall off the healthy-eating wagon or skip a workout, she says she has to look no further than her wrist for inspiration. "I just look down at my bracelet that says, 'What would Lance Armstrong do?'"

Moving into Action

I hope that now you are inspired and ready to get started. So, what you need to do next is write down your goals. You need your dream goal (something you can only imagine achieving in an ideal world), your long-term goals (things you should be able to achieve with a lot of work), and your short-term goals (things you can accomplish right away). Now, starting with your short-term goals, write down what exactly it is you need to do to make that happen. If one of your short-term goals is to just start exercising and eating better, then you need to write down things like buy running shoes, set up workout schedule, and work out! Think of what you need to do to start making these things happen. Go back through the fifty secrets of skinny chicks and use these to help build out your list. Then, do this for your long-term goals as well. Leave your list of things to do for your dream goal for after you've reached your long-term goals. OK, so now you have a "to-do" list. So, start doing it! As you do each thing, draw a line through that part of the list. Once you've got everything set up, for example, new groceries purchased, proper equipment in place, you need to just start doing it. Do it. Don't think about it, just get moving.

It's a good idea to create a workout schedule to follow. You can place this on your fridge and check off each workout as you go so you can see how much you've accomplished. It's also a good idea to keep a diary of the food you are eating. Again, refer to all of the secrets to make sure you've got all of your bases covered.

Tips for Getting Out That Door

* Put your workout clothes on as soon as you get home from work to help avoid getting stuck on the couch.
* Carry a water bottle around with you all day to help keep yourself in an "athlete" state of mind.
* When you can't stand the thought of going out for a workout, just put your workout shoes on. Tell yourself that's all you have to do, and if you still don't want to go, you don't have to. Once they are on, you'll probably go.
* Remind yourself of how great you feel after a workout. Remind yourself of how crummy you'll feel if you skip your workout.
* Buy sexy, sporty clothes for hanging out around the house. This will help you to maintain that "active woman" mentality.

Keeping with It for Life

The key here is to remember nothing in this book is about the short term. I once had a friend ask me why I didn't run nine miles at a time instead of six miles. I told her that it was because I knew I could never maintain that kind of commitment. You need to decide what you can manage for the long term and commit to it. There are plenty of secrets in this book to help you make that possible. This isn't about dieting; it's not about doing something for a short period of time to get a certain result and then going back to what you did before. What you want to do is create a new healthy lifestyle that you can live with, for life. Maybe twenty years from now you'll decide feeling fit and fabulous isn't that important to you anymore. You may want to loosen up the reins at that point. But even then it won't be healthy to start eating whatever you want and sitting around all the time.

Heart disease is the number-one killer of women and the prevalence of an unhealthy lifestyle, particularly as we get older and more sedentary, is why. The reality is that gluttony and inactivity just aren't options. You won't feel well, you won't like the way you look, and your self-esteem will be diminished. It's just not worth it. So, this is something you need to do for yourself, to whatever degree is right for you. Building a healthier body will make you happier and more confident, allow you to have a higher self-esteem and body image, and help you to charge into your future with all your might. You owe it to yourself to make this change. Seize the day. Make it happen.

Index